(A Novelist/Editor's View)
By Robert L. Bacon

No-nonsense, Concise Answers
to

HOW TO WRITE WHAT PEOPLE WILL PAY TO READ!

**Hundreds of Writing and Publishing Issues
You Must Know**

so

People Will Pay to Read Your Book

HOW TO WRITE WHAT PEOPLE WILL PAY TO READ!

To My Mother, Bettymae, who when I was growing up would come back from the bookmobile every other week with a shopping bag full of books.

*She was an angel on Earth
in so many ways.
RIP*

TABLE OF CONTENTS

On Publishing **203**

Introduction

If you are a writer who is seeking information from a person with formal credentials such as an MFA from Iowa State and a fellowship with Jane Smiley (whom I respect and adore as a writer), or a brilliant soul who holds a professorship at Columbia and writes bestsellers on the side, my background in this regard will be a huge disappointment.

I came into editing in a roundabout way. During the first year after I moved to South Florida I attended a series of author meetings conducted by a local literary association, and over time a sizable number of participants voiced an interest in formal workshops for writers. No programs were available in the immediate area, and no one suggested anything structured other than an occasional assemblage held at a church or in someone's den.

I had just finished conducting a reading program for seniors, so I contacted a local library about offering a series of workshops with a focus on writing prose at a level that would appeal to a major royalty publisher. My proposal was accepted and for the next three years I facilitated developmental, intermediate, and advanced workshops under the sponsorship of The Palm Beach County Library System. I later mentored a group of youngsters at a school for gifted children before moving to central Florida, where I currently reside with my wife of forty-one years and a lot of flora and fauna.

I never had any intention of editing for a living, as I didn't believe I was remotely qualified. But I was constantly asked to critique this or edit that, and my compliance—however reluctant it might have been—became the genesis of my current vocation, as writers said I was providing substantially more pertinent information than they had previously received from other editors, and my rates were much lower. Authors were also getting hits on the query letters I was designing for them. So I developed a bit of reputation as a go-to guy for a query that produced results.

To help build my editing business, I began providing a free Newsletter for the stalwarts who braved my writing workshops, in hopes these folks would recommend my services to others. What began in June of 2009 with an article on writing, and sent solely to my workshop attendees, by January of 2015 was broadcast to writers in forty-five countries. My monthly Newsletters remain free, and anyone can subscribe by scrolling to the bottom of any page on my Web site at theperfectwrite.com and filling out the simple two-step form.

The premise behind my Newsletters remains the same, and this is to provide information on writing prose at a level people will pay to read, and to explain the nuances of the publishing industry as I've come to know it during the past two decades as both a novelist and an editor. In line with my first broadcast, in each Newsletter I continue to provide an article that I design which pertains to either writing or publishing. It's only at the prodding of subscribers to my tripe that I've assembled these individual articles in a single volume.

Before reading the first topic related to publishing, it's important to recognize that the industry has changed dramatically during the past five years. I had always been adamantly opposed to self-publishing because of what I viewed as widespread abuse and writers paying fees as exorbitant as their aspirations. I found it sad to see folks come to writers' conferences with their books in shopping bags, then leave with their sacks still full and with crushed egos to boot. I'm still not ready to give a pass to print self-publishing, as alligators continue to abound. But since the digital arena is inexpensive, and readily available, I've relented and encouraged writers to move ahead with their dreams via this medium. And since this book begins its "life" as a self-published e-product, I'm eating my own pudding while offering one caveat about editors in general.

The universal editors' lament is that the profession is known for its subjective behavior—and sometimes this is practiced to extremes. In reality, all any editor can offer is an opinion, and it must be treated as such. The rules of writing are broken all the time. And while it seems that only the superstars can let their POVs switch around or write a prologue, I'm of the opinion that every author should create what he or she desires. My job is solely to explain what I've learned to be extant, and then let the writer make the decision whether or not to accept my advice about what I've determined to represent quality syntax.

My hope is that I will have made this last thought apparent in the material you will be reading, should you be brave and venture onward. Even though there are some elements of writing that I'm firmly against violating, an occasional adverb such as I just used doesn't diminish my opinion of a work or its author. Yes, it would be better to write "...I'm adamant about not violating...." But what's wrong with writing what one feels at a given moment in time? So, settle back. And if you're of the age that an adult beverage is legal, grab a glass of one and see if some of what my Newsletter subscribers believe to be of value might benefit your writing as well.

For ease of reference, should anyone ever want to come back to something (heaven forbid), I've placed the topics in alphabetical order and separated the prose-writing content from what pertains to publishing. I'll look at adding a supplement to this material at the end of each year, and if it's not a huge issue logistically I'll provide the addendum at no charge to those of you who were kind enough to purchase this first edition of HOW TO WRITE WHAT PEOPLE WILL PAY TO READ!

My final remark before the body of articles is that very little about writing is incontrovertible. When I begin any of my writing workshops I tell participants to challenge everything I say, not by standing up and vociferously denouncing each of my remarks, ha ha, but by researching anything they might question to develop a personal understanding related to their individual needs. I suggest the same mode of action for those of you who slog through what follows, because as editing is heavily weighted on the opinion side of the ledger, my drivel on these pages—regardless of the topic—is therefore far from sacrosanct. However, if you should see something in this material you like and want to apply it, by all means take advantage of the newfound information and let your writing journey continue with unbounded enthusiasm.

On Writing

Action Does Not Always Constitute Plot Movement

One of the most serious issues facing many writers is the ability to maintain the action throughout the narrative. Unfortunately, the mere creation of a dramatic occurrence does not guarantee plot movement.

The literary critic for The Palm Beach Post, Scott Eyman, has written many outstanding books on the legends of the cinema. In an article he wrote some years ago pertaining to a trend in filmmaking that was conceived to sustain an audience's attention span, he stated: "Action has become confused with movement." I was so taken by what I felt was an exceptionally acute and accurate comment, I asked for and received his permission to cite his line, since I am of the opinion this issue applies equally to crafting a novel.

There Is a Time When You May Have to Kill Your Babies

In writing, a glaring fault occurs when an otherwise perfectly good section having nothing to do with the plot has evolved to the stage of rendering the entire scene superfluous—but the writer doesn't want to lose the material. As harsh as it sounds, to paraphrase Faulkner, this is the time the writer may have to kill his or her babies. But not many who write their gems want to do it, at least not without a battle of intestinal tumult that often reaches epic proportions.

Whether Exposition or Dialogue, Lateral Movement Is Equally Deadly to Advancing the Story

No aspect of a narrative is immune, and to imply the problem is found more in exposition than dialogue is likely inaccurate, but flat scenes seem easier to identify in the latter. In a book, stagnant dialogue in a dining vignette, for example, although much less dramatic, is not dissimilar in effect to a fight scene or an explosion or a car chase ridiculously positioned or overused as a plot element in a movie. In leaving the theater and asking why a particular scene was in the movie, this is no different from a reader saying that a passage of exposition or a run of dialogue had nothing to do with the storyline of a novel.

Writers of Books Don't Have the Luxury Filmmakers Possess

But moviemakers have an advantage, since their medium is visual. A lot can be remedied in a couple of minutes and a few scene changes. A novel requires much more time to regain the reader's confidence after a lull in the narrative, and it requires much less effort to put down a flawed book–that might take another eight hours to read– than to hang around the theater for a half-hour until the movie ends.

It Is Impractical to Write Around an Ineffective Scene

It sounds simple, but this is the whole megillah: For anyone desiring publication by a bona fide royalty publisher, all of the words have to be focused toward the goal of advancing the plot. If not, revise or cut the superfluous narrative. It is impossible to write around material that does not advance the plot, no matter how brilliant the rhetoric might be. When a writer accepts this, the task of transitioning prose becomes easier, sometimes exponentially. And the overall narrative is more effective.

Action That Does Not Advance the Plot – Examples of Incidental Rhetoric That Retard the Flow of a Narrative

Avoid These Amateur Writing Mistakes

One classic faux pas is the unnecessary setup to a phone call. If Tom wants to talk to Bill, begin the call with Tom or Bill talking on the phone, not the picking up of the phone and then waiting for the ring or anything else that has nothing to do with the content of the call, such as this:

> Tom walked to the phone. He picked up the receiver in his left hand and punched in the numbers with his right index finger.
> On the second ring Bill answered, "Bill here."
> "Hi, Bill, this is Tom."
> "Well, hello, Tom. How are you?"
> "I'm fine, I hope you are too."
> "Yes, I'm feeling good."

Another Scene Never to Write Is the Greeting with a Receptionist

> Tom walked into the waiting area to Bill's office and approached a woman who was sitting behind a desk in the middle of the room.
> "Miss, my name is Tom Miller, and I'm here to see Bill Jones. He's expecting me."
> "One moment, please."
> The woman picked up her phone and pressed a button on her console. "Mr. Jones, Tom Miller is here to see you."
> "I'm expecting him. Please send him in."
> She nodded to Tom, who had remained standing in front of her. "Mr. Miller, Mr. Jones can see you now."

Nothing Can Shut Down a Novel Quicker Than Describing Mundane Activity

Each of the prior examples illustrates serious writing deficiencies, and unless there is high anxiety attached to either scenario, such as Bill's coming back from the dead or being overly cautious in an attempt to conceal his affair with the receptionist, neither incident should be played out for the reader. To state that Bill called Tom is all that is necessary before proceeding to the dialogue. Likewise, a phrase indicating Bill met with Tom is all that's required to move the story to a start of a run of dialogue.

15

Search for Writing That Retards Pacing—and Eliminate It

When reviewing a manuscript, it's always helpful to approach each scene with the attitude of deleting anything that is not absolutely necessary to the narrative. And while this might seem harsh, since there is always material that is supportive of the whole, there is generally a great deal that can be cut, and especially if a passage should be representative of either example in this article. The ability to recognize and delete incidental rhetoric is essential for anyone wishing to be considered a serious writer.

Adjectives – Their Overuse and How This Inhibits Quality Prose

It seems as though everyone has had an English teacher in high school who wanted things described in the most florid terms possible. This enthusiasm for abundant description was often championed in college too, and we commonly read material from MFA superstars that illustrates dogged determination to accentuate every noun with some form of embellishment. And while writers are warned about adverbs, adjectives don't evoke anywhere near the same level of disdain. But adjectives are just as detrimental to quality prose as their routinely maligned counterpart.

The Rules That Apply to Adverbs Also Pertain to Adjectives

The same as the "correct" verb's eliminating the need for an adverb, the "right" noun does not require adumbration. In describing an Amazon, is it necessary to state this is a large woman with ferocious tendencies? Doesn't the word "Amazon" convey all of this by itself? It's comparable to writing that skilled artisans built fabulous domiciles in Italy. Is there such a thing as an unskilled artisan? Of course an Amazon and an artisan can indeed be accentuated, but in the examples does either benefit from the modifier?

"Very" and "Much"

I've never had the problem with "very" and "much" that some educators profess (but I'm not an educator either, ha ha). I believe something can indeed be "very" good and we can all do with "much" more of something, like money, but the elimination test should always be utilized before using either of these words. Simply, read the sentence, clause, or word with and without the respective adjective. If the message does not read appreciably better with the adjective, omit the modifier.

When Are Adjectives Definitely Not Necessary?

The strength of the nouns in a passage can have everything to do with whether or not an adjective adds to the message. Take a look at the following: "A big gray German shepherd chased after an agile young man with blond hair who was wielding a black Louisville Slugger baseball bat and had just robbed the elderly Armenian owner of the Mini-Mart grocery store on Waverly Street." Now read this: "A dog chased a man who had robbed a grocer." It's up to the writer to determine to what degree each noun needs to be enhanced.

Is the dog important to the story? If so, does the reader need to know it was a German shepherd? What about its color or size? A German shepherd could be chasing the crook just as well as a big German shepherd. Or a big gray dog might be important, since a big gray dog of undetermined breed (should it not be known to be a German shepherd) might have been "policing" the neighborhood. Or the German shepherd could be owned by the grocer and everyone on the block knew of this animal and that it always protected its owner. Analyze all of the adjectives in that bloated sentence to determine the way you think it should read, based on your interpretation of the scene.

As with the Strength of the Noun, the Significance of the Word Determines the Necessity of an Adjective

I have often cited this horrible sentence I read in a book published by a Big 6 imprint in the mid '90s: "He held a green garden hose as the yellow taxicab came up the concrete driveway." Has there ever been a more overwritten sentence?

Think about the green garden hose and ask yourself if a garden hose is ever thought to be any other color. And even though taxis come in a rainbow of colors, unless this one was other than yellow, isn't this the color most people associate with a cab? Finally, unless a driveway is full of potholes, or there is some compelling reason to discuss its composition, why would it be necessary to mention the material from which it was constructed? This is all that's needed to convey the message: "He held a garden hose as the taxi came up the driveway."

Find the Best Nouns and Use Them

For all of the antediluvian mishmash in many of our old primers, this is one maxim that's incontrovertible. Think of all the single words that could be used to describe a big mean dog. "Cujo" was the consensus when I asked this of some grade-schoolers a while ago. But there's always Hellhound, or the original Hellhound itself, Cerberus. Even "beast" can be the ideal word choice in many settings.

Trim a Draft of Every Adjective and Then Replace Only Those That Are Essential

I've suggested this to my clients as well as to those folks for whom I critique their opening chapters as a service. If a writer will take out every adjective and then go back through the draft and replace only those modifiers that are deemed crucial to the sentences in which they originally appeared, the narrative will be tighter and a better read. Always!

Adverbs – When They Should and Should Not Be Used In a Narrative

I remember when I first read information on writing a query letter that rule number one was never to use an adverb in the text. Anywhere! I also recall being told when writing dialogue never to use an adverb attribute, such as "he said hurriedly." And I recollect being admonished after I started writing seriously that I shouldn't use adverbs in my manuscript but instead seek verbs that conveyed the desired meaning without the need for modification.

Why Have This Element of Grammar If It Can't Be Used?

If adverbs are such evil components of syntax, why have them at all? Were they the terrible incarnation of morphed adjectives that lazy authors everywhere conjured up to bail them out of a writing malaise? Or, maybe, do they serve a useful purpose when, if used, they don't automatically label a writer as indolent, inept, or befuddled?

What's Wrong with Speaking Rapidly?

John rubbed his hands together, tugged at his collar, and said rapidly, "I don't know what happened to the money." This author is demonstrating—by John's physical actions—that he's nervous, and isn't a rapid speech pattern a natural component of apprehensive behavior? Should John's short line of dialogue have been crafted to illustrate he was speaking briskly, expeditiously, speedily, swiftly, hastily, hurriedly, precipitately, urgently, excitedly, quickly, feverishly, hotly, fleetly, energetically, frantically, or heatedly?

Considering the material that preceded his speech, does any word other than "rapidly" better convey what the author intends? The closest word is "quickly," but this can imply that he began talking right away and not that his delivery was rapid. Writing gurus can argue that John's antsy actions indicate he might be inclined to speak fast, but unless the author stated this up front, how better to accentuate the man's discomfort than by alluding to his rapid delivery?

The writer could have written this: John rubbed his hands together, tugged at his collar, and said slowly, "I don't know what happened to the money." John could simply have been cold in the office and the starch in his collar was bothering him. His slow delivery might indicate he wasn't nervous but was stating a fact in a resolute way. To take this a step further, what happens to the meaning of the run if it's written in a sterile fashion? For example: John rubbed his hands together, tugged at his collar, and said, "I don't know what happened to the money." He appears nervous, but can the reader be certain? An adverb attribute is one of the few ways to give the reader the necessary information, and in this instance "rapidly" is certainly the most precise and concise word to convey the author's intended message.

Adverbs Aren't the Worst Things to Happen to The English Language

I ask again, in the prior exercise does any one of the dozen and a half adverbs I offered as substitutes express John's mood more definitively than "rapidly"? But of greater importance to the thesis of this paper, can the same clarity of purpose be conveyed *without* an adverb modifying the attributive phrase "John said"? Of course another sentence or two of setup could be crafted and poor John's state of mind would be obvious, but what better way to do this than with the adverb "rapidly" complementing the attribute "he said"?

Don't Get Carried Away with This

What I've just written shouldn't be assumed to provide carte blanche that a writer should now feel free to litter a manuscript with adverbs at every opportunity. My contention is that a well-placed adverb in a run of narrative is just as valuable as any other word that is used to its best advantage. But words such as "smilingly" and "tiredly" should never be used–even though both are in dictionaries–as it must be understood that almost any adjective can be made into an adverb by adding an "-ly." Consequently, while my article might provide some writers with newly found freedom, serious constraint must always be practiced.

As with adjectives, which should be used only after seeking the best noun to meet the author's needs, adverbs have a place in our language, but only after the best possible choice of a verb is sought.

Backstory (Flashback) in a Narrative – Three Effective Techniques Other Than Dialogue

Some people have said that the best way to display backstory, or flashback as it's also commonly called, is via dialogue--or not to write it at all. However, for the purpose of this article, the assumption is that backstory is critical to the ongoing development of the plot, and the three additional methods for presenting flashback material in exposition are within parentheses, via italics, or as an aside by way of a "remembrance."

Parentheses Never Seem to Make the Right Impact

I have long espoused that the parentheses should never be used in fiction, and I still believe this. First and foremost, a parentheses, by its very nature, is used as an aside to indicate something of lesser significance, and therefore would seem to contraindicate the need for backstory. Simply, if this aspect of the narrative is so important, as stated earlier, write it into the normal sequence of events. Now this last remark is a stretch, but if backstory is deemed necessary, why relegate it to second-class status as a parenthetical expression? Plus, from a purely pedestrian view, when a long run of backstory ends with a parenthesis, isn't it irritating to be "told" via the closed parenthetical mark that what was just read had not happened in real time?

Long Italics Can be Annoying

I once wrote an entire story in italics, as have other novelists. A couple of authors' works have been successful, but that's about it. After a few pages of italics, readers tend to become annoyed. And I've even found that italics beyond a couple of paragraphs can be too much. I look at this like reading stream-of-consciousness writing. Unless parked under Faulkner, Joyce, or Woolf, a little bit goes a long way.

Offering a "Remembrance" Is Often an Effective Method

Backstory for me seems to work best when the character begins with a short muse and then a full scene follows. This can be anything from a couple of sentences to a long chapter. Either way, something with this sort of setup: John looked across the barren field at the rusted chassis of the old Chevy truck, now seeming like it had died while planted up to its rims in the hard ground, and he remembered the first time Mary came into his life. It was a similar dreary Kansas afternoon in late November, ten years earlier. "Hey," a soft voice had called from over his shoulder, a decade in the past. He turned and saw a woman who....

No One Size Fits All

I'd create something such as what is in the preceding paragraph—in the three ways I've described—and see how each style sets up with what is written before and after it. Maybe the dreaded parentheses is the answer, or a half page of italics will do the trick. But if more than a few paragraphs of text are required, I'd consider a "musing" ahead of any other treatment.

Backstory in a Novel – How to Write It and Where to Position It

Some time ago I was asked to write a piece on techniques for displaying backstory (or flashback, if this is preferred) in a novel. That article focused on formats such as italics, parentheses, or a simple writer's aside. Later, it was suggested I address how to specifically use backstory in a novel, and that is what this article is about.

A Prologue Is the Most Obvious Medium, But Also the Most Dangerous

The simplest location for backstory is in a prologue, as this generally deals with what has occurred in the past. The problem is that prologues are often frowned upon by agents and publishers because they feel this "explanation" gives away too much of what is going to happen in the story, hence lessening the inherent poignancy of the plotline.

The Next Most Obvious Option Is Via Dialogue

In the earlier article I purposely didn't include dialogue because that article dealt with format techniques to display backstory. But, what one character says to another is the most convenient way to depict the past without being accused of "telling" rather than "showing" the action. And "telling" rather than "showing" is one of the primary reasons the publishing industry as a whole eschews backstory.

Stream-of-Consciousness Writing Also Works

Most people would agree that it's really hard to write like Virginia Woolf or William Faulkner, which might be the understatement of the century. But some people try. And if a writer is brave enough to give it a go, stream-of-consciousness writing will enable a character to express the past.

Interior Monologue Is Easy—Sort of

Short bursts of interior monologue deftly inserted between spits of dialogue can work quite well. However, this too requires a good ear and being especially alert to unintended POV shifts. POV problems seem to crop up most often when interior monologue becomes lengthy, so it's generally best to keep these runs brief. But, again, this is a great place to offer information to the reader that is significant to the fabric of the narrative.

Entire Chapters Can Be Devoted to Backstory

I've seen instances when writers have used an entire chapter of backstory to lend clarity to what is now going on in a story. But in the overwhelming number of instances, in my opinion, it would've been much better to "show" the event in real time, early-on in the narrative, and then build from it.

Then There Is the Denouement

The denouement doesn't always have to occur at the very end of the story, and a prime example is in A THOUSAND ACRES, a book I cite often because I feel it's brilliant in a great many respects. One of these is the subtle way Jane Smiley lets the reader in on why her protagonist, Ginny, has had severe emotional struggles throughout her life. The method by which this information is interjected—and where in the story—is a testament to Ms. Smiley's immense talent. Without critical backstory handled in this manner, in my opinion the book would not be sitting as a model for outstanding contemporary literature.

Chapter Length in a Novel – Why Consistency Is Important

A Time When Size Really Does Matter

"When is this chapter ever going to end?" This is a common rebuke heard by many a weary soul. The quality of the story may not have diminished, but the chapter is not consistent in length with the rest of those in the book. And the reader is uncomfortable. No time was allowed for the person to relax with the words.

Consistency with Chapter Length Is Important

Harry Crews, an ex-professor whose writing is far-removed from the mainstream, dissected Graham Greene novels related to how many chapters they contained and the length of each. Crews had a number of reasons for doing this, and it can be suggested that a writer should look at his/her own work as Crews parsed Greene's to create visual continuity that can affect pacing and even tone.

Genre As an Influence

When reviewing chapter length, a number of issues must be considered, not the least of which is genre. A writer of Literature, such as Pat Conroy, will have different chapter parameters from a Mystery author like James Patterson, with the separate and distinctive narrative nature of their disparate story styles influencing chapter length.

Clever Techniques That Provide the Perception of a Shorter Chapter

If a writer finds a chapter, for whatever reason, too long, there are techniques that can be used to shorten the perception of its length and provide the reader with some breathing room. One effective method, if there are multiple scenes in a long chapter, is to break up the chapter internally by adding an extra line space to indicate a shift in the scene, though evident, is not so great that a new chapter is desirable. The other device is to use a series of dots or other symbols such as * * * or # # # between an extra line space to indicate that a shift in the direction of the scene is substantial but still not enough that a new chapter is deemed appropriate.

Prudent Reasons for Section Breaks

It should be kept in mind that section breaks must have distinct functions—such as denoting the passage of time, a change of setting, or a point-of-view shift. Correctly positioned, they indicate transition points that would otherwise confuse the reader by their absence. But just as section breaks enable the reader to take a deep breath, too many of these breaks, or if they are ill-placed, can bring into question why these changes of direction were deemed necessary. The story will appear choppy and therefore a poor read.

The Ultimate Test for a New Chapter

If you believe a chapter might be too long or bloated, apply a simple concept: If you were getting tired of reading the chapter, wouldn't the reader likely be feeling the same way?

Characters Significant to the Plot Must Change for the Story to Be Effective

One of the main principles behind sound plot development is the change a major character must experience for the storyline to be effective. And make no mistake about it, this character must be different at the end of the story from what the writer presents at the outset. Yet the ability to show the changes in believable ways is just as important as the modifications themselves.

THE ELEMENTS OF SCREENWRITING, by Irwin R. Blacker, Provides a Solid Template to Follow

In my creative writing workshops I often allude to books on screenwriting to help writers structure their novels in a technically correct manner. Irwin R. Blacker's THE ELEMENTS OF SCREEN-WRITING offers superb advice with respect to the principle characters' requiring change, and he explains ways this can be accomplished.

Changes to a Character, While Essential, Cannot Be Sudden

One of the most important issues Blacker points out is that writers often show a character's shift in persona occurring too abruptly. I will occasionally ask a writer to look at his or her draft and pinpoint the exact location in the story where a major change occurred with one of the primary characters. If the writer can go to a single paragraph in the narrative, this lets me know that the change wasn't subtle enough–and too much happened at one time.

Gradual Changes Also Move the Plot Along

The biggest downfall to a sudden change is that it doesn't give the character and/or plot a chance to adequately develop. And the pacing will often flag, as one seems to have an inverse relationship to the other, especially if too much of a change occurs too rapidly. Small changes that take place as the plot moves along are important (read "crucial") because they enable the reader time to develop a relationship with the character(s), and the significance of this cannot be stressed strongly enough.

There Is a Point When the Reader Must Know the Change Has Taken Place

Although I just wrote at length about subtlety, at some point in the story the change in a character must be obvious to the reader. The skill in presenting these subtleties so they ultimately develop in dramatic fashion can make or break a story.

When does Gregor Samsa, and therefore the reader, realize there is no possibility of his returning to his normal body? When does Pierre realize his life will never be the same, even if he can reclaim his position with the royal family in Russia? How about the Reverend Dimmesdale's realization that he can no longer endure Chillingworth's prodding? Or Raskolnikov's acceptance of the reality of his crimes during his gut-wrenching confessions? And, in a more contemporary vein, Meggie's acceptance of her life after the birth of a son she never reveals to the priest who fathered her child?

Find a Pace for Each Character

Studying the sort of outstanding material I just referenced can give writers a feel for the pace of each character's development in their own work. By translating the concept of change to their personal narratives, authors can learn to sense when something should be foreshadowed and to what degree. Handled properly, the ultimate result will be both dramatic and obvious in the mind of the reader, which should be every writer's goal.

Classic Authors' Styles Are Not Always a Good Idea to Emulate

I recently critiqued a spate of unpublished manuscripts that were well written for the most part except for what I refer to as "literary retro," and I thought it might be a good idea to address what my phrase encompasses.

It's a Lot More Than the Overuse of Commas

For many readers and writers, the most obvious instance of "dated" writing is material with excess comma usage that is indicative of the respective styles of Henry James, Jane Austin, and other Victorian-era authors of classical literature. But the problematic issues with antiquated writing are much more extensive than abundant commas, and include placing a character's thoughts in quotations, combining different tenses, and awkward POV shifts. And many of the worst offenders are recipients of literature's most prestigious awards.

A Prime Violator at Placing Thoughts in Quotations

Kafka wrote THE METAMORPHOSIS approximately 100 years ago. The work's value as a dream-narrative is indisputable, but the author's quoting of thoughts can be misconstrued as an acceptable technique—when it is not. Bob thought, "What can I do now?" is going to rapidly send a manuscript to the slush pile; whereas, Bob wondered what he was going to do next, while not scintillating writing, would not in itself most likely discourage an agent or publisher from continuing to read the draft.

Even Recipients of Literature's Most Prestigious Awards Are Guilty of Verb-Tense Errors

In Bernard Malamud's THE FIXER, for which he received a Pulitzer Prize, in a couple of instances the author shifts from past to present tense in such an uneven way that it stops the reader. Knut Hamsun, a Norwegian writer—who won a Nobel Prize for Literature in 1920—wrote HUNGER, and any who read it can readily experience the problems with shifting tense. I can only assume that the Nobel committee thought this was stylish at the time, but anyone parsing the work today would not be advised to consider writing this way and expect any chance of being considered by a major royalty publisher.

Saul Bellow and POV

In THE VICTIM, Saul Bellow inexplicably shifts POV in two instances so abruptly that I had to read both passages several times to figure out who was speaking. Anyone familiar with Mr. Bellow knows he won a Pulitzer Prize for HUMBOLDT'S GIFT and was also the recipient of the Nobel Prize for Literature. But while he got away with these POV indiscretions, none of us would likely be as fortunate with our own efforts, so it would be prudent not to be influenced by THE VICTIM, lest we become one.

Good Writers Don't Copy Bad Examples

It is traumatic when someone who has studied classical literature begins serious writing and soon learns that much of what was thought to be acceptable is not. This is why many mentors will recommend to their students, once they read the past masters, that it's a good idea to spend a comparable amount of time with the current ones. Regardless of a person's taste (or distaste for my selections), reading successful contemporary authors such as Joyce Carol Oates, Stephen King, John Grisham, Barbara Kingsolver, James Patterson, Colleen McCullough, Dan Brown, Sue Grafton, Nelson DeMille, and Pat Conroy will demonstrate the value of correctly placed quotation marks, maintaining tense, and paying strict attention to writing in a consistent POV.

A Thought on Structure As Well As Stricture

It behooves a writer to study what successful contemporary material looks like, not just stylistically but from the perspective of conventional formatting; however, there are of course exceptions in this latter environment too. In Charles Frazier's wildly successful COLD MOUNTAIN, he employed em dashes, a technique I hadn't seen in so long (since I'd read James Joyce, to be specific) that I'd forgotten what they were called. Regardless, I don't suggest trying this or other nontraditional methods to set up text any more than it's beneficial to violate current strictures in an attempt to draw awareness to one's writing.

Comma Usage –
What Is Correct and What Is Not

The comma is one of the most highly debated forms of punctuation, simply because its use is often a function of inflection and for this reason can be viewed the same as opinion. Simply, one person likes where a comma is placed and another person doesn't. But there are clear-cut issues for which many writers take a lot of leeway, and this article will address some of the more obvious miscues involving comma usage.

A Comma Precedes a Conjunction, It Doesn't Follow It

Here's a typical example of sentence construction I noticed recently: John went to the bistro and had several drinks but, since Mary didn't show up, he left. Here's essentially the same sentence, except with "and" instead of "but." John went to the bistro and had several drinks while waiting for Mary and, since she never showed up, he left. Clearly in both instances the comma should precede the conjunctions.

There really isn't wiggle room in these illustrations, but for whatever reason I find some writers trying to set off "since Mary never showed up" as a separate clause when it isn't. Perhaps a way to look at this is if the word "however" was substituted for the conjunctions in both sentences. If the word was now "however," would anyone not use punctuation (a semicolon and a comma)?

To Comma or Not to Comma Is Often the Question

A comma has to come before "too" or "also" if either of these words is placed at the end of a sentence. Ms. Milsey in fourth grade taught me this, so did my high school English teacher, and every English course I took in college reinforced these earlier positions. Some educators can become downright nasty in their justification. Current grammar experts, however, tend to eschew a comma preceding "too" or "also" at the end a sentence.

Commas to Set Off Proper Names

Commas are generally necessary to set off proper names, but it's important to understand the context in which a proper name is placed. "Go see Mark," is not the same as "Go see, Mark." And, while this illustration is a no-brainer, here's one that's not: "I want to talk to you, Mark." Even though proper grammar requires it, for the sake of fluency in many instances the comma is eliminated. Just as "Oh well" might be an author's preference instead of "Oh, well." It all gets back to what I said at the outset of this paper about inflection.

Commas With Proper Names Can Be Very Complicated

This one can cause writers to tear out their hair. "My son, John" requires a comma before "John" (and after if in the middle of a sentence) should the person "speaking" have only one son. But if John has brothers, then the line is correct without the comma. I have found no good way to keep this rule straight except to think more is less; meaning, if what's modified signifies more than one, eliminate the comma(s).

No and Yes Require a Comma–At Times

"Yes, I want to go," and "I'm certain that, no, it is not a good idea," are examples of "yes" and "no" in sentences in which a comma is necessary to set off each word. Yet I commonly read these words without a comma (or commas as the case may be). However, a sentence such as "I won't take no for an answer," doesn't require commas around "no."

A Short Compound Sentence Doesn't Need a Comma

"I have to go and I need to go now" is fine, even though it's also correct to write "I have to go, and I need to go now." The second example is especially prevalent if the writer wants to emphasize the phrase "I need to go now."

Commas in a Series Are Always Up for Debate

One of the ongoing contentions is the use or nonuse of running commas. Here are two examples and you can judge which you prefer. "The old man left the boy, the dog and the cat." or: "The old man left the boy, the dog, and the cat." Tomato/Tamato, but take a look at this long sentence without the running (read "last") comma: Ms. Milsey in fourth grade taught me this, Mr. King in high school followed the same rule and the English courses I took in college also applied the identical standard.

Only the reader can decide if sentences with running commas are easier to read than those without. I suggest always setting off the last element with a comma when it's a component of a series of contiguous long clauses. Then to assure consistency throughout the narrative I advise setting off the short clauses and phrases, as well. For me, running commas solve a lot of issues; however, this topic is hotly contested and has been forever.

The Best Way I Know to Determine If a Comma Is Necessary

The old standby: Read the sentence out loud. Note where you have to pause. If a comma is not already placed at the point of the break, see if inserting one makes the sentence read more fluently. Likewise, if a sentence's flow is broken up unnaturally by a comma, it might be beneficial to eliminate the punctuation.

And while there can be serious conjecture about many aspects of comma usage, as several subsections of this article pointed out, there are a number of instances in which a comma cannot be eliminated or placed and enable the syntax to maintain its integrity. It's important not to lose sight of the grammatical scenarios that for all practical purposes are inviolable.

Conflict in a Story –
Its Meaning and Significance

To have any chance of engaging the reader, the number-one challenge is to create conflict as soon as possible and make it powerful enough to propel the story. The famous editor Irwin R. Blacker feels it's so important that he quotes Aristotelian theory, which I've bastardized as follows: If the conflict is not great enough to change the central character, the reason for reading the book has been removed. Simply, if the conflict is not powerful in the mind of the reader, the story is dead out of the box.

What Exactly Constitutes Conflict

Last year I took time away from my adult creative writing workshops that were sponsored by the Palm Beach County Library System to work with kids at a school for gifted children in my community. These youngsters were great fun, and I began with the same elements I discuss in my adult programs, and one was defining conflict. And that conflict, in and of itself, isn't always something which is earthshaking, let alone dramatic. During an early session, one 9-year-old girl, who was shy to begin with, read her opening paragraph from an exercise I'd given the group. She finished her material, which involved a puppy that was left in a box on her porch by person or persons unknown, and asked me—while displaying a terribly sad look—"Not much conflict, huh?"

I said she was far from correct in her self-deprecation. The abandoned dog in her story created all sorts of scenarios: Who left it? Why? Did the person who found the puppy like it and want to keep it? If the animal was discovered by a little girl, would her parents let her have it? The list went on and on. When we were finished, she had more conflict options available to her than any of her classmates via their respective material.

There's Rising Conflict, Peaking Conflict, and Falling Conflict

In my opinion, "conflict theory" can foster overanalysis at times, but once conflict is established in a story, it needs to crescendo. Will Mom and Dad let me have the puppy? If they do, how much time will it take from my other activities?

Conflict should also run full circle: Wow, my parents say I can keep the dog. He's great and I named him Fluffy. I've had him a week now and he's my best friend. But I still don't know who left him outside, and this really bothers me. I never took the time to care about much before, but now I feel responsible for things. Mom even says I'm keeping my room neater and taking more of an interest in people too. I'm not as shy anymore, either. And Mom and Dad seem to be paying a lot more attention to me. Is it possible Fluffy has something to do with this?

Conflict Must Change a Major Character

In the last few lines, the conflict is falling, but it must descend to a level that brings the protagonist and antagonist together at the end. In our imaginary tale, the little girl walks by the den one night and hears her mother and father talking without their being aware she's listening.

The mom says to the dad, "It sure seems like the money we spent taking Cindy to Dr. Nichols was worth it. I had no idea she was suffering from a case of such low self-esteem." The dad replied, "That little mutt has helped you and me too. We seemed to have gotten so caught up in our jobs that we were neglecting Cindy. It's strange it worked out this way, since I didn't accept the doc's diagnosis in the beginning and you didn't either." His wife smiled at him. "It's amazing how he could know that placing a little dog in a box and letting Cindy find it would make such a difference in her life." He returned her smile and took her hand. "It's made a difference in all our lives."

Here's a case of the primary conflict's being resolved in the denouement while several peripheral conflicts were "satisfied" along the way, as well.

And Then There's Too Much Conflict

If the conflict in a story requires more than a sentence to define, the plot is likely too complicated. Sounds silly, but think about the most complex tales out there and how succinctly the main conflict is presented. Most conflict can be defined in ten words or fewer. Try the "ten words or fewer" exercise for your favorite novel as a test.

Some Rules for Conflict Are "Absolute"

* Conflict must always be "shown" and never "told" to the reader.

* "Final" conflict should place the protagonist and antagonist together in the same theoretical room. However, If they aren't directly involved with one another to establish the conflict, those around them must be the catalysts who pull them into the scene.

* Unresolved conflict makes for very unhappy readers.

Contractions and Their Use
to Create More Fluent Dialogue

With an Ear for the Reader, Understand the Value of Contractions for Realism in Dialogue

A major hindrance to realistic dialogue is the inability to recognize the value of contractions to enable fluency. Dialogue quickly becomes stilted due to the nonuse of contractions, and the narrative tends to read like dissertation material or a legal brief. Unless the character is not familiar with spoken English, or if the writer wishes to create and maintain an accent, it is generally advisable when constructing dialogue to utilize contractions.

Early On, We Learn to Avoid Writing Dialogue Like People Actually Speak

Related to dialogue and creative writing, from the first sentence of the initial lecture we attend or book we read, the adage is the same: for dialogue to work, it must not be written in the exact way we speak; conversely, dialogue normally would not be spoken in the same syntax in which it is written. Unfortunately, this is a difficult element to comprehend for a lot of writers, and poorly conceived dialogue knocks out manuscripts quicker in the eyes of many agents and publishers than any other factor.

Read the Line Fast, First Without and Then With the Contraction(s)

If a writer reads the line of dialogue fast—first without a contraction(s) and then with—and applies the intended inflections along the way, a good sense of pitch can be ascertained. When multiple contractions are a possibility in a sentence, this "fast-read technique" not only helps to determine if contractions will benefit the dialogue but where, since many times a contraction works well in the first spit of dialogue yet not later in the same sentence, or vice versa. This of course also applies to exposition, but the evil noncontraction as a contributor to stilted rhetoric tends to be more marked in dialogue—and imminent death for a manuscript.

It's All About Pitch

Most people have favorite authors they like to read purely for pleasure. If we ask why, we're generally told it's because those writers are easy to read. Pick up someone's work you enjoy relaxing with and start parsing just the dialogue out loud. (After I wrote this line, I pulled down books by Barbara Kingsolver, Larry McMurtry, and Colleen McCullough to support my point.) You won't have to search for the contractions; they'll find you. Now take a sentence and read it instead with two-word substitutes for the contraction(s), paying attention solely to the new pitch of that sentence. I don't have to guess if there was a negative impact, and in many instances I imagine it was profound.

Good writing happens for a reason, and the proper utilization of contractions in dialogue is a powerful stepping stone for improving prose-writing skills.

Contractions – More on Their Use

One of the more difficult tasks facing any fiction writer is the proper application of contractions in the narrative. A set of standards applying to exposition that is often different from those which pertain to dialogue makes this particularly perplexing.

Start By Reading the Material Aloud

Anyone who routinely reads my articles is aware that reading material aloud is what I always suggest as the first requirement for determining good writing, regardless of whether it's exposition or dialogue. Unquestionably, authors listening to their own prose is the best way I know for them to assess the fluency of their material. If not combining two words that form a common contraction causes an undesired pause in the delivery, this is the best indicator I can think of that a revision is in order.

Emphasize a Sentence Element By Not Using a Contraction

It's especially good not to use a contraction if it is deemed important to add emphasis to something, the same as I did in this sentence. I wanted the second "it is" to draw attention to my belief that it is indeed beneficial to use a contraction to add emphasis. Conversely, I didn't feel "It is" held any significance as a lead-in. Keep in mind, it's not the "it is" that's important but the degree of influence the writer wants to place on a sentence element.

Noncontracted Words Influence Dialogue As Well

Some fine editors, especially those who work mostly with nonfiction, have issues with dialogue because they expect to see it written in a "perfect" way. Ignoring that an author can't effectively write dialogue the exact way people speak any more than folks can talk comfortably the same way dialogue is written, contraction use and nonuse is critical to the way a run of dialogue is perceived.

Contracted and noncontracted words can provide a wealth of information. Here are two of the simplest but purest examples: "That isn't what I meant," and "That is not what I meant." In the second short sentence, is there any doubt that the speaker is more intent? Does it require underlining or italicizing "is not," or an exclamation point at the end of the sentence, to indicate the speaker is vexed?

Contractions Can Indicate a Casual Atmosphere

I publish a Newsletter that many subscribers have told me is like receiving a letter from a friend. In large measure, I believe this feeling is because I use a great many contractions in the narrative. My thought is that contractions make the material more pleasant to read and at times will lend a lighter air to some serious topics. I've found this to be my best approach to many facets of prose writing, and the placement of contractions is a critical component for shaping tone as well as pitch.

An Issue to Be Aware Of

There seems to be a penchant to tag "-'ll" to the back of an inordinate number of words, spawning disasters such "that'll" or "it'll." I even recently read "somebody'll" and in another draft "brother'll." It's one thing if a writer is trying to illustrate a speech pattern or a dialect, but quite another when creating an altogether new amalgamation of words.

Contrivance Issues – The Impact on the Credibility of a Narrative

The Problems with Contrived Writing Cannot be Overstated

Someone recently asked me about the meaning of contrived writing, and when I was coming up with some flagrant examples this brought to mind a wonderful crossword puzzle phrase: deus ex machina. I couldn't remember how to pronounce it, so I went to dictionary.com and an elegant female voice enunciated it with what I assume to be the perfect inflection. And the correct delivery is critical to express the gravity of this devilishly problematic writing nightmare, which is "any artificial or improbable device resolving the difficulties of a plot."

The Meaning of Contrived Writing Must be Clearly Understood

Some people assume "contrived" relates to material that is "obvious." This, too, is certainly a meaning, but in the context of this article contrived writing relates to anything that would not occur without some sort of miraculous intervention. What makes contrived scenes particularly difficult to reconcile is that a substantial number of genuinely superb writers have resorted to fantastic good fortune to preserve their plotlines. Unfortunately, this weak writing seldom saves the story. It's important for a novelist to consider that many readers will put down a book for good when a scene's resolution comes across as beyond fortuitous.

We Might Expect Superman to Break Down a Door and Save the Editor of The Daily Planet, But Not to Do So on The Nightly News.

I refer to the writing of impossible scenes as the "Marquez Syndrome." ONE HUNDRED YEARS OF SOLITUDE is a terrific story and in large measure contributed to Gabriel Garcia Marquez' Noble Prize for Literature. But did the story require the mysticism? For me, it detracted from an otherwise perfectly executed saga. But this wasn't contrived, just a vignette he employed in the tale. Some writers, however, have taken his technique to heart and utilized preternatural events to cover a plot point instead of writing relevance into the scene. Contrivance is much easier than going back in the narrative and creating a setup for the overall plot element, with some authors forgetting that a single nonconforming thread can dog an entire story.

Even the Bard Wasn't Immune

But Shakespeare had an excuse. Other than CORIOLANUS and a couple of other not so egregious exceptions, he apparently was forced for a number of reasons to stick pretty close to a two-hour time frame for his plays. Yet, in my opinion, he made a mockery of the audience and later the reader with THE TEMPEST, a play that is one of his most acclaimed, and from which I remember several movies being made in just a short stretch (PROSPERO'S PAPERS, for one). With the ship's being destroyed and the survivors stranded on the island in the opening act, the plot is horribly and irreparably vitiated when at the one-hour-and-fifty-nine minute mark the vessel is found to be intact. Even though the storyline was pure fantasy, the catalyst for the wrecked ship's sudden "appearance" in relatively sound condition was due to the play's needing to come to an end, not Prospero's conjuring.

Not Many Can Claim the Skills of Marquez or Shakespeare

Since most of us don't possess their genius for writing, or dozens of titles under our belts and an international following, we're probably better served if we write our scenes—and most certainly our story finales—with acceptable possibilities. If anyone should remember the ending to the television series DALLAS, this is a prime example of what constitutes a contrived scene—and how devastating it can be to an entire body of work. Contrived scenes are a certain sign of lazy writing, and as harsh as this sounds, one of the best ways to guarantee never being considered for publication.

Dangling Modifiers and the Problems They Create

When I was in grammar school, dangling modifiers were referred to as dangling participles, and I never understood what my teacher was talking about. All I knew was that sidewalks couldn't walk and trees shouldn't talk if they weren't in a cartoon or if I wasn't writing a metaphor. "Walking down the street, the skyscraper looked over the bay as I turned the corner," or some such mishmash was generally provided as the example to learn from.

Not Beginning Sentences with Words Ending In "-Ing" Sounded Like a Good Idea

I decided that the easiest way to sidestep the problem was to never begin a sentence with a word ending in "-ing." But then I learned what a gerund was and that shot my idea all to pieces.

First and Foremost, Understand It's a Matter of Linkage

Any misplaced modifier implies a linkage problem, although for the purpose of this paper I'm discussing modifiers that are considered to "dangle" at the end of a sentence. Before considering anything else, analyze just how close your phrase is to what it is you're intending to modify. Sometimes this can be corrected by inverting the order, but more commonly a simple comma placed prior to the offending "dangler" will solve the problem.

Restructuring the Sentence

Last year, in my Newsletter no less, I sent a mailbox and not a letter to Belize. I wrote something like this: "Eduardo placed a letter to his mother in a mailbox and sent it to Belize." There are an inordinate number of ways to write this correctly, but a simple remedy would be: "Eduardo opened the mailbox and placed a letter in it that he'd written to his mother in Belize."

The Comma Is Often the Big Equalizer

In the overwhelming number of instances in which dangling modifiers occur, they can be neutralized with a comma placed before the offending clause, indicating it does not modify what it immediately followed.

In this sentence as written, the problem is apparent: "The lovers swayed to the bedroom locked in an embrace." But if a comma is placed before "locked," the lovers are correctly swaying in an embrace and not the bedroom, hence: "The lovers swayed to the bedroom, locked in an embrace."

Identify What Is Being Modified

The key to not falling into the dangling modifier trap is to recognize what is being modified. Once the antecedent is identified, the sentence can be structured correctly.

Dashes Defined By Variety and Application

The dash is indeed one of the most valuable forms of punctuation writers have at their disposal. But it's misused in a way that's diminished its value. First and foremost, it must be understood that the most common form of dash, referred to as an em dash, is formed by two hyphens contiguous to one another; or, via today's word-processing programs, a single line approximately twice the length of a hyphen. Regardless of the configuration, both are defined as an em dash.

The Different Forms of Dashes

THE CHICAGO MANUAL OF STYLE (Edition 14), in sections 5.105 through 5.119, lists the various forms of dashes: the en dash, the em dash, the 2-em dash and the 3-em dash. These sections in TCMOS also explain the various uses for these dashes, but before discussing the one definition that causes the most problems, it's important to detail the numerous styles for this punctuation and their suggested applications in standard prose.

The En Dash

The en dash should be slightly longer than a hyphen, but before word processing most typewriters only allowed for a hyphen to substitute for this particular dash. This form of dash has manifold uses, including connecting numbers to dates, time, or other reference numbers: 2002-12; 10:00 a.m.-12:00 noon; and pages 14-23. But, and this is confusing, we usually see these examples I just cited via a dash that doesn't often seem different from a standard hyphen, the latter which you find in these examples because I don't use en or em dashes in their proper configurations because of the problems they can cause for word-processing software.

En dashes also supplant the hyphen if one element of a compound adjective is open ended (what a horrible mishmash of rhetoric), which means there is a "Chicago-New York train" and a "post-World War II era" as examples. Please note that in both of these examples I also used a single hyphen to indicate an en dash. As I stated in the prior paragraph in this section, in correct typeset the en dash should be slightly longer than a hyphen. Technically, an en dash should be equal to the width of the "n" in the typeset of the material in which it is used. Under the same parameters, the em dash should be the width of the letter "m," hence how the meaning for both was derived.

Applications for the Em Dash

Em dashes are used for amplifying. TCMOS offers a subtitle that states the em dash is also used for "explanatory and digressive elements." I believe that most writers would be safe to stick with "emphasize," as to me the other definitions are ambiguous. Simply, em dashes are used to set off material a writer wants to highlight for a reader: "John got up—it was the first time he had moved out of bed all day."

Em dashes are also used in tandem around phrases a writer wants to emphasize: "John got out of bed—the first time he had moved all day—but soon went right back under the covers." If commas were used instead of dashes, the reference to John's action wouldn't create the same impression: "John got out of bed, the first time he had moved all day, but soon went right back under the covers."

Em dashes are commonly and rightly used to indicate an interruption in conversation, and there are some other instances in which an em dash can be applied, but these are more than a little confusing for many writers, as this would encourage authors to abandon commas, semicolons, and colons, which I wouldn't want to condone. But these options are explained in sections 5.108-5.110 of TCMOS, should anyone be interested, as well as in section 5.116.

The em dash has also been used instead of quotation marks by noted writers, who include the likes of James Joyce and William Faulkner in their ranks, and in more recent years Charles Frazier of COLD MOUNTAIN fame. But unless an author can write like Joyce or Faulkner or Frazier, I'd eschew this technique when creating dialogue and stick with quotation marks.

The 2-Em Dash and the 3-Em Dash

The 2-em dash is used to signify missing letters in a word, such as in "What the h----l are you talking about?" This can be via two sets of hyphens as illustrated in the example or two long em dashes as provided by word-processing software.

The 3-em dash is used to signify missing words, such as in "What in ------ are you talking about?" This can be created with three sets of two hyphens as shown, again contiguous to one another, or three single-line em dashes. Note that if the 3-em dash is used there should be a space before and after.

Both of these forms of punctuation are seldom used today, but they are correct and can certainly be placed in prose should this be desired.

So Where's the Misuse of the Dash?

The best must be saved for last, and once again TCMOS provides a resource for the confusion. Section 5.106, next to its subtitle "Sudden Breaks and Abrupt Changes," reads: "A dash or pair of dashes is used to denote a sudden break in thought that causes an abrupt change in sentence structure." TCMOS provides a series of examples, with the first one coming the closest to the definition: "Will he—can he—obtain the necessary signatures?" Mills asked pointedly. (Yes, TCMOS's example included the grotesquely unnecessary adverb attribute, and I didn't use the correct punctuation to cite this phrase because I found it potentially confusing.)

The definition in this subsection in TCMOS allows wide latitude and the impression that a dash can be used to indicate a pause in the narrative. Indeed, a dash can pause text, but it still accentuates—and that's the rub. To be specific about this, if a writer desires a pause, should a mark designed for emphasis be used? It can't work both ways, and writers must understand that for all of a dash's numerous varieties and manifold uses, a pause is not one of them. And in no reference manual I could find does it state that a dash pauses text to indicate missing words—only that words were omitted. When dashes are used, words are skipped and the narrative continues, whether it's dialogue or exposition. Nothing is paused.

Derogatory Material – Issues to Consider When Writing Something Unfavorable About a Real Person

Novelists sometimes have a great story on their respective hips that they're bursting to tell, but a character in the tale is fashioned around a real person with negative traits. So the question is, what's the best way to write about an unflattering characterization that happens to be true?

William Goldman Stated It Best

For anyone who might not be familiar with Mr. Goldman, he wrote BUTCH CASSIDY AND THE SUNDANCE KID, WHEN HARRY MET SALLY, and THE PRINCESS BRIDE, among many other fine works. He mentioned in one of his memoirs that he'd written something which wasn't necessarily unflattering about a man he'd known years earlier, but for whatever reason the person took umbrage.

Mr. Goldman soon suggested that no one write anything negative about someone—if the text might be identifiable in any way with the person who's being written about—until that individual is dead! As strong as that might sound, I think it's great advice. And to take this one step further, the family of the deceased person can also be offended, and if it's felt that the material was libelous, there could be a legal challenge from these relatives as well.

Even the Most Innocuous Implication Can Be Misconstrued

Who wants to gamble with the way someone's waffle might have gone down on a given day? I know a writer who had to print a retraction because he misstated a man's occupation from 30 years earlier. And this wasn't as if the fellow was the president of a company and he classified him as a clerk. This offended party was a medical technician and the author wrote that he was a lab technician. Both professions at the time carried the identical pay grade, and each continues to be viewed as a prestigious position. Go figure, but the man was dismayed because he felt that the lab technician title was debasing in some way.

More Serious Scenarios Can Occur

If all it amounted to was a retraction, most writers wouldn't be too concerned about what they wrote about anyone. But if a character can be readily identified as the one depicted in the story, and the person feels libeled, let the fireworks begin! If a writer is considering someone as a template for a character in a story, and this person for example was a notorious shoplifter as a young boy in Chicago, my suggestion is to make the character a middle-aged woman in Tuscaloosa who reads fortunes. Seriously, it's not worth the risk. Remember, if the person who's being written about knows the writer, this individual will be acutely aware of whom the author is modeling the character.

Wait Until the Person Is Deceased—and Then Look Further

I touched on this earlier. Even after the person is dead, I'd take a hard look at the individual's family and assess how the negative material might affect them. Only after every hoop is jumped through, and all the questions fully satisfied, would I then venture onto this turf. And I'd constantly ask myself if it's worth besmirching this person's name or family to try to sell my novel—when an imaginary character, adequately removed from the real individual and lineage, would serve my purpose just as well. Please think about this, as leaning to the cautious side of this equation might save a lot of grief and money down the road.

Description in a Narrative – When Is There Too Much Information?

I'm getting the question about too much description more and more of late. Writers become concerned about material that for them comes across as overwritten, and they want to know if there are guidelines which can be applied to determine a reader's tolerance.

Why We Dislike a Book Isn't Always Easy to Pinpoint

Whenever I think of material that is rich in detail, Jody Picoult and Tom Clancy come to mind, as I consider each to be a true artisan at the craft of writing fluent prose.

Yet, I've read many rebukes from readers and critics who find their writing to be everything from laborious to just plain boring. When readers make these sorts of remarks, I always wonder how invested they were in the work to begin with. I'm going to guess, not very.

I Believe It Comes Down to Timing As Much As Anything

It's not unheard of to be pleased with a work later in life that wasn't enjoyable the first time around. I remember hating HAMLET in high school but loving it in college. The same with THE SCARLET LETTER. I despised it in junior high but liked it immensely when I read it as an adult.

When we read a story can have as much bearing on our feelings for the material as any other factor. Many readers will have a greater appreciation for a quite detailed story when they also have the time to take in the width and breadth of what was written. Perhaps this sounds absurd because it's such a basic premise, but I think it has merit.

The Attention Span of the Reader Is Important to Match to the Narrative

I can't imagine anyone in a hurry wanting to read a Tom Clancy novel, any more than the same individual would be interested in breezing through CRIME AND PUNISHMENT or THE WINDS OF WAR. Those books provide an enormous amount of detail, and the reader should assume this by the word count if nothing else. The same with works by Pat Conroy or James A. Michener. If someone wants a quick read, in my opinion these aren't the authors to select. And once into the opening chapter of a book, with rare exception, it doesn't take a large amount of reading to know what to expect the rest of the way.

But What If There Is Just Too Much of a Good Thing?

How far into the capillaries should Ms. Picoult or Mr. Clancy be allowed to take us? No doubt, there is a point when enough is enough. But when we're sufficiently wrapped up in a storyline, do we really care? Or, better yet, do we even think about it? It again gets down to how engaged we are the story. If we are enamored with the material, we can't get enough of it; if not, anything beyond the basics is aggravating.

One Person's Manna Can Be Another's Poison

I've been to book signings at which a person in the audience asked if the author would consider writing more fabric into his characters' backgrounds. But a half-hour earlier, someone had buttonholed me in the parking lot to lament how irritating he'd found the same author's writing–because he provided way too much detail about his characters (yes, I wondered as well why this individual came to the signing).

What Does All of This Prove?

Probably not much. However, I've learned a quick way to fix the problem when a story becomes bogged down with minutiae. By ignoring the exposition, including the interior monologue, and reading just the dialogue, I can sidestep the superfluous text while still keeping the plot in focus. In very few instances have I had to go back to the exposition to check for "missing" information. So when you've had enough of Brenda's pining for Flynn or Agent W's bomb-disabling technique approaching the one-hour mark, try moving on to just the dialogue. You might be surprised at how well this works.

Developmental Arcs – What They Are and Ways to Develop Them

Transitioning Narrative and Developmental Arcing Are Not Synonymous

Effective transitioning is the utilization of various techniques that enables a reader to move comfortably from one plot point to another. A developmental arc is more detailed and involves a character or plot element that needs to evolve for the story to maintain or gain strength. Developmental arcs often require extensive narrative, sometimes over many chapters, and at times can span the width and breadth of an entire work.

Using Arcs to Develop a Character for the Reader

If a writer is ever told that a character needs a developmental arc, this can be as simple as adding family history to the narrative, showing how the character lives in his or her physical environment, or providing the character's thoughts on social issues that have relevance to the novel. Of course this can and often does require in-depth writing, but a lot of times strategically integrating snippets of these elements within the fabric of the story is all that's necessary to make a character engaging for the reader.

Using Arcs to Develop Characterization for the Reader

As with the requirements for a character to achieve "redemptive" status, characterizations can be treated in a like manner, although purists will argue that developmental arcs only apply to people. However, historical references, physical descriptions of any pertinent aspect of the storyline, opinions of a plot element via interior monologue; any or all of these techniques can be utilized to create solid development arcs. Simply, any link that can build the story for the reader is a candidate for use in this capacity.

What Is Not Enough and What Is too Much?

If people are reading your early drafts and telling you they would like to know more about a character or a story element, this is a clear indication that more work is necessary to "flesh out" certain aspects of your material. Unfortunately, lay readers don't often look at these areas the way a professional does, or these people can often be too close to the writer and therefore not comfortable expressing their candid opinions.

Overzealous attention to detail can be just as much of an issue. But it seems it's generally not as hard for a friend to tell a writer to back off rhetoric than it is to intimate that the author needs to add to it. However, this applies solely to potential arcing material, and my comment is not meant to imply that a sheer volume of words can provide a developmental arc for anything.

It's All About Balance

Finding the equilibrium point for a story is an art form, and as much as anything why certain writers are better for certain readers. Which means that developmental arcing is a matter of degree, and like most everything in fiction writing, highly subjective. Still, if a writer is receiving lay reviews on his or her own work that indicate the characters aren't adequately developed or the characterizations aren't portrayed with enough depth, it would probably be a good idea to get a professional critique from a reputable editor who has experience with the genre in which the novel is written.

Dialogue – How Not to Begin It in a Novel

The First Rule Is Still the First Rule

The very first thing that everyone learns about writing dialogue is that we can't write exactly the way people speak any more than we can speak in the identical manner in which people write. Yet I read material all the time in which good writers forget, or stretch, this maxim.

Let's Begin with "Well"–Or Let's Not

Anyone who's old enough to remember Ronald Reagan's speeches–and he was nicknamed "The Great Orator"–is aware of how often he'd begin a line with "Well" and then an extended pause. It was his trademark, and so well-known that comics copied it in their routines, and even the single word "well" would have a crowd in stitches. But "well" doesn't work when writing dialogue because it soon turns into a tic.

One "Well" Per Narrative, Please

There are indeed times in the dialogue of a story when "well" is perfectly acceptable. Just not at the start of every sentence spoken by a character, or worse yet by a number of characters. Someone saying one time, "Well, I'm just not sure about that," is a lot more palatable to a reader than a character's, "Well, you need to go see Jerry," followed by, "Well, I can see where that could be important," and then, "Well, how did it go?"

If writers will read their dialogue aloud, the superfluous nature of "well" and its redundancy, if this word is used, will quickly become evident.

"Oh" Is the Next Culprit

As someone said once, "If 'Well' doesn't get you, 'Oh' will." And this is true. In everyday speech, people are constantly saying, "Oh, come on," or "Oh, I don't know," along with an inordinate number of other phrases that start with "Oh." Start a half-dozen lines in a story with "Oh" and the reader is usually long gone before the next half-dozen.

Then There Are "Ah" and "Er"

"Ah" and "er" do nothing for dialogue, and while I don't like the use of ellipses in a story, I'd rather see them any day in lieu of an "ah" or an "er." Anything that retards the flow of speech is bad, and these particular words are two of the major culprits.

Combine These Examples for a Very Mushy Rhetorical Stew

It's very common for someone to say, "Oh, well, ah, I guess so." But please don't write it out this way. Instead, if you feel the pause is necessary to express to the reader, write something such as: Joan paused to think about it. "I guess so." Or: Joan hesitated, then said, "I guess so." Or even a simple: Joan paused. "I guess so." This is an instance when a pause is just that, and the halt in the action defines what would have been said via "ah" or "er."

"Hey" Has Only One Use in Dialogue

It's common to see dialogue begin with "Hey." This is another word that's used as often as any to begin everyday speech but should not start a sentence of dialogue unless the character is yelling, "Hey, don't walk out on me!" or "Hey, is Pete down there?" It's not a word to use in standard runs of dialogue such as, "Hey, you know me," or "Hey, you know what I'm saying." (However, if you're writing like Damon Runyon, "Hey, you know me," was a particular character's comical speech pattern, and this is a different issue altogether.)

Phrases Such as "You know" and "I mean" Should Be Avoided

Even when writing slang these phrases should be avoided, as they tend to slow the reader. The best way to view both phrases is in the same way we're admonished when it comes to our personal speech, and this is to eschew their use. It only requires a few times of coming across "you know" or "I mean" before the readability of the story is seriously affected.

"Listen" Is Perhaps the Worst Offender of All

How many times when we're on the phone do we tell someone to "Listen," as if the person isn't already doing that, ha ha? People love to use the word, but it has no place when writing dialogue.

Hear Dialogue Read Aloud to Ferret Out Superfluous Wording

If the person reading the dialogue is hesitating, this usually means the text needs to be revised. I think it's fair to state that the following doesn't read smoothly: "Listen, ah, well, er, I mean, oh, hey, you know?" When one finally gets through that sentence, a question to ask is why would anyone really want to talk like this? Yet people indeed do—and all the time. Just don't write it this way unless it's a one-time line to show a character's nervous behavior.

Dialogue – Interior Attributes That Are Unnecessary

"Dear" and "Honey" Should Lead the Pack

In normal conversation, how often does a person address a significant other by "honey" or "dear"? Of course these words are used often as terms of affection, but are they applied to the beginning of each sentence that's spoken between two people, no matter how much either person cares for the other? Hardly, yet I'm often sent dialogue flush with either word or both.

Sometimes These Words Are Effectively Used for Identification

Skilled writers can use "dear" or "honey" or "love" or other handles of affection to let the reader know who is being spoken to when there are more than two people in the conversation, but it doesn't occur that frequently in most runs of dialogue.

A Paucity of Usage Is All Most Readers Can Tolerate

To illustrate just how overbearing the constant "outpouring of love" can be, I have only to point to THE WINTER OF OUR DISCONTENT, Steinbeck's account of Ethan Hawley's relationship with his wife, Mary, and others. On page one, he begins by referring to Mary as "Miss Mousie," "darling chicken-flower," and "ladybug." On the last page of the penultimate chapter (none of his women are in the finale), Hawley addresses his latest flame, Ellen, as "snookum," and finishes the fusillade with, of all words, the banal "darling."

I always wondered if Steinbeck wrote "darling" at the end to show in a sublime way that constant reference to any element can play on the reader, especially since this tic "supplement" seemed to be designed with such purpose.

A Way To Keep "Dear" and "Honey" at Bay

Collectively, words of affection are perhaps one of the few instances when an author can write from the perspective of volume exactly the way people speak (ignoring Steinbeck's bulbous parodies in the work I just cited). Outside of the bedroom, or if one spouse or the other is trying to impress a house guest, how often is a term such as "dear" or "honey" uttered in the course of a day? There certainly are exceptions, but for effective dialogue authors would be wise to write terms of endearment with the low frequency in which they are spoken in everyday life by most people. And this won't mean we will love our significant other any less.

Dialogue Techniques to Remedy the Overuse of Speaker Attributes

When Two People Are Speaking, Less Is More

It's always crucial to make certain the reader knows who's speaking, but when it is just two people it's not necessary for one to identify the other in every other sentence: "John, it's wonderful to see you again." "Martha, I'm so glad you feel that way." "Why, John, I didn't know you cared about me." "Martha, I care about you a lot."

This reads like something that's made up be comical, but here's the same material without the speaker identification in each line, set up by a simple phrase to begin the segment: Martha sat down next to John and said, "It's wonderful to see you again." "I'm glad you feel the same way." "Why, I didn't know you cared about me." "I care about you a lot" In this, is there any question as to who's speaking once it's identified that Martha began the conversation?

A Character's Actions Can Indicate Who Is Speaking

"Darn, this crate is heavy." As Don pushed the heavy cargo in a cart, his foreman bumped into him as he was coming around a corner, almost knocking him down. "I'm sorry, I didn't see you making that turn." Don smiled at his boss's comment and got a tighter grip on the handles. "I've been doing this for so long, I know what to expect." His boss nodded. "I guess, but I still should've been paying more attention to where I was walking." He looked at his watch and then to Don. "Why don't you stop in my office later today when you have a minute? I might have a new job for you." "Really?" "Yep, I believe your attitude earned you a promotion."

In this material, there's no question about which character is saying what. And as with Martha's sitting next to John and initiating a conversation that doesn't require additional speaker attributes, a character can do common things, such as look at the other person, to indicate who's speaking. Jack glanced at Joe. "You sure we can do this?" His brother shook his head. "Nope." Or something like this: Joe threw his shovel into the dry riverbed. Jack heard the blade grind against a rock. "You don't look none too happy." He glared at him and pushed up his Stetson. "I ain't."

Multiple Speakers Create the Need for Speaker Attributes

When there are three or more people speaking, direct speaker attributes, such as Don said or Martha said, must be used with greater frequency. But if the same two speakers are exclusively involved in an exchange, once they are identified for the reader it's not necessary to treat this as any different from the two of them talking to each other with no one else around. This only changes when another character enters into the dialogue.

Analyze the Way Your Favorite Author Handles Speaker Identification

This is the suggestion I always give in my creative writing workshops. If you like Cormac McCarthy or Nora Roberts or Nelson DeMille or Clive Cussler or James Patterson or Elmore Leonard, grab one of their books and study how a major writer structures speaker attributes and interior monologue so the reader always knows who is who. You will see a lot of good old-fashioned "he said" and "she said," but you'll also notice some masterful skill at adding variety to this most important aspect of writing effectively for what is a most sophisticated audience—you.

Dialogue to Enhance Characterization

It is important to recognize all of the various writing components that can be utilized to develop and enhance characterization. Yet while dialogue is definitely one of these elements, it is often reduced to a lesser status. Here is a typical textbook definition that, via the specific omission of dialogue by name, diminishes this writing medium as a valuable means for crafting characterization:

Characterization is the process of conveying information about characters. Characters are usually presented through their actions, dialect, and thoughts, as well as by description. Characterization can regard a variety of aspects of a character, such as appearance, age, gender, educational level, vocation or occupation, financial status, marital status, social status, cultural background, hobbies, sexual orientation, religious beliefs, ambitions, motivations, personality, etc.

While dialect is mentioned, and this reference certainly indicates the use of dialogue, the insinuation can hardly be described as comprehensive. Perhaps nothing can more adequately place the reader in the mind of a character than the dialogue attributed to that individual. Nor can we learn any more about an environment, whether physical or social, than through reading dialogue.

A Contemporary Novel with 100-Percent Dialogue

For an exercise in excellence in this medium, regardless of how one feels about Stephen King (as a writer, I regard him as a super genius), DOLORES CLAIBORNE is an extraordinary example of the use of dialogue to tell a story. And in this instance the entire text consists of a monologue by Dolores—and without one word of interior monologue or a single adverb attribute.

Reading Suggestions That Demonstrate Outstanding Dialogue

GOD'S LITTLE ACRE, THE SOUND AND THE FURY, RABBIT RUN and TORTILLA FLAT are all classics that contain extraordinary characterizations portrayed through dialogue. For purely contemporary readers, anything by Elmore Leonard will be of benefit; however, GLITZ may be the book to parse first.

Many find creating good dialogue to be the most arduous aspect of their writing. And it is hard to argue that straight dialogue can be inherent with problems. But when a writer considers dialogue as a means of communicating characterization, then the task can be much less daunting and a perfect way to present a story with great depth and definitive focus.

Dialogue to Enhance Pacing

It would be nice to relate that writers seldom have pacing issues. And as any novelist knows, the story's tempo is often—as it should be—on the forefront of an author's mind. But sometimes a story just doesn't seem to be moving along at the right speed.

In the writing workshops I've facilitated over the years, budding authors often asked about ways to better pace their material. One of my suggestions has been to insert dialogue if the scene is flagging. This, of course, isn't always possible or even practical. However, I find this option is available more often than it isn't. And this is another reason why learning to craft effective dialogue is important (read "paramount") to any writer's success.

Dialogue Can Promote "Showing" and Eliminate "Telling"

Another of the greatest benefits of developing dialogue skills is that this element often ameliorates the dreaded "show vs. tell" contention. This is because dialogue automatically creates action, as the characters are speaking. As a by-product, dialogue also encourages the writer to maintain an active voice (and write around potential passive tense; i.e., "have been," "had been," "would've been," etc.).

Reading "Out Loud" What We Write Is Never More Important Than with Dialogue

In discussing dialogue in general, it is critical to understand that we can't write like we talk any more than we can talk like we write. It is the ability to write between the two that makes for quality dialogue. And the best way to determine if the goal has been met, as in all writing, is to read aloud what was written.

And if it sounds bad the initial time we read it, no matter how many more times we traipse through it, the material isn't going to get any better. What will happen by rereading is that we will memorize the lines or the pattern of the dialogue so we can read it more fluently. But the person reading it for the first time is not going to have the author's patience or persistence. Hence, if we stumble the first time we read it, rewrite it!

Steinbeck and Leonard As Models of Great Dialogists

I wrote an article, "Four Authors of Classical Contemporary Literature Defined the Craft of Writing Perfect Prose," and stated that it's hard to dispute Steinbeck's brilliance as a dialogist. In the medium of dialogue, if he is not considered the quintessential classicist, few would dispute that he is certainly near the very top of the craft. However, from a purely contemporary standpoint, many find Elmore Leonard the current standard-bearer, and I find this difficult to argue, as he's one of my favorites as well. Pay attention to the way both these brilliant writers use dialogue to pace their scenes.

Publishers Often Consider a Writer's Dialogue Skills First

As an aside to dialogue as a pacing tool, regardless of whomever and from whichever era a writer chooses to study material, many of today's renowned publishing-house managers have documented that dialogue is often the first aspect of a novelist's ability they consider when contemplating a work for publication. That, in itself, should tell anyone the significance placed on dialogue.

Editing –
The Five Most Common Errors an Editor Sees

I'm often asked about the most common errors an unpublished writer makes. While it might seem hard to answer, I've looked at so much material over the years, regardless of how disparate the narratives might be, there are certain issues that always come to the forefront.

What aren't the Big Five?

I want to provide an answer that will be accurate and make sense, because I'm confident no one is interested in reading about issues related to punctuation, POV shifts, tense, voice, and misplaced modifiers. So here's my perspective of what would prevent a manuscript from being considered prose that only a friend or family member would pay to read.

The Bugbears

If I parsed 100 drafts and totaled what I deemed to be the five most common major flaws that writers must avoid, the list would likely be topped by inadequate conflict, followed by poor pacing, unengaging characters, elliptical transitioning, and weak developmental arcing.

Work to Eliminate The Problem Areas

If a writer can design conflict and present it quickly, this will motivate the reader to keep going. But if the story flags or the characters are uninteresting, no amount of conflict is going to maintain a reader's attention. And if the writing from scene to scene is choppy, or the entrance and exit of characters should be too abrupt, this spells doom for a story. Additionally, if the characters and/or characterizations aren't adequately fleshed out, this will foul a narrative.

Short and to the Point

This article may indeed be brief, but the five issues are anything but quick fixes. A writer needs to parse his or her draft and pay close attention to each aspect of the five areas I've referenced. If one or more or more of the elements I've broached are suspect, a revision will be necessary for the material to be accepted by a quality agent or a bona fide royalty imprint.

Ellipsis Use –
What Is Correct and What Is Not

One of the most misunderstood and therefore misused forms of punctuation is the ellipsis. It's erroneously applied so often that it falls into the same category as the parentheses, which teeters at the top of the bungled punctuation list and is seldom dislodged except by the ellipsis as the chief syntax violator.

First, the Definition of the Ellipsis As It Pertains to Language

Dictionary.com defines an ellipsis as the omission from a sentence or other construction of one or more words that would complete or clarify the construction. The second meaning is a mark or marks such as ------, . . . , or * * * to indicate an omission or suppression of letters or words. (Note the triple em dash as the first mark, which is almost never used today.) I ask, does it say anywhere that an ellipsis indicates a pause? Oh, and the Oxford English Dictionary also references the omission of words—and provides not one additional definition.

Romance-Genre Writers Created Their Own Meaning for the Ellipsis

Seriously, anyone who reads Romances can easily assume that "…" indicates a pause, which is unfortunately a horrible influence on a great many writers who are interested in crafting correct syntax. I'm hardly the one to imply ellipsis misuse does or doesn't have importance, but the mark should be understood so it can be utilized properly if it's a component of a sentence's construction.

Where Does It End?

Here's a sentence of dialogue I pulled from a Romance novel:* "Well, the truth is . . . because you're a. . . a maiden lady." Huh? In reality, these three dots should each signify missing words. But missing what words? Perhaps: "Well, the truth is you're a big, ugly tramp because you're as far a cry as a female brothel owner is from a, a maiden lady." Or should it read this way: "Well, the truth is that you're more than just a pretty face because you're even more special as a, a maiden lady."

* This example is in no way meant to impugn either the author or the publisher of this work; it is solely to illustrate my perception of a grammar issue.

What's Wrong With Allowing the Dialogue To Speak For Itself?

"Well, the truth is, because you're a, a maiden lady," doesn't read a bit different to me from the run with the two ellipses. But if the author felt so compelled to indicate a pause(s), wouldn't interior monologue have been a better choice than the dual ellipses? For example: "Well, truth is." The old doc scratched his ragged whiskers. "Because you are." He stopped again, as if to search for help. "A, a maiden, lady."

Use the Ellipsis to Indicate an Omission, Not a Pause

"She did do it, but she... I just can't tell you the rest," is overstating the point, but it's an instance in which an ellipsis is the correct way to write the passage. An ellipsis denotes missing words, not a pause in the text, regardless of whether it's dialogue or exposition.

When using an ellipsis within a sentence, the acceptable mark consists of three dots. But when the ellipsis ends a sentence, use four dots, letting the final one serve as the period. And, yes, a question mark would be used if the sentence was constructed in the form of a question and an exclamation point if the material was exclaimed.

One Final Remark

If a person looks up "ellipsis" in three-dozen dictionaries, a half-dozen will offer a definition that includes the word "pause." It's my opinion that these references should be construed to imply a pause due to missing words, not a pause in and of itself, regardless of the way this might be worded.

Ending a Story Effectively –
The Value of Setting Up a Storyboard

During writing workshops I'm often told by participants of the difficulties they are having with crafting a suitable ending for their respective novels. When this issue is raised, if the writer hasn't already done so, I always suggest setting up a storyboard.

Just What Is a Storyboard?

A storyboard is a diagram, either simple or complex, that if properly designed will contain a start, a middle, and an end. Consequently, in an of itself, it enables a writer to concentrate on "filling in" each element. But it is also much more, since it provides a template from which to also create developmental arcs for both the characters as well as the scene depictions that are critical to the storyline.

Some people say they can start a project and come up with an ending later. Others say this is bull, and in stronger terms. I don't know what is the correct answer, but I do know many writers, and some quite good ones, who have discontinued a project because of frustration over not being able to "close the deal."

If It's Not Already Determined, a Storyboard Forces a Writer to Consider a Conclusion

A writer can lay out the characters and the plot points via a simple macro format that establishes the major elements. Once the plotlines are established, any degree of layering can be used, from the most basic to something that looks like it was generated by an astrophysicist at NASA. And by its very dynamic, a storyboard motivates the writer to come up with a conclusion.

A Storyboard Can Be As Simple As the Example to Follow and Still Be Quite Effective

Joan meets John. Joan marries John. Joan is miserable. Joan shoots John. Joan escapes to Alaska. Joan changes name to Jenna and marries man who becomes governor. Joan/Jenna is blackmailed by ex-best friend from back home who is aware of her past. Joan/Jenna plots to kill ex-best friend, who was secret lover of husband Joan/Jenna killed and has been planning revenge. Ex-best friend anticipates Joan/Jenna coming after her and sets trap.

If a storyboard is laid out to this point, most people can easily come up with a feasible scenario for an ending. If nothing else, setting up a storyboard can be a sound way of creating a working model with at least the guise of an achievable conclusion. Perhaps not what it will be in its final form, but an ending nonetheless, and a finale that the whole of the narrative can be written toward.

A Book on Screenplay Writing Can Be an Invaluable Aid for Understanding How to Design a Storyboard

Early in my developmental writing workshops I recommend a couple of books on screenwriting that I've found to help writers struggling with an ending for a story. SCREENPLAY by Syd Field is my favorite, followed closely by THE ELEMENTS OF SCREENWRITING by Irwin R. Blacker. Both books have been around a long time and reprinted ad infinitum.

Field's book includes a wide array of diagrams that can help writers with continuity issues. Because when a writer sees his or her plot via a storyboard, it's not only a wonderful source of motivation but a reliable means to keep the narrative on course, as well. And Blacker says, "When the conflict is resolved, the story ends." Perhaps not earth-shattering words at first pass, but within them is the key to solving plot problems for many authors. If Blacker's keen insights are applied, writers will learn ways to effectively enable their stories to reach a satisfying conclusion.

Ending a Story –
Ways to Craft a Solid Finish

A great deal is written about the importance of a strong opening for a novel, and especially if a fantastic hook can be created in the first paragraph or two. And much effort is devoted to the significance of a terrific title. But little time is spent discussing a brilliant ending. Yet doesn't a powerful finish to a story deserve equal attention? There are several options and techniques that respected writers have utilized to leave the reader with a lasting impression of a work.

The Poignant Ending Is Example Number One

Some years ago I was discussing powerful endings for novels with a long-time mentor and friend of mine, Noel King, who I'm sad to say has recently passed away. My erudite friend mentioned that he'd never found anything more dramatic than the ending of A FAREWELL TO ARMS, in which the lieutenant must leave his wife's body as it lay in a hospital bed after she hemorrhaged to death, also losing their unborn child in the process. Hemingway wrote: "It was like saying good-by to a statue. I went out and left the hospital and walked back to the hotel in the rain."

I might also offer the ending of THE FIXER, by Bernard Malamud as an example of an incredibly powerful finish: "Some, as the carriage clattered by and they glimpsed the fixer, were openly weeping, wringing their hands. One thinly bearded man clawed his face. One or two waved at Yakov. Some shouted his name." In THE HUNCH-BACK OF NOTRE DAME, I have never forgotten Hugo's line describing Quasimodo's remains when they were touched: "When an attempt was made to loosen him from the skeleton which he clasped, he crumbled into dust." And I still recall my grief at the ending of Kipling's THE LIGHT THAT FAILED: "Torpenhow knelt under the lee of the camel, with Dick's body in his arms."

Love Conquering All Seems to Be a Certain Path to Success

At the opposite extreme is the Shakespearean approach to his comedies, in which love conquering all is the overriding theme. A Romance writer almost always provides a satisfying ending via the heroine getting her man. Or on occasion vice versa. Along these same lines, a writer of commercial fiction can be relatively comfortable if he or she can craft a story that fulfills the reader's aspirations for the protagonist, regardless of the trials and tribulations along the way.

An Open Thread Is Often a Great Mechanism to Close a Novel

If we think about some of our most widely read contemporary authors, the opportunity at the end of a story to provide the hint for a sequel is never overlooked. James Patterson does this as well as anyone, and a good reason why so many people come back for more of his material. (He has 31 #1 New York Times bestsellers as of this article, which is a record, and not bad for someone who many in the literati deem to be a poor writer.) Thomas Harris did a spectacular job with open threads to end each book in the Hannibal Lector series, especially the finishes that involved the brilliant psychopath's always eluding the authorities. The world of literature is full of stories that begat stories, some of which were flagrantly presaged. Regardless, this is a terrific way to close a novel, but it requires skill so the reader doesn't feel shortchanged.

Which Brings Us to the Denouement

Here is arguably the most common but quite often most difficult type of ending for a lot of writers to pull off well. I often judge the skill of the writer, and hence the quality of the story, by how much the author has to explain at the end for the reader. In some cases, a detailed denouement is indeed necessary to provide the reader with a fuller understanding of some of the less significant but nonetheless still important plot elements. But if handled poorly, a lengthy, multi-leveled denouement can be a sign of either lazy writing or the self-exposure of the limitations of the author.

Select a Closing that Will Make the Reader Remember Your Story

The ability to create a memorable closing brings me to GONE WITH THE WIND, and Scarlett saying: ". . . after all, tomorrow is another day." Here is a book with more than 300,000 words that is filled with the richest of characters and the grandest of characterizations, yet if I asked 100 people who read the book–regardless of how many decades ago–to recite the last line, the majority would be able to do so, or at least come close.

Give the Same Effort to the Ending As to the Opening

Experienced writers are always considering ways to motivate people to read their next book. There is no better method than by providing a satisfying ending to their current work, regardless of the technique that is used. And I'm convinced that notable writers spend as much time on their endings as they do on their openings. It only makes sense.

Exposition Within Dialogue

Write to Advance the Dialogue, Regardless of the Length of the Exchange

Anyone who has read my Newsletters for any period of time has noticed how often I've suggested that writers at all levels should acquire a copy of Browne and King's SELF-EDITING FOR FICTION WRITERS (they owe me a holiday card). One of the exercises they suggest in their "Easy Beats" chapter is to break up a long run of dialogue in THE GREAT GATSBY by inserting exposition at various points. They offer some examples, and for many years I assumed someone moving forward in a chair or scratching a beard or pulling on a chin would be suffice to give a reader the desired "breathing room."

READING LIKE A WRITER, by Francine Prose, Offers Excellent Advice

A wonderful friend of mine gave me a copy of revered academic and outstanding fiction and nonfiction author Francine Prose's READING LIKE A WRITER. One of the many things I took away from her book was that "scratching" and "pulling" and "moving" and "looking around" do not advance a narrative. Exposition within dialogue should be used to a vignette's advantage—and not just as filler.

To illustrate in my feeble way what Ms. Prose is contending, I'm going to write a dialogue exchange both ways; one, as many of us write when we start out; and, two, how the same material can be designed when exposition is written with purpose.

Exposition Written Without Purpose

"Nancy, I can't understand where all the money is going." Frank stared at his coffee cup. "We've been in the hole to the tune of five hundred to a thousand dollars every month since the first of the year. That's six months."

Nancy fiddled with her spoon. "Groceries seem to go up every time I go to the store, and the kid's school expenses are through the roof."

Frank ran his hand through his hair. "I don't know what to do. It looks like we'll have to dip into our savings just to pay our bills."

"Sweetie, we don't have any savings to speak of." She took a deep breath. "Do you think you might ask your dad to help us?"

Frank looked up and faced his wife. "You know how tight he is."

"Maybe if he knows how desperate things are, he might loosen up his purse strings."

"What do you mean, 'how desperate things are?'" He tugged on the collar of his shirt.

Nancy put her hand on her husband's shoulder. "What I mean is, if we don't get our financial situation straightened out soon, I'm going to leave."

"You don't love me anymore?"

"It's got nothing to do with love. I just can't take this any longer."

Exposition Written with Purpose

Frank shuffled the past due notices from one hand to the other and tossed them on the breakfast table. "Nancy, I can't understand where all the money is going. We've been going in the hole to the tune of five hundred to a thousand dollars every month since the first of the year. That's six months."

"Groceries seem to go up every time I go to the store, and the kid's school expenses are through the roof." She picked up the bill from the dentist for their daughter's braces and waved it in her husband's face.

Frank snatched the dentist's bill from her, mad at himself for letting his emotions get the best of him. "I don't know what to do. It looks like we'll have to dip into our savings to get through this."

"Sweetie, we don't have any savings to speak of. Do you think you might ask your dad to help us?"

Frank had already asked his father for help and was refused, something he'd not discussed with his wife. "You know how tight he is."

"Maybe if he knows how desperate things are, he might loosen up his purse strings."

"What do you mean, 'how desperate things are?'"

Nancy put her hand on her husband's shoulder, but her touch was cold. "What I mean is, if we don't get our financial situation straightened out soon, I'm going to leave."

"You don't love me anymore?" She'd threatened to leave him before, but this time even though the words were the same they sounded different.

Nancy jerked her hand away. "It's got nothing to do with love. I just can't take this any longer."

Advancing the Scene Can Add Valuable Character Dimension

I realize that someone can say that all I did was flesh out the vignette, but is that really true? What I did was provide dimension; so, instead of vapid actions, the reader learns particulars about Frank and Nancy's relationship. I'm not into exercises, but just to humor me, how much do you know about this couple by way of the second example that you didn't know via the first? I'm going to guess quite a lot.

A Simple Way to Keep Exposition in Dialogue Exchanges Focused

The easiest method I've found for writing exposition with clout is to create a micro storyboard. In essence, just a few notes that tell what the dialogue exchange is intended to accomplish. In what I just wrote, my desire was for the reader to know that Nancy was in control of their marriage, a marriage that was often on shaky ground, and Frank was incapable of taking charge of the situation any more than he could convince his father to lend a hand. In the first example I provided, how much of this would be evident to the reader?

Writing exposition within dialogue exchanges with purpose will provide a more satisfying reading experience and elevate the writer in the eyes of the reader. This is one aspect of writing that's difficult to argue.

Etymology and Its Importance
When Writing Period Material

Timing Is Indeed Everything

I recently had the pleasure of editing a draft for a longtime client whose storyline took place in the 1600s. I found the plot immensely appealing, and everything was moving along swimmingly for me until I decided I'd better check some words to make certain they were in the lexicon of the period.

"Hooligan" Made Complete Sense

Since the tale involved an English protagonist during the King James Era, I assumed the use of "hooligan" was a nonissue. But a little bird told me to check the word, and I was stunned to learn it evolved in 1898 via a London newspaper article and was attributed to the "lively" Houlihan family (whatever that was supposed to imply).

It Got Worse

My client's protagonist endured many major calamities at sea, one of which left him injured and hallucinating. I was certain that "hallucinating" was a word ascribed to the drug culture or perhaps the morphine days of the 1800s at its furthest stretch. Stunned again. The word developed from Latin—circa 1595—right within the timeline of my writer's story, and therefore perfectly acceptable.

"Fellow" Was a Given, But "Guy" Really Threw Me

"Fellow" originated around 1050 or before. And since most everyone has heard of Robin Goodfellow from Shakespeare's AMND, it's fair to assume that "fellow" was certainly around in the 1600s. But do many people know that its counterpart "guy" wasn't in use as a name for a person until the early 1800s, and spawned by the enactment of Guy Fawkes Day as a national holiday in Great Britain?

What Makes the Word "Guy" Confusing Is Twofold

Here's what I found fascinating about "guy." The actual "Guy Fawkes" event, in which this man and his co-conspirators tried to blow up Parliament, occurred in 1605, but the word was not coined in the U.K. until the early 1800s. And then it meant "a weird person." In the U.S. at that time, few people knew of Guy Fawkes or his "Day," and in the 1900s "guy" became what it is today, another name for "fellow."

But to compound the problem of determining the correct chronology for "guy," the word was originally coined in the mid 1300s to refer to a guide rope or apparatus used to steady something. Ever heard the phrase "throw me a guy line"? I used to think someone misspoke, really wanting to say "guide line." Regardless, both are correct, but the issue with "guy" is that it was a word in the 1600s, just not one that referred to a "fellow." Tell me that's not a pistol with a barrel protruding from the bottom for someone simply trying to write a good story without getting shot in the foot.

It's Impossible to Look Up Every Word

If someone is writing material involving a contemporary setting, other than the most recent slang—which nobody cares about anyhow and is best to avoid—all words are in play. However, words in existence at the time of the story I've referenced become a problem if analogous for example to Elizabethan-era vernacular depicting Victorian-era culture. I doubt many word historians would get too bent out of shape in most instances about a decade or two of unintended "crossover," but 250 years is a legitimate issue.

Fiction Writing Techniques Defined in Literary Classics – Reading Program Designed to Improve Skills

This is a reading list for my Intermediate Workshop Series I facilitated that was sponsored by the Palm Beach County Library System. And the last time I provided these suggestions for a workshop group, it was spread over 15 months. With an eye toward balancing the word count in a reasonable manner, I segregated the material into three sections (hence, five months to complete each section). Obviously, the important issue is to read and learn from the material, not the time frame associated with accomplishing this.

If a serious writer will read (or reread) these novels, I don't think it would be immodest to state that this person's writing can only become more proficient. So, to good reading and better writing, here is the list, along with a brief explanation of the purpose and rationale behind suggesting this material.

PURPOSE

Reading from these selected works will provide the background necessary for understanding the nuances of form and structure.

READING RATIONALE

One of the most daunting problems with any structured reading program is currency. For this reason, every selection in the following group is contemporary, in that none of the material was published prior to the 20th century. Although not limited to these, selections will encompass treatments related to Style Nuance, Story Threads, Pacing Elements, Theme-Development Techniques, Dialogue Cant, Paragraph Style, Chapter Patterning, and Punctuation Subtleties.

"First 5-Month Reading Program"

Group 1 - Read one from group

1) A CURTAIN OF GREEN, by Eudora Welty. Seventeen short stories, some of which will stand your hair on edge. Not horror, but what I refer to as pure noir writing even though it doesn't fit the traditional bleak-and-present-danger definition. Ms. Welty won a Pulitzer Prize and about every other award one can win for literary achievement.

2) SHIP OF FOOLS, by Katherine Anne Porter. Another Pulitzer Prize Winner. A deep story that exposes human frailty amongst a host of other things.

3) AN AMERICAN TRAGEDY, by Theodore Dreiser. Since I am from Indiana, I had to select one Hoosier writer. Just kidding. Mr. Dreiser's story is a treatment of what happens when there is a hole in the social fabric.

Group 2 - Read one from group

1) GOD'S LITTLE ACRE, by Erskine Caldwell. The book is one of the all-time bestsellers. In his lifetime, Mr. Caldwell's books exceeded 80 million in sales. This story illustrates cant and how dialogue develops depth of characterization.

2) THEIR EYES WERE WATCHING GOD, by Zora Neale Hurston. Oprah made her famous, but a member of the literati rediscovered her much earlier, sadly, well after Ms. Hurston's death. Many feel that the novel begins with one of the most brilliant opening paragraphs ever written. She also wrote a metaphor for the ages, which I won't describe in the hope you will read the book. Again, this is a treatment of how cant in dialogue creates characters we remember forever.

Group 3 - Read one from group

1) GLITZ, by Elmore Leonard. Known as much for his skill at pacing as for his dialogue, this is my favorite of his works from the perspective of the storyline; liking it so much that I've read it three times.

2) THE DA VINCI CODE, by Dan Brown. The best-selling single novel of all time. And for those who have enjoyed finding fault with it, I have not heard anyone disparage its pacing. As one might have surmised, this group of stories is about pacing.

3) ANNE OF GREEN GABLES, by Lucy Maud Montgomery. Perhaps thought to be a weird placement with the other works in this group, yet with a child's short attention span nothing exemplifies the need for great pacing than when writing in the Children's genre.

Group 4 - Read one from group

LONESOME DOVE, by Larry McMurtry. He won a Pulitzer for this work, and it is an example of fluent prose writing at its best. Also not a half-bad story, ha ha.

THE POISONWOOD BIBLE, by Barbara Kingsolver. One of my all-time favorites. A "layered" story with a fabulous history lesson as a by-product.

THE THORN BIRDS, by Colleen McCullough. Another book that is an example of fluent prose writing at its very finest.

Each of these novels demonstrates what the phrase "writing re-demptive characters" means.

"Second 5-Month Reading Program"

Group 5 - Read one from group

ONE HUNDRED YEARS OF SOLITUDE, by Gabriel Garcia Marquez. A story that traces many generations of a family from its beginning until its ultimate demise. Mr. Marquez won a Nobel Prize, in large measure for this work.

THE FORSYTHE SAGA, by John Galsworthy. Another Nobel Prize winner. A multilayered treatment of a complex family tree, along with the perfect illustration of creating conflict between the lead characters.

Group 6 - Read one from group

USA, by John Dos Passos. A novel in trilogy form that at first pass is a history lesson which details the Socialist movement in America after WWI and beyond the Great Depression. But it is much more of a literary treatment than a historical novel. The format for inserting material so the reader can sense the cultural perspectives of an era was unique to anything I had read until RAGTIME.

RAGTIME, by E.L. Doctorow. Multiple inserts on the order of USA, but all of the threads are carried throughout the book, making it impossible not to become fully invested with the various characters.

Group 7 - Read one from group

THE CONFESSION OF NAT TURNER, by William Styron. Another Pulitzer Prize Winner. I've discussed this novel in our workshops because the entire work is written in backstory (or flashback, if you prefer), demonstrating that it can be done.

THE COLOR PURPLE, by Alice Walker. Still another Pulitzer Prize recipient. This work is presented in its entirety in epistolary form, meaning a series of letters, and is another exceptional example of stylistic variation.

DOLORES CLAIBORNE, by Stephen King. I'm presenting this book to demonstrate Mr. King's skill at writing dialogue. This book is 90,000 words of pure monologue—without one adverb attribute. In my opinion, this is the quintessential example of characterization developed via dialogue, and for this reason it's well worth studying.

Group 8 - Read one from group

TO THE LIGHTHOUSE, by Virginia Woolf. Once it's recognized that this is stream-of-consciousness writing, it is not as difficult to understand or accept as a style. Some believe this technique enables a writer to become more creative.

THE SOUND AND THE FURY, by William Faulkner. Should you choose to read the novel, read it from the beginning with a Norton's Criticism to develop a better understand how Faulkner uses Benji to expand the stream-of-consciousness concept.

"Third 5-Month Reading Program"

Group 9 - Read one from group

HOT SPRINGS, by Stephen Hunter. Great tale, in my opinion, by a very skilled writer. Big change of pace from the recent material. Again, pay particular attention to the pacing.

CONDOMINIUM, by John D. MacDonald. He's famous for the Travis McGee series, and if you should choose to read this book you will be rewarded with a lot of fabric that is easy to read, again demonstrating the value of writing prose in a fluent manner.

Group 10 - Read both

THE BLACKBOARD JUNGLE, by Evan Hunter. Hugely popular story that is important because of the visceral nature of the writing and the surprise ending.

KISS, by Ed McBain. Ed McBain is the pen name under which Evan Hunter writes his 87th Precinct novels. The purpose of each of these suggestions is to detect the subtleties in the style of both novels written for different genres by the same author.

Group 11 - Read one from group

THE JOY LUCK CLUB, by Amy Tan. The story and the writing illustrate ways to present a foreign culture through the eyes of several characters.

THE RIVER SUTRA, by Gita Mehta. Another instance of bringing the reader into another culture.

THE GOOD EARTH, By Pearl Buck. She did not win a Nobel Prize for nothing. For anyone who's never read this story, it's not the Pollyanna that might be assumed by the title. An incredible work of art expressing some harsh aspects of Chinese society, and that there can be children in any culture who do not respect what their parents have had to endure to provide a better life.

Group 12 - Read all three

THE STRANGER, by Albert Camus.

THE VICTIM, by Saul Bellow

STEPPENWOLF, by Hermann Hesse

What I find so exceptional about these novels is that this is the same storyline treated in a different way by three people who have each won a Noble Prize for Literature. See how this triumvirate of brilliant writers handled the identical theme.

Group 13 - Read one from group

BEACH MUSIC, by Pat Conroy. If you can stomach a dysfunctional family at its worst, this story brings out some of the best writing anyone could ask for. Just don't expect a warm fuzzy feeling when you finish it. But the characterizations are spectacular, and you'll learn something from reading this book.

BREATHING LESSONS, by Anne Tyler. Again, a Pulitzer winner, but this time a story without a redemptive character, proving once more that someone can write against the grain and be successful. The importance of this book is its brutal honesty.

A THOUSAND ACRES, by Jane Smiley. Another Pulitzer Prize winner. Conflict expressed at its dramatic best. The easiest of the three books in this group to read. And I wish I had Ms. Smiley for a neighbor.

Fleshing Out a Character in a Novel

One of the first remarks many writers hear from an agent, editor, or publisher is the need to flesh out certain characters. Most of the time the request is easy enough to understand, but there is often a great deal of confusion about the best way to accomplish this.

A Textbook Definition of Characterization

Characterization is the process of conveying information about characters. Characters are usually presented through their actions, dialect, and thoughts, as well as by description. Characterization can regard a variety of aspects of a character, such as appearance, age, gender, educational level, vocation or occupation, financial status, marital status, social status, cultural background, hobbies, sexual orientation, religious beliefs, ambitions, motivations, personality, etc.

Yes, Characterization Covers a Lot of Ground

As everyone recognizes from the scope of the list, characterization is a broad platform. And this in itself is why fleshing out a character can be viewed as a daunting process. But the task should be considered part and parcel to the integrity of any character written into a storyline. So what is the best way to do this?

Two Choices Are Available—the Burst or the Subtle Presentation of Information

There is no way to reasonably imply that a sudden burst of information is not a good idea, since this is one of the few methods by which a peripheral character can be presented to a reader. Consequently, upon a secondary character's introduction, a few sentences that provide detail are often all that's necessary. Here is an example:

Akeem Walker had attended college on a basketball scholarship but was cut from the team. The coach cited his lack of height, since he was 5-feet-11-inches tall. But with his exceptional athletic skills, and bulldog-like build and demeanor to match, his family wasn't buying it. They thought drugs were involved, since Akeem exhibited wide mood swings whenever he came home. Three divorces in ten years hadn't assuaged their opinions, which were supported by his frequent run-ins with the law, most stemming from his use of narcotics. But now the game had changed, since he'd been charged with possession of heroine with intent to distribute and jailed five blocks from where he'd grown up in the Bronx.

The reader now knows quite a bit about Akeem, and anything else can be expressed by his actions if he should resurface in the story.

Fleshing Out a Major Character Is Often an Ongoing Process

It seldom seems to work when an author tells the reader everything about a major character at one time, since the character's actions then have to constantly exceed what was depicted if the reader is going to maintain interest. Here are examples of material that could be provided along the way to help flesh out a significant character:

1) Not even panting hard, John placed the 350-pound barbell back in the support. 2) He carried his young baby as if she were a carton of eggs, and he smiled at his wife and kissed her cheek, careful not to smudge her makeup. 3) John once again looked at his watch and

swore. He was never late. 4) John glanced in disgust at his dress-shirt's frayed cuff. 5) John kicked the side of his stalled car, which he'd wanted to replace, but with another new baby his money was…. 6) John adjusted the sight on the rifle and pressed the trigger with the same control he maintained when caressing his child. 7) Now John could have the things he had always wanted.

Each step of the way the reader learns something new about John. He is strong, loves his wife and daughter, is fastidious, is financially strapped, has a temper but can stay under control when he has to, his family is keeping him from meeting his perceived needs, and he's willing to resort to crime to get what he wants. Developmental arcing that builds as the story unfolds is the key to creating strong characterizations which satisfy the reader.

The Boundaries Are Limitless

Some people contend that readers can indeed learn too much about a character, but for those of us who like in-depth writing on the order of Jody Picoult's, we don't find this to be the case. The more we learn, the better. But, then again, we're seeking detail in a writer of this style of work. The same is true if we read a Pat Conroy novel. And while Mr. Conroy enables the reader to learn about his characters more often through actions and dialogue rather than interior monologue, both of these remarkable writers provide an exceptional experience, albeit with different techniques.

Use What Works Best

Most writers know their strong suits (as well their limitations, whether they choose to admit them or not), and it's important to craft stories by utilizing what works to the plot's—and therefore the author's—greatest advantage. And for most everyone's work, this involves analyzing the degree to which the characters are presented to the reader. This is what is meant by character dimension.

At different points in a narrative, it never hurts to ask, "How much does the reader really know about John or Mary or Lee or Maria?" Then, should it be thought that more information would be beneficial, it's simply a matter of going back, or moving forward, and fleshing out the character(s) via what's considered the most effective technique for each situation.

Fleshing Out a Scene in a Novel

This a companion piece to the material I'd recently written on techniques for fleshing out a character. And while certain components are the same, many techniques for crafting fuller scenes are quite different.

Consider Fitzgerald's Technique of Loading Up the Start of the Narrative

In creating a lasting scene for the reader, it can and often requires a substantial setup. Literature's greatest writers have earned their reputations by possessing this ability. In my opinion no one was better at crafting an opening scene that was strong enough to carry an entire story than Fitzgerald. For me, the start of TENDER IS THE NIGHT is as good as it gets. I have never forgotten Fitzgerald's description of the cupolas atop the old villas along the beach, which he likened to rotting water lilies.

Then he spends a couple of hundred words on other physical scenery and people who inhabited this area on the French Riviera, before settling on a mother and daughter—the point when the real magic begins. Readers already feel they know Rosemary Hoyt even though she's just been introduced. This is what fleshing out a scene is all about, because soon afterward the reader has no problem accepting everything about Dick and Nicole Diver, since they enter the story as homogeneous plot elements.

Hemingway Used a Paucity of Words to Say a Great Deal

Hemingway used what some describe as terse writing, yet he was able to craft such skillful exposition that his narrative style won him both a Pulitzer and Nobel Prize for Literature. His short stories are wonderfully emblematic of his skill. THE SNOWS OF KILIMANJARO is a perfect tale to study, since the physical scenery is the story, which starts with a page of dialogue broken only by a brief description of some birds that are referred to as filthy. The single word "filthy," which the reader learns is a metaphor having nothing to do with unsanitary conditions, sets the scene, and ultimately the mood, for the entire piece.

Scene Development and the Physical Setting

Everyone has a favorite writer for one reason or another. If a person likes tremendous depth in both characters and the scenes that surround them, Jody Picoult, Pat Conroy, and Barbara Kingsolver come to mind for many of us. But for pure scene creation, I'm going to suggest someone who is not often considered these days, and this is Emile Zola. Read NANA but forget about the protagonist and just focus on how Zola sets up his story from the perspective of the physical environment. The streets, the shops, the weather, the attitudes of the people; each element creates a powerful image as the story moves along.

It's Solely a Matter of Imagination, Since Fleshing Out a Scene Can Take Any Direction

Fleshing out a scene might require the description of a village, the interior of a building, the heavy perfume people are wearing at a Broadway opening, a little boy's tattered clothing, the street argot a gang of ruffians is using, an old man's gait, the sounds of the night, the heat of the day, the cars on the street, the commotion in a mall during a holiday, a somber-sounding wind, the bitter cold, a baby crying incessantly, a roar from inside a stadium, a cacophony of explosions from afar, the musings of a philosopher sitting on a park bench, the attitudes of the townspeople after an election, the poor design of an intersection, a pastor's avuncular disposition, the lawlessness of the inhabitants in a border town, the joyous atmosphere at a wedding reception—ad infinitum.

Fleshing Out a Scene Is As Much About Tempo As Anything

The most important thing to take away from this article is that the opening scene can set the mood for the entire story. And if a writer will read some of the material I suggested in this article, this will enable a solid understanding of the different options that are available to maintain or advance the desired characterizations along the way.

Gerunds and Gerund Phrases Defined

First, what is a gerund? Dictionaries seem to also use this brown-paper-bag definition, so I'll stick with it as well. In the simplest of explanations, it's a verb that functions as a noun.

Gerunds Are Generally Easy to Spot

They always end in "-ing." This is one of the few rules in all of English that's absolute. And most often they are found at the beginning of a sentence, but this isn't always the case, so this is far from definitive. [To be clear on the "-ing" statement, many components of common syntax can qualify as gerund phrases in one way or another and don't have an "-ing" in them. For a comprehensive look at this, I suggest studying pages 24 through 47 in A HANDBOOK OF ENGLISH GRAMMAR by R.W. Zandvoort. Anyone who parses this material will notice that Professor Zandvoort fits a seemingly inordinate number of clauses into a plethora of gerund categories. But for the purpose of my short paper on the topic, I'm referring to the gerund bearing "- ing" that begins a sentence and not the gerund phrase. Hence, in my definition all gerunds do indeed end in "-ing."]

Here Are Some Examples of Gerunds

1) Dribbling helps a basketball player develop good hand/eye coordination. "Dribbling" in this instance functions as a noun and is the subject of the sentence. 2) Running is great exercise. "Running" is considered as an event in and of itself and therefore takes the form of a noun, just as the dictionary definition indicates it would.

What About Gerund Phrases?

These can be a little trickier to isolate at times, but if we take the first two examples that follow and reduce them to their respective "gerund denominator," it becomes a less-daunting exercise. 1) Dribbling fast and switching hands helps a basketball player develop hand/eye coordination. "Dribbling fast and switching hands" is a phrase that serves as the name of an activity, albeit a compound one, while still performing the role of a noun. 2) Running long distances can be good for your heart. In this sentence, "Running long distances" is looked at as an event unto itself and therefore accepts the role of a noun.

Gerunds Aren't As Uncommon As They Might Seem

Close readers will notice that much current material contains gerunds in the possessive form because of the word "being" within the construction of each respective sentence in which this element occurred. And in many quarters it's considered desirable to incorporate "being" in a gerund phrase, but it must be accepted that this isn't always possible.

Revise the Sentence Without "Being" and the Possessive Gerund No Longer Exists

Take this grammatically incorrect sentence that many people, including yours truly, think sounds just fine: "It was because of Richard being held by the police." This should be written: "It was because of Richard's being held by the police." But the latter construction is awkward, so it's perhaps best to revise this to read: "It was because Richard was held by the police." In this syntax, the gerund phrase is eliminated and word impropriety becomes a non-issue.

Then there's "him" and "his" that also fall into the gerund arena. Here is the wrong construction: "I'm not happy with him dating my daughter." This can be repaired by substituting "his" for "him," thus: "I'm not happy with his dating my daughter." ("His" of course is possessive.) One might argue that "him" reads better, and the best way to fix this once and for all is to write: "I'm not happy that he's dating my daughter.

Gerunds Have Fostered Considerable Debate

I realize that the latter half of this article became quite complicated, but for practical purposes the first two subsets in this paper contain the information that's most necessary to digest. However, for any-one who's ultra inquisitive, when gerunds are used incorrectly they create what grammarians call a "fused participle," and there are two well-documented disparate schools of thought from bastions of the King's English. On one side there's the iconic H.W. Fowler, and the other position is championed by C.T. Onions (yeap, that was his name, and he's quite famous in grammar circles) and Otto Jespersen.

I gets down to which syntax has been "influenced" the most to the point of acceptance. As indicated by this article, my contention is that if text becomes too complicated or cumbersome to read, it's best to revise it and avoid the gerund issue altogether, especially in the possessive form.

Interior Monologue –
What It Means and How to Use It Effectively

A correct definition of interior monologue is the presentation of a character's immediate thoughts expressed in first person. Different techniques can be used to accomplish this, but regardless of the method used to convey a "thought," the idea is conceptually the same.

Stream-of-Consciousness Writing

The first and most obvious way to design interior monologue is via stream-of-consciousness writing set off by italics, and for readers who can be patient enough to parse material to develop an appreciation for the genius of the writer, Faulkner is in my opinion the undisputed master at utilizing italics. Yes, at times it can be a major brain drain to work through his narratives, but once the jigsaw puzzle is assembled it's often a masterpiece to behold.

I've decided that the most effective way to describe creating stream-of-consciousness from a stylistic perspective is to write out the character's thoughts as if the person has Tourette's syndrome, and I in no way mean this indelicately related to anyone afflicted with this malady. But a primary premise of the disease is that a person "speaks" what is on his or her mind without couching anything, and this compares favorably with my definition for SOC. Here's a run of SOC material integrated within a dialogue exchange:

"Harold, you always say the nicest things *you've never told me the truth about anything in your whole damn life*. Honey, I don't know when I've ever felt closer to you *I'd divorce your lazy ass in a minute if we didn't have the kids*. You want to take in a show tonight? *You cheap bastard, you wouldn't think of taking me out for a nice dinner. You are lower than pond scum* I'm so happy to be married to you."

The Simple "He Thought" or "She Thought"

The next technique follows along the lines of Virginia Woolf, who simply tells the reader that the character's "thoughts" are forthcoming and then provides the lines in the same font. Hers is a simple technique, and it works fine for me except when the point-of-view has been clearly established. In these instances, the use of "he or she thought" is superfluous, and my suggestion would be to write the desired narrative in italics without any form of attribute.

Virginia Woolf Is Exemplary for Analyzing the "Thought" Technique

Here are two brief runs from TO THE LIGHTHOUSE that illustrate Ms. Woolf's technique: "It was like that then, the island, thought Cam, once more drawing her fingers through the waves." This wouldn't seem significant or even different from normal exposition if not for the material in the preceding chapter in which this line appears: "(The sea, without a stain on it, thought Lily Briscoe . . . .)" The advantage of this style is obvious, as it allows the writer to switch points-of-view without confusing the reader. [Please note that the parentheses were part of the original text, and I wanted to remain true to it, but this punctuation has nothing to do with interior monologue.]

The Colon with Italics to Set Off Interior Monologue

The use of a colon and italics to set up interior monologue was used throughout GONE GIRL. However, the italics in my opinion makes the colon excessive, as what follows is clearly in John's POV and there--fore automatically in his thoughts.

Example one: John thought: *I haven't been that obvious, have I?*

Example two: John thought: I haven't been that obvious, have I?

My contention is that the second example is adequate; or, as with Ms. Woolf, a writer can simply set up a vignette with "he or she thought" and write for hours without again alluding to the text as "thoughts." But this type of writing is very hard to pull off, even by some of today's most acclaimed authors.

Care Should Be Taken With Interior Monologue, But Its Correct Use Can Be Golden

So if a writer is going to venture into interior monologue as a technique, it's probably a good idea to tread lightly, offering only an occasional snippet in italics to bring the reader into the mind of a character. Or, as Barbara Kingsolver has said--and I believe she has forgotten more about writing than I will ever know--don't write interior monologue at all.

However, it's been said that the primary reason people continue to read is because literature is the only medium which truly allows entry into—and therefore an understanding of—the minds of the characters. So whether an aficionado of Faulkner or Woolf, the main desire for a reader engaging their narratives is often predicated on how expansively these writers, in their own brilliant ways, expressed their characters' innermost feelings.

And, at the hands of an adept writer, what better way is there to accomplish this than via interior monologue?

Literature Written by These Four Authors Defined the Craft of Writing Perfect Prose

From academicians to book critics to lay readers, each is often eager to recommend a list of authors who will provide aspiring writers with a sound foundation from which to build. Any suggestions should be revered, but it would be ridiculous for one person to state that her/his idea of quality prose is better than another's.

However, there are four aspects of the craft of writing that many who understand literature would argue have never been better addressed: Steinbeck's perfection with dialogue, Faulkner's depth of characterization, Hemingway's precise narrative style, and Fitzgerald's palpable creation of mood.

Steinbeck's Brilliance As a Dialogist

One of the quickest ways to appreciate John Steinbeck's brilliance in the realm of dialogue is to read TORTILLA FLAT, THE WINTER OF OUR DISCONTENT, and OF MICE AND MEN. Accents are often hard to maintain in a novel without eventually grating on the reader, yet Steinbeck's last line of dialogue in TORTILLA FLAT is as fresh as his first. THE WINTER OF OUR DISCONTENT provides a perfect medium for demonstrating his range. And it is then a simple step to OF MICE AND MEN to gain an understanding of Steinbeck's genius in the art of writing divergent dialogue at an extraordinary level.

Faulkner's Genius with Characterizations

The mere mention of William Faulkner can cause many to quail. But a lot of Faulkner aficionados, of which I am included in this group, feel he is unchallenged in the realm of characterization. Many erudite souls recommend ABSALOM, ABSALOM as an ideal example of why Faulkner rules the world of characterization, and one needs to read only the first paragraph in the initial chapter to realize the reason for this praise. Another suggestion is that serious writers read THE SOUND AND THE FURY. The characterization of Dilsey the maid is, in my opinion, a masterpiece.

Hemingway's Impeccable Pitch

With simple words, Hemingway's narratives are so powerful and his depictions so poignant that he is credited with creating a unique style. An efficient way to experience his skill is to read THE OLD MAN AND THE SEA. What is often overlooked about Hemingway's crisp, concise style is the quality of pitch his technique provides. His passages of perfect pitch in themselves can be important to analyze by anyone desiring to become a better writer.

Fitzgerald's Mastery of Mood

Mood, like voice, is one of those magical areas that is easy to recognize but impossible to define with much accuracy. But whatever mood happens to be, it can be experienced in the works of F. Scott Fitzgerald. In THE GREAT GATSBY, THIS SIDE OF PARADISE and TENDER IS THE NIGHT, there is an unmistakable mood that is so sentient the reader easily and pleasantly becomes enveloped by it. In just the opening paragraph of TENDER IS THE NIGHT, the mood for the entirety of a story is set in place. Whatever Fitzgerald's voice was, he found it. And whatever mood is, he created it with exceptional flair.

There are numerous other writing elements, and subcategories of each, that anyone serious about becoming a novelist must consider. But for those who desire an understanding of what many regard as the four pillars necessary for developing proficiency at writing quality prose, especially if the interest is to have a book signed by a major royalty publisher, it is difficult to argue against studying the distinctions of dialogue, characterizations, narrative pitch, and mood established by Steinbeck, Faulkner, Hemingway, and Fitzgerald, respectively.

Metaphor Use to Enhance a Narrative

When discussing metaphors, which simply implies that something is written that has another connotation, I can't help but think of Joseph Conrad and his depiction of James Waite's character in THE NIGGER OF THE NARCISSUS. Waite was crafted as a homonym for "weight," and the name in and of itself expresses a deep and lasting metaphor, as this has long been associated with the "white man's burden" as felt by the English. And the constant banter of the ship's crew is considered by many academicians as a reflection of mankind "as a whole." Heady stuff, indeed.

And Then There's Moby

Melville has always been one of my favorite and least favorite writers. I loved BILLY BUDD but I absolutely loathed MOBY-DICK (and still do), and I always felt that Hemingway wrote THE OLD MAN AND THE SEA to show the world the way MOBY-DICK should have been written (which is a topic for another time). However, by Melville's own design, the whale is emblematic of God and therefore a perfect example of a metaphor that also serves as an allegory.

When Metaphor Is Undeniably Allegorical

Faulkner's A FABLE, for which he won both a Pulitzer Prize and a National Book Award, is the perfect allegory, since in this brilliant narrative a father sacrifices his son for the greater good. However, any metaphor with a spiritual or religious meaning can be classified as an allegory, and it doesn't need to involve the prime tenet of Christianity to qualify.

A Metaphor Does Not Have to Incorporate the Entire Story

A single passage can contain a s, and this is what we find more often than an entire narrative having broader ramifications. "The tractor-trailer lay upside down and crumpled in two, its engine some- how still running but rasping intermittently, and with tires facing the sky as fuel spewed from its ruptured tanks, coating the roadway," is an obvious comparison to an animal that's severely injured and bleeding to death, but this might have no implication whatsoever to the overall meaning of the story.

Metaphors Sometimes Occur Naturally

I've never been of the opinion that every writer sets out to write a metaphor. Often, some literary pundit will assign "metaphor status" to a section of a work and the writer is canonized, yet the metaphor was never a part of the author's planned creative process. I've talked to many authors who have received accolades for metaphors they never knew they had created as such. However, whether a metaphor was by design or developed by happenstance, if it indeed fits a scene or a storyline, achieving this is often emblematic of a quite accomplished writer, and the importance of this literary skill set should neither be diminished nor dismissed.

Metaphor vs. Unacceptable Exaggeration

I remember the first partial manuscript of mine an agent requested, 20 or so years ago, and how destroyed I was when it was sent back full of remarks written in red pencil. (Yes, in those days some agents would routinely edit a few pages and return them, along with their comments. This still happens today, but very rarely.) The predominant complaint this agent had with my writing was that many of the things I assigned to my characters were not humanly possible.

It Began With "I Held My Heart in My Hand"

I don't know where I came up with this goofy phrase. I probably heard somebody say it and thought it accurately expressed a person's deepest emotions. Regardless, it was pointed out that a person couldn't hold his or her own heart unless this occurred after a heart transplant. I know, dumb but true.

Can a Jaw Really Drop to the Floor?

If a person got knocked down or fell down, his or her jaw could of course drop to the floor. But standing and becoming in awe of something wouldn't allow this to occur unless this was written around an animated character with no physical limitations.

What About Idiom?

We've all read something to the effect that a character's ability to anticipate danger approaching from behind was so uncanny that the person must have had "eyes in the back of his head." Of course no one can have eyes in the back of his head, but here's where idiom bears its complex face and deems this allowable. And carrying equal weight with idiom, "must have" is what will save this from being deleted by an editor, since these words imply a logical conclusion. I know, it's insanely complicated.

"Save Grace" Sparingly

Phrases with antecedent modifiers, such as "It felt as if my jaw had fallen to the ground," and "It was as though I were carrying a ton of bricks on my back," are perfectly acceptable once in a while. And this means once in a great while. As soon as I read a couple of phrases in a client's draft like these I just referenced, I delete the rest.

How Much Is Too Much?

My rule is two per 100,000 words, and I'm dead serious, or at least as serious as I can be about anything in the complex world of writing material people will pay to read, because these phrases in and of themselves can become a tic in a hurry. Should a writer receive a rejection from an agent or publisher with the word "overwritten" in it somewhere, the sorts of phrases I alluded to can often be the justification for the comment.

This Sometimes Goes Too Far

I remember reading that a person couldn't walk through the trees, as technically this was impossible. Come on. The same with someone walking through or into a house. Only The Hulk or some such creature could walk through a house, and anyone walking into a house would likely have a bloody nose and skinned knuckles. But we all know what walking through or into a house means, and I believe a modicum of common sense needs to prevail—lest very few things could happen as described.

For example, "The car turned into the driveway" isn't possible unless by some automated assistance or the steering wheel's being locked in place. Yet we all know the car is being driven by someone. Likewise, do car lights coming towards something require clarification that they're attached to a vehicle that's in turn being driven? I remember Fitzgerald's line about a car's lights weaving their way through the fog in THIS SIDE OF PARADISE. It remains part of one of the greatest descriptive vignettes I've ever read, and I'm so happy Charles Scribner wasn't a stickler for "absolutism" in this instance (or throughout the whole book, for that matter, ha ha).

"Correctness" Can Lead to Some Very Boring Text

Isn't John's "pulling his car in the driveway" implying that he's physically towing it in some way? And that the car is being pulled right into whatever the driveway is made of? The distinction between what's allowable and that which isn't is often quite blurred. My advice is to stick with what makes sense, without tincturing the phrase to make it acceptable. And ignore the ridiculous pedants; however, during the past few years I have found my characters walking through doorways more often than into houses, and this is probably not a bad idea.

Metaphors Created Unintentionally

It always amazes me when I read the way academia has canonized a writer by alluding to the incredible depth of the person's writing, claiming that so much of this author's prose contained brilliant metaphors describing some "condition" pertaining to that era, and especially something with political import.

Dante and Voltaire

It's impossible to argue that Alighieri's INFERNO is not a scathing rebuke of the Medici family and their long and widespread oppression of the Italian populace. Likewise, CANDIDE is a striking example of using prose to ridicule religion and just about everything else in a society the author believed had gone wildly off kilter.

Hugo and Hawthorne

Hugo's characterizations of cultural hypocrisy in both THE HUNCH-BACK OF NOTRE DAME and LES MISERABLES are exceptionally depicted. And I place THE SCARLET LETTER not too far below either of Hugo's lofty ascensions. But the pier becomes shaky, in my opinion, when one travels to Melville.

Melville

The academic community seems to have taken every line of the whale's story and made it sacred, with the animal possessing Godlike implications in everything it did. I never found this to be the case, and I parsed the story very carefully (much of it several times). And while BILLY BUDD is the obvious metaphoric allegory, how much beyond Billy's sacrifice for the common good does the tale really go?

Thackeray and Porter

Perhaps no two authors wrote more obvious metaphorical material than Thackeray with VANITY FAIR and Katherine Anne Porter with SHIP OF FOOLS, as the titles themselves clearly express the nature of each story. However, in parsing the other works I just mentioned, is it reasonable to believe that each line, vignette, or scene credited as a metaphor was really written by each of these great authors with that intention? I hardly believe this.

I've often extolled Joseph Conrad's virtues, as I'm of the opinion he's in a class by himself at writing similes that work. And he's not far behind the best when it comes to metaphors, as well. In analyzing THE NIGGER OF THE NARCISSUS, I recently discussed James Waite's name as oft-heralded at being synonymous with "the white man's burden." And I also mentioned the academic view of the ship's crew's constant chattering as indicative of society's bemoaning social issues. For me, the crew was simply mumbling about Waite's fate, and not a mote more was on Mr. Conrad's mind when he wrote the line.

Academicians Seem Eager to Jump the Gun

Many people who study literature are quick to look for anything possible to assign metaphor status. I'm of the opinion that many writers aren't considering metaphors as a conscious component of their narratives, and what occurs is often the by-product of an academician's active mind during analysis of the text. For this reason, it's my contention that metaphors often occur accidentally. And this is uncontested, because what author doesn't want to accept credit for something considered clever, whether or not it was intentional?

Narrative Fluff – Avoid Unnecessary Information

Editors routinely discuss transitioning with their clients, as the way a story hangs together is one of the most crucial aspects of writing fluent prose. Transitioning elements determine not only readability but everything from plot believability to story continuity. Often a single word, placed in the proper location, can create the ideal scene from the perspective of all the nuances I just discussed. But what determines what does and doesn't need to be included in a narrative?

Eschew What's Obvious to the Reader

I read a novel by a popular author who decided his readers needed to know when his protagonists had to void their bladders. I'm eternally thankful that the writer spared us a detailed report of the actual events, but we still received an account of each trip behind a bush. I'm not making this up, and I can only assume this writer was trying to provide a sideways stab at humor, but because of the serious nature of his material otherwise, it didn't work for me.

Likewise, Don't Write About Issues That Have Nothing to Do With the Scene

Readers can assume that a garage door was shut before the hero or heroine entered the house, as well as the kitchen lights were turned off as a character leaves to enter another room. This is no different from answering the phone. Someone can simply write that "John answered the phone" and move on to the actual conversation.

Or the same activity could read like this: "John heard the harsh cacophony of the ringer inside the old, white, oblong phone hanging on the wall in his kitchen. He pushed himself up from the lounge chair in the living room and walked briskly to grab the receiver, noting the location of the furniture along the way so he wouldn't bump into anything. As soon as he reached the phone, he placed his right hand firmly on the black handset and removed it from the cradle, pulling upward and outward in one swift motion. He swallowed and took a deep breath, holding the mouthpiece directly in front of his lips, but not so close that they might brush against it. He wasn't at all nervous about who might be calling him, so in a pleasant tone he said, "Hello."

Some Things Can and Should Be Taken for Granted

The same sort of laborious writing describing answering a phone can apply to any normal activity. I read a paragraph in a novel recently that was just as silly as the one I wrote, but in that instance it depicted a person entering a car. Instead of the character driving away from the scene of the crime, I was told that he entered the car through the driver's-side door, placed the key in the ignition, started the engine, shifted the transmission in gear, and then pressed the accelerator. That really was more information than I needed to know, although I appreciated the tutorial, as I'm getting old and tend to forget how to get my own car going.

Some Aspects of a Scene Must Be Explained

Writers often find it bewildering that an editor will consider one issue important while deeming another trivial. The answer is that it relates to either scene transitioning or story continuity or both. And determining what's important and what isn't, and acting on this prudently, can make or break a story.

Nonfiction or Fiction As a Category – If Some Aspect of a Book Is True, Which Is It?

I'm often told by participants in my creative writing workshops that the material they've crafted is fiction but contains some nonfiction elements, and I'm asked in which category their work should fall. I remember what I read that another editor said in response to this question: "Even the wildest science fiction tale has to have some elements grounded in reality as people know it or no one would accept the work's premise."

A Novel Is Always Based on Various Degrees of Plausibility

As the editor related, the creatures from the planet Bublitzko had to have certain plausible characteristics or readers would put down the book. If, for example, they were bigger in size than the universe, readers would back away, since nothing as we know it could be larger. And humans certainly couldn't see them, as each Bublitzkoain would be impossible to distinguish. But if the Bublitzkoians were our size but never required nourishment in a traditional manner because their systems were sustained by light from their sun—which is fading and the reason they've chosen to colonize Earth—readers might well approve of this.

It's Fiction Even If the Story Has True Components

Once it's accepted that a scenario could occur, it doesn't matter that Aunt Eloise *really* threw a plate of food at her husband at the dinner table when everything else in the chapter was the product of the writer's imagination. If a story is written as part truth and part fiction, then it's classified as fiction, although some books are written as if they were documentaries. In my opinion, one of the most skilled writers of this sort of material was Gore Vidal (who died in 2012), with BURR as a glowing testament to his ability to bring a tale to life as if it had happened exactly the way he wrote it.

Don't Agonize Over an Insignificant Issue

Writers are often vexed when editors revise something in a narrative that was written exactly as it had occurred in real life. Editors then have to remind authors that the editing suggestion was due to a problem caused by the scene as it was designed—and that their story is a work of fiction. At times I'm afraid it's either accept an editor's advice or face revising a large segment of the draft. And whether or not Eloise tossed the chop suey at Charlie underhand or rifled the plate past his head is not going to make or break the story, hard as this might seem to believe.

Novel Length –
What Is Correct for Each Genre

A while ago I read a paper that offered guidelines which ran from a page for flash fiction to 60,000 words as the starting point for a work to be considered novel-length. I'm not remotely qualified to comment on flash fiction, but it seems 60,000 words is an acceptable metric for a narrative to be classified as a novel.

If the 60,000 Number Is the Starting Point for a Novel, What Is Considered Too Long?

When I began querying my initial novel 20-plus years ago and called a few agents (not a good idea, even then) to get a feel for the market, I remember the first words out of several of their mouths: "How long is your manuscript?" I thought it was quite odd to ask this without knowing one thing about the story. But when I began editing for a living, I often found myself requesting–also early in the conversation–the same information. What follows are a couple of reasons why.

The Interest in Length in Many Cases Relates to the Cost to Print the Book

It's very hard to get many agents to consider a mammoth work from a heretofore unpublished author because they know submissions editors will balk at considering something that is essentially a tome. This doesn't mean the "new" author of a book with a high word count cannot achieve success, but large books cost more to print and consequently often retail for more money.

Following this thinking, it's hard to entice readers to pay an additional amount for something written by an unknown author. Certainly e-publishing renders the increased-cost argument nugatory, but until the industry reaches a point at which nothing will ever be printed, the contention regarding word count will likely retain some degree of validity.

Traditional-Length Stories are What the Public Desires

Commercial Fiction in the 80,000- to 90,0000-word range seems to be what appeals to the general public, since this provides an 8- to 10-hour read for most people, and it's the ambit a great many agents and publishers recommend their authors' works fall within. Of course a book could be 55,000 or 120,000 words (or whatever), but the

80,000- to 90,000-word model provides a good framework, especially for an unpublished writer trying to break into the business.

It's Always Important to Understand There Are Exceptions

A single factor normally determines why publishers allow exceptions, and this pertains to an author's following. This implies the writer was published in some medium previously and has achieved considerable success. And the publisher is gambling that the next book will sell, regardless of its size. I could be very wrong, but if J.K. Rowling had written the first installment in her series at the length of some of her later works in the oeuvre, we might never have heard of Harry Potter.

One Rule and a Summation

The rule is: there isn't one. But as I constantly write, unpublished authors have to jump over a very high bar, and it's constantly being raised. So it's imperative to make an agent's or publisher's work—as it applies to evaluating a manuscript—as comfortable as possible.

Some of the positions maintained by agents are purely personal and even regrettable. But regardless of the reasons for agents' and publishers' purported biases, writers have to be prepared to work around those that are extant. Yet I must mention that I recently spoke with a highly regarded submissions editor who said she has never found word count to matter, irrespective of the genre.

I realize this article is fraught with contradictions, but the publishing industry is tough enough to crack without trying to circumvent what are considered the traditional word-count metrics by many if not most of those who make the ultimate decisions regarding the fate of a story.

Opening Chapter in a Novel – Writing a Powerful Hook Is Essential

Nothing is more critical than the first few lines of a story, since this will often influence whether or not a reader will continue with a work. And a great opening is never more important than for the budding author who is trying to acquire an agent or publisher and later, of course, attract an audience.

Writers like Dickens and Woolf Provide a Mighty Lofty Pedestal

It would be wonderful if lines like "It was the best of times, it was the worst of times," or "Mrs. Dalloway said she would buy the flowers herself," were on the forefront of our thinking when we first sat down at a keyboard. The reality, however, is that this is not how it plays out for most of us mere mortals. But there are ways to attract attention without having to conjure up the catch phrase of the century.

Think Along the Lines of Larry McMurtry

Larry McMurtry opened A DEAD MAN'S WALK by telling the reader about a naked 200-pound prostitute, nicknamed The Great Western, walking down the street while carrying a huge snapping turtle. Who wouldn't want to find out why this woman was involved with this seemingly inane activity? The same as a feminist would immediately be impressed with Clarissa Dalloway's opening salvo.

But What If It Requires Time to Set Up the Introduction to the Story?

This is when it gets sticky. Yet not impossible to remedy. A suggestion is to find the single most prominent element of the entirety of the opening and maneuver this to the top of the first page, and then write from that point forward. This might seem difficult, if not impossible, but with a little practice it can be done.

A good exercise is to write a page on a random topic–not considered previously–then locate the most significant facet of the text and place this as the lead sentence. Now rewrite the page with the narrative following this new opening. It might not be a bad idea to do this several times, each with a new topic, and then apply this technique to your novel's opening.

The Opening Requires the Same Effort As the Book's Title

It's prudent to apply the same effort for the opening as was expended to come up with the title for the work. Often, however, much more time is spent on determining the title. If this should happen to be the case (from the perspective of the amount of time spent on each), it could be suggested to reverse the process. A solid opening, whether it be a single paragraph or several, will eliminate the need to try to create one-line intro's like "Who is John Galt?" or "They call me Ishmael," which happen on only the rarest of occasions for even literature's most esteemed scribes.

Paragraph Construction – How to Design the Perfect Paragraph

First, Consider Length

I've found the initial issue to contend with is size. Some writers, especially when starting out to create a serious work, ignore paragraph length altogether. I often see material of Faulknerian proportions and wonder if the writer had ever read anything as bulbous in the genre in which he or she was writing.

An executive editor with a major publishing company told me years ago that most readers don't like long paragraphs. And this was before this editor had read the first page of my manuscript! I took the comment to heart, and I advise authors to write a lung full. Meaning, just before reading a paragraph, take a deep breath. When the air runs out, it's time for a new paragraph. This of course doesn't apply to everything, and this might even seem a bit silly, but I've found it's a sound way to approach runs of exposition from the perspective of word volume.

A Start, a Middle, and an End

A perfect paragraph is much the same as a perfect chapter. Both require the same three components. And while I'm referring to a paragraph that's a run of exposition and not sprinkled with dialogue, the same methodology can apply if there's substantial interior monologue interlaced with speech.

The ideal paragraph should begin with a hook to captivate the reader. Conflict of some sort must occur in its middle, and the paragraph would close with a full explanation or a teaser to encourage the reader to stay with the story.

Here's an Example of the Concept of a Perfect Paragraph

The sharp noise from the gunshot awakened John from his sleep at the same moment he felt the hot air from the bullet whizzing by his head. Since the report wasn't loud, it had to be a small caliber. But it could still kill him, there was no mistaking that. He felt his cheek and it was wet. The bullet had done more than just fly past him. He yanked up the mattress to provide what little protection it would afford, when a round hit the middle of it. Stuffing flew in his face and blinded him as he dodged behind the bed and felt in the dark for the revolver in his nightstand.

Hardly great writing, but this paragraph provides the reader with a start, as John's being shot at. The scene escalates as he realizes that the bullet has grazed him and he's bleeding. Then the passage ends as he is seeking cover just before he's shot at again, and barely making it as he feels around for his weapon. Did the paragraph pique your curiosity as to what will happen next? If so, the text achieved what a solid paragraph is supposed to accomplish.

Think of Each Paragraph as a Mini-Chapter

As I stated up front, every paragraph can't be written to meet the mini-chapter requirement, but the more often this can be accomplished the better the story will read in almost all instances. And it's easy to "reverse engineer" the process. Meaning, if the paragraph is too long, it can be broken into components.

In the example above, John could be shot at while he's lying in bed and talking on his cell phone. Everything can play out exactly as I've written it, except for short runs of dialogue spliced within the overall narrative.

Add your own dialogue to what I wrote and see if the scene doesn't read the same and the paragraph's three main components don't remain intact. I always advise clients to design a start, middle, and an end when crafting paragraphs they know beforehand will contain considerable exposition, since material developed in this manner will inherently please the reader.

Paragraph Length in a Novel – Why This Is Important

Almost 20 years ago, an editor who was between jobs, and soon thereafter became the editor-in-chief of a major publisher—where she remains today—took on the project to critique a novel I had written. But before she'd read one page of my manuscript, she warned me about paragraph length; simply, I should be certain my work was written for the most part in short paragraphs.

Paragraph Length Is of Prime Significance to the Readability Quotient

At first I thought it an odd, out-of-place comment, especially since she'd not yet received my manuscript. But then I thought about the Thriller genre in which the book was written and decided to parse the average paragraph lengths of authors whom my style most closely patterned. I was pleased that my word count was, on average, not abnormal. But it was not until I began facilitating writing workshops many years, and many novels, later that I fully understood why I was given the admonition.

Paragraphs That Are Too Long Can Kill Pacing; When Realistic, Try Inserting Dialogue

One of the first problem areas I noticed with material from budding writers involved run-on paragraphs. This occurred in dialogue as well as exposition, and it destroyed the pace of the narrative quicker than any other factor. While long paragraphs wear out the reader, there are simple ways to remedy this. And not always by breaking up the material into multiple paragraphs of continuing exposition. One is to insert dialogue, as there is no easier way to break up a long paragraph than for a character to say something. However, this is not always feasible, so the question is, "Where should the paragraph be split?"

How Long Is Too Long? Apply a Simple Test

We are trained that a paragraph should start and end a thought. But since sometimes thoughts can be substantial, try this exercise: While you're reading a paragraph you've written, consider its length as if it's invested in your breathing process. If your breathing suddenly becomes labored, and you're still reading the same paragraph, determine the point that caused your breathing to strain and begin a new paragraph with that sentence. You might have to rearrange a few words, but when you read the new shorter paragraph, check how much easier you are now able to transition to the next paragraph. And how much more comfortably you happen to be breathing. You may have improved the manuscript and the health of your readers at the same time.

[In another article I mention taking in a deep breath—and when the air runs out so should the paragraph. The exercise suggested in this piece accomplishes the same thing but will keep many writers from turning blue, ha ha.]

Plot Authenticity –
Its Importance to a Narrative

I recently wrote an article on plot believability and was asked if this was the same as plot authenticity, since both seem to imply the same thing. In some respects they are alike, but in other ways they are dissimilar. Believability relates to the feasibility of situations occurring in the manner in which they are depicted; authenticity involves the specific characteristics of a scene as the reader believes the events would take place.

The Authenticity of a Happening

In a scene in an operating room, would a surgeon be allowed to continue to botch one operation after another when everyone on the medical staff knew the doctor was incompetent? Would a cop be allowed to shoot an unarmed person and go back on the street the next day? Could a lawyer—solely by the threat an injunction provides—prevent a spouse from stalking the man who was having an affair with his wife?

Now make logical conclusions based on what you just read. Could the same doctor in the earlier example remove the wrong limb and simply cover it up? Would a police officer make the mistake of shooting an innocent bystander for a second time in his career and be left to remain on the job in the same capacity? Would an attorney be foolish enough to think that a court order is going to keep a crazed spouse away from a cheating counterpart when a prior client was murdered under similar "paper" restrictions?

Competent Characters Displaying Incompetent Actions Won't Work

Assuming it's a human, once a character's profile is crafted for the reader, it's critical to understand the way this person's actions are going to be perceived. Among other elements, perceptions can be determined by the character's appearance, personality, and employment. For the purpose of this paper, let's take these three traits as a starting point. If we're wanting our character to be suave and debonair, this person can't be 50 pounds overweight and a slob at the dinner table. Should our character possess a legitimate gentle disposition, this person wouldn't do well as a sadistic murderer with no conscience. An FBI agent who is a long-time Agent-In-Charge wouldn't be indecisive, forgetful, and prone to making the same mistakes over and over. Yet I've read drafts with these sorts of misrepresentations.

Consider the Global Nature of the Narrative

If the lead character is a crown prince and the son of the richest man in the world, and this person is kidnapped, how extensive would the search likely be? And if this child were thought to be on foreign soil, how many people in that country's police—and military—would be searching for the lad? I'm suggesting it would be no less than the quest to find Bin Laden right after 9/11. It's important to sometimes "size" a character's activities so they don't appear too large for the storyline to handle.

Authenticity Is More Than Perception

Authenticity also means how scenes play out in the timeline in which the story was written. To this point, if an author is writing about the FBI or CIA or the NYPD, it's important to understand the way these outfits operated during the entire timeline of the narrative. If writing a period piece, the technology must also fit. Cell phones can't show up in 1975 any more than a commercial jet can be flying tourists from New York to Paris in 1955.

Check the "Facts"

And this means looking further than Wikipedia or the first link to the subject that's provided by an Internet search engine. I'm not criticizing any particular sourcing medium, but anyone can post on Wikipedia, as it's really nothing more than a sophisticated blog. And while Wikipedia can be a fine starting point, I strongly suggest checking with reputable encyclopedias and other sources that pertain directly to the subject. When I do research for my own material, I commonly make phone calls. For example, about 20 years ago I called Sikorsky Aircraft in Connecticut to make certain a helicopter I cited in a story was in fact deployed in 1960, which was the time of my narrative. I learned it wasn't in operation until the following year. Perhaps not a big deal, but the sort of thing savvy readers of Military Thrillers pay attention to, and my book fit that category to a tee.

For that same story, I called the State Department in D.C. to find out what the lobby in the building looked like in 1960. It required a few phone transfers, but I was put in touch with a woman who was a receptionist in 1960 (I also learned the building was under major renovation). In the overall scheme of things, the barren walls and bank of elevators on the left meant nothing to my story, but I felt good about describing the scene as it would've appeared to someone entering the dual set of doors to the building on C Street at that time in our history.

Authenticity adds to the richness of a tale, and while the correct helicopter appearing in a particular time frame might never sell a story to a publisher on its own, a lack of accuracy can certainly keep a book from being accepted by knowledgeable readers. And that does matter.

Plot Believability –
Its Importance to a Narrative

As an editor who specializes in fiction, I quite often have clients lament about my criticism of a plot element that I find implausible. The general response is, "It's fiction, so why should it matter?" First, just because a narrative is fictional, this doesn't mean the story elements should not be factual. Second, all fiction is grounded on fact to some degree, and even the wildest fantasy has to contain characterizations the reader can relate to with respect to their legitimacy.

Once Again, to the Planet Zegrebnon

I wrote an article not long ago in which I stated that even the most outlandish science fiction requires accurate physics to make scenes work for readers, since the scientific community understands the various disciplines. For example, a space alien couldn't be in multiple places at the same instant. Even traveling many times the speed of light, if that were possible, would entail nanoseconds (or whatever) to differentiate location. An extraterrestrial entity might appear to be in several places at one time, but the author couldn't tell the reader that the being was indeed in more than one spot at an identical moment.

Let's Get Back to Earth

If a person is tossed into the Bering Strait, I know from "Deadliest Catch," and a tour guide of mine while on a fishing trip in Alaska, that a person has about four and one-half minutes before hypothermia occurs. And while a human might make it for a half-hour, the person would have substantial health issues if still alive after being in the water for that period of time.

However, there is a documented case of a man who survived for longer than six hours in 45-degree-or-colder water after his ship wrecked in 1984. Studied by scientists from all over the world, he was overweight and his body fat was two to three times thicker than the norm and solid like that of a seal. I think it's fair to imply this fellow was unique. And that's the point. Can a writer expect readers to accept that a character could negate insurmountable odds when only one person in recorded history is purported to have done so?

This has nothing to do with hypothermia. It could mean rowing a heavy boat on a lake against a gale wind and in two hours making it ten miles. Or incapacitating a burglar in the dark (I know the movie, too, but you get my point). Or never having fired a gun and hitting multiple people with single shots in a speeding boat on rolling seas. Then there's tossing a bullet in a fire so it will go off at just the right angle and hit the bad guy. While this list is of course endless, readers' attention spans aren't.

All Writers Must Understand and Respect Their Audiences

If it's a Police Procedural, the person buying a book in this genre will likely be hip to the way law enforcement operates. When the bust takes place, the writer had better understand what cops say and do. And what they can't say and don't do! Also, a reader's acceptance factor is not like what occurs when watching "Nikita" on TV, a show that has all sorts of female assassins with martial arts skills enabling them to take down men three times their size. At the time of this article, only one woman in the entirety of our Armed Forces is rated at the highest level for hand-to-hand combat. This means she also possesses jujitsu skills that enable her to effectively fight a man on the ground. Again, only one female in the whole of our military!

Fully Grasp the Limitations of Every Character

Even Superman and Wonder Woman have limitations. Since we create our characters from our imaginations, it's important not to get carried away and want to live vicariously through their actions. Make chase scenes realistic, love scenes acceptable, physical attributes identifiable for the average person, etc. The more accurately fiction is written, the better it is.

The Feasibility/Plausibility Test

Even though the words "feasible" and "plausible" are often considered interchangeable, someone whose name I've sadly forgotten wrote something along these lines: "If it's feasible, this means it can be done under normal circumstances; if it's plausible, this means it could be done, but only under the most unlikely of situations." To keep the reader engaged, I suggest staying with feasible scenarios and avoiding scenes that are unlikely to occur except by sheer luck. Think of the man from Iceland who swam for six hours in 45-degree-or-below water and survived. Would you believe it?

Plot Elements Should Not Be Revealed Prematurely in a Narrative

Prologues Can Be a Major Problem

I'm often telling my clients not to write prologues if they reveal too much of the actual story, and instead to write this material into the narrative as backstory if it's deemed that important to the setup. This advice is most assuredly of the standard brown-paper-bag variety, but writers often feel they must "prepare" the reader for what is to come, and this is generally not a good idea.

"Conditioning" the Reader Is Seldom Necessary

Readers commonly don't require as much guidance as author's might think. They're more than capable of figuring out things without a helping hand. They certainly don't need to know every detail of the millennium-long war between the Gribdons and Calgothians prior to starting with the main narrative.

Telling of What's To Come Takes Away from the Suspense

It's sort of like reading the end of the story first. Anyone who's ever done this, and I don't know who hasn't for one reason or another, has essentially destroyed the reading experience for that particular work. Knowing this, would it make the best sense to tell the reader that a particular event is about to occur?

Eliminate the Conflict, Eliminate the Story

Exposing story elements also eliminate or drastically reduce conflict, and what is any plot without this component? The more heightened the conflict—and the inherent intrigue this creates—the better the chance the reader will remain engaged in the narrative. If there is one "given" to good storytelling, this is it.

Hints Are Okay; Telling Too Much Isn't

And that's the key. I personally enjoy a story with well-crafted cliff-hangers. The millions of people who read James Patterson's material apparently do also, as his cliffhangers "juice" many of his thin plots. But a cliffhanger shouldn't explain what is to happen; or, even worse, describe an event that doesn't take place.

Never Foretell a Scene That Doesn't Occur

Bogus setups remind me of the serials from the '50s that showed the hero or heroine in the throes of imminent death, only for me to find out in the next reel that nothing close to the peril in the preceding scene had occurred. I always felt cheated, sometimes so much so that I gave up on that series. I highly suggest avoiding anything that comes close to this sort of gross impropriety.

Remember, Even a Little of What We Imply Will Go a Long Way

Regardless of just how much foreshadowing an author might want to provide for an upcoming plot element, a little bit goes a long way toward lessening the reading experience. So unless the writer is highly skilled at crafting "teasers," it's best to let the natural progression of the story play out without any peripheral prodding.

Plot Holes –
How They Can Destroy a Story

As an editor, I find nothing more uncomfortable than having to tell a writer about a flaw in a draft that pertains to a plot hole. And often I'll be asked to define this tear in the fabric of a story that makes a section of the narrative so unrealistic that it affects what I refer to as the reader's "acceptability quotient."

Plot Holes Can Crop Up Anywhere

The tendency is to assume a plot deficiency occurs only at the end of the story, and while this indeed does happen, it's often easiest to remedy with a denouement. The problem I've found, however, is that the more elements revealed at the end of the story, the weaker the overall plotline. If I'm reading a couple of pages of plot resolution at the very last of a narrative, I generally suggest that the writer go back and work on these elements so they're brought out and resolved within the framework of the text.

Types of Plot Holes

The most obvious plot hole is anything that requires a deus ex machina to save the day. I always hate when an otherwise good story requires a preternatural event to reconcile a plot element. But plot holes are more insidious than purely contrived events. How do characters make it cross country in a day in an automobile? Or heal from horrific wounds in three days? How does a year pass in a story and the only person who is affected by this is the lead character?

Chronology Is a Factor Never to Lose Site of

Time is a big deal, and it contributes to plot problems as much as anything. When a year passes, everyone in the story is impacted by this. What did they do during that year? Quite commonly, even the best writers can't effectively fill long gaps, and it's a reason I suggest writing tight timelines whenever possible, and especially with Mysteries and Thrillers.

Inconsistency Creates Plot Holes

Readers don't have to know that characters go to the bathroom, eat every meal, answer each phone call, etc., but if a character has a lisp on page 4, it can't have been cured by the middle of the next page. Mary can't be two months pregnant in June and have a baby that has gone full term by August. Tom can't be fired in December but working for the same firm in April, without an explanation. A boat that's destroyed in a storm can't reappear in the final scene—with the reader told that the craft really wasn't dashed against the rocks as first reported. Shakespeare could get away with it; the rest of us can't.

Not Finishing Threads Can Cause As Many Problems As Anything

It certainly is easy to take a run at one Pulitzer Winner, INDEPEND-ENCE DAY, by Richard Ford. But my reason for disliking this book has nothing to do with anything I saw on the review sites or the opinions of people I respect who read the book. My reason was because the thread regarding the murdered realtor, which Mr. Price brought up twice, was never tied up for the reader. In my opinion, it was the only true plot element in the entire story, and it was ignored. (If you haven't read the novel, it has no plot, just the idle ramblings of a neurotic malcontent during a three-day Fourth of July holiday. If you like Virginia Woolf, you'll likely enjoy this; if not, you might want to stay away.) As to my point, I don't see how this open thread could have escaped the editors at Knopf, but it did.

Major Writers Get Away With Plot Holes, the Rest of the World of Writers Can't

Disregarding my reference to THE TEMPEST, in THE EYE OF THE NEEDLE, how is it that a man as meticulous to a fault as Der Needle would leave a door unlocked so his landlady could walk in on him while he was on his radio transmitting to the Germans? This occurring when the entire story was a testament to this assassin's extreme caution with everything he did?

Everyone has plenty of examples of the sorts of missteps I just mentioned. Established writers are cut a lot of slack for reasons that boggle the mind of most authors trying to get a start in this business. But a major requirement, like it or not—for anyone striving to attract a mainstream publisher—is to provide material devoid of inconsistencies that create holes in the narrative.

Point of View in Writing – A Clear Definition with Examples

Let me state flat out that the importance of understanding and writing consistent POV cannot be overstated, as this is one of the first elements agents, publishers, and professional editors notice, since shifting POV is considered not only a deficiency but a sign of amateur writing. No one can guarantee that a writer will become published by a major royalty imprint, but I am certain of issues that will discourage this possibility. And the unskilled shifting of POV is one of the fastest ways I know for material to end up in the slush pile.

Some Highly Skilled Writers Can Indeed Shift POV Effortlessly

There are of course exceptions. Some highly skilled writers can shift POV seamlessly. But their POV shifts are done sparingly and generally at high-tension plot points in which the writer is not concerned with the movement because the scene is so powerful that the other character's view is necessary. And not expressing that POV would hinder the scene.

I wrote an article on POV in which I illustrated an instance in which I felt the shift was not only acceptable but desirable. So the issue is not confused, I'm not going to include the article at this time, but will mention that E.M. Forster said that POV shifts are fine—as long as nobody notices them (his remark made me laugh too). The difficulty for most writers is that POV shifts are most often not only noticeable, they are overwhelmingly detrimental to the narrative, as well.

Even Some of Literature's Most Famous Writers Have Made POV Mistakes

It does not require close reading to find problematic POV shifts, and even some of literature's most famous writers err. For a developmental writing workshop series I facilitated, I reread Saul Bellow's THE VICTIM, since I use it in one of my syllabuses and wanted to refresh my memory on an aspect of the plotline. I noticed two instances in the story in which Mr. Bellow shifted the POV, and to the extent that it required me to reread both passages, one several times.

A callow youth might read something by a famous author that contains jarring POV shifts and assume this sort of writing is acceptable. I'm sorry, it is not! Especially if a writer has hopes of being published by a bona fide royalty press in today's highly selective literary marketplace.

A Clear Explanation of POV

If POV is foggy, perhaps this will make it clear: A character whose POV the scene is written around (maybe it would work best to consider this the "lead character" for this illustration) can demonstrate actions and express thoughts. Every other character in the scene can demonstrate actions but never thoughts, since the thoughts of another character in the same scene automatically reflect that person's POV–and what is referred to as shifting POV once the scene's initial POV is established by a character. How POV is maintained for the reader–related to which character's thoughts are controlling the scene–is the key to POV consistency. To repeat, the first character whose thoughts are expressed dictates the scene's POV.

Along this line, it is important to keep another issue in mind. Even though this lead character can show actions and thoughts for the reader, he or she must couch the viewing of others. This means that the lead character can state whatever he or she desires–but can only "suppose" what is going on in anyone else's mind. Hence, we read phrases in which the lead character says that it "seemed," or it "appeared," or it "looked" like something was occurring related to another character or circumstance. Again, for POV consistency, once the lead character in a scene is established, no other character can express an opinion via interior monologue about anyone else. Only the character "controlling" his or her own POV can express "thoughts," and then only about his or her own emotions.

Examples of POV–The Right and Wrong Way

Here, now, are examples of the same scene with John and Mary written three ways. The first is in John's point of view:

"Hi," John said to Mary. He gazed into her eyes, more nervous than he had ever been in his life.

"I'm happy that you came by," Mary said, her voice sounding positive to him.

John, uplifted by her tone, experienced a sudden burst of confidence that he hadn't thought possible. But as he continued to stare at Mary, she blinked several times before turning away. He could only guess at what had caused her sudden change in comportment.

He took a deep breath and his voice was shaky. "Do you want to talk about it?"

Mary kept her head down. He heard what he thought was a muted sob, then she looked up at him and seemed to force a smile. "No. I thought I could but I can't."

Since the scene is written around John's POV, he can state his positions because he knows for certain what he is feeling. His thoughts are "leading" the scene. But he cannot know for certain what Mary is feeling. He cannot know, for example, that she forced a smile, only that she seemed to have forced one. It is only after she says "no" that the reader can infer that John might have made a correct assumption. If the last spit of dialogue read, "Yes, I thought I couldn't, but I can," this could mean that her smile wasn't forced but was one of subtle satisfaction with her decision. What follows is the same scene in Mary's POV:

"Hi," John said to Mary, as he gazed into her eyes.

John's anxiety was obvious to Mary, since his voice had cracked. "I'm happy you came by," she said in a soft tone, hoping this would provide him with some degree of self-assurance.

John seemed uplifted, and appeared to experience a sudden burst of confidence that pleased Mary. But as he continued to stare at her, she blinked several times before turning away. She hoped that he wouldn't misinterpret her actions, because it was she who now needed to gain composure.

He took a deep breath, but his voice was still shaky. "Do you want to talk about it?"

Mary kept her head down, hoping he wouldn't know she was crying inside, but then she looked up and forced a smile. "No, I thought I could but I can't."

Here Is the Same Scene with the POV Shifting Back and Forth—and the Consequences

"Hi," John said to Mary, as he gazed into her eyes, wondering if she really wanted to see him.

"I'm happy that you came by," Mary said, her voice soft, and thinking she should've been more aggressive, since he'd made everything so awkward.

John, however, was uplifted by her tone, and experienced a burst of confidence that she hadn't thought possible. Then he'd noticed a change in her comportment as she looked away to consider what to say next. He needed time to think and she wished he were someplace else.

Mary kept her head down and made what sounded to John like a muted sob. Then she looked up and forced a smile. As they stared at one another, he dreaded the words: "I thought I could but I can't."

This example is overkill, but I've read material just as bad, and it demonstrates just how devastating inept POV shifts can be. Lack of speaker designation is the most common issue with POV shifts, as depicted in the last paragraph, since the reader is unable to determine who was speaking.

A Final Bit of Advice

As I mentioned earlier, there are exceptions to strictly maintaining POV via one character. But if a writer is trying to find an agent and become published for the first time by a bona fide royalty publisher, I strongly suggest avoiding POV shifts.

Point of View –
The Reason It Matters to a Narrative

I normally don't get too concerned when people discuss the vagaries of what it requires to write well, regardless of how off-base I think some of the comments might be as they pertain to a particular subject. But I'm motivated to get involved when an element of writing is discussed with fervor and a decided bias, yet with a blatant lack of understanding for the topic.

Why Can't POV Be Written in Any Way One Sees Fit to Write It?

Last year I was taken to task by a young writer who'd written a piece he'd submitted for "approval" via a critique blog. I don't generally respond to this sort of thing, but as I read his material I noticed distinct POV shifts via four characters in what was a short opening chapter of 500 or so words. I wrote this fellow that his writing was fine except for the POV issues. I was sent a brisk note that "since *he* was the creator of the material, in who else's Point of View could it be written"?

It Would Be Funny If It Wasn't So Serious

I laughed off his callow sarcasm, tried to explain what Point of View entailed, even providing some resource material to support its importance, then quickly moved on after I found I was stoking rather than extinguishing a fire. I thought little more about POV misconception until I noticed one of my articles on the subject posted on a Web site for writers. Several people were kind enough to state that my explanation of POV was indeed better than the original one that fostered the blog's thread, but then each contributor tried to diminish the validity of POV.

This rankled me, especially when the moderator of the blog went on to support my contentions yet was just as quick to offer that POV shifts really don't matter much one way or the other. She admitted, however, that she also had difficulty at times with POV. This should have told readers the value of her opinions on this subject, but the coup de grace was when she closed her post by stating that POV was important only to agents, editors, and publishers–but not to readers.

It Isn't True That POV Matters Only to Agents, Editors, and Publishers; It Matters to Readers–Most of All

If I'd ever read a position that justifies why amateur writers accepting advice from other amateur writers is a road map to disaster, that was it. Agents, editors, and publishers are not an exclusive club infatuated with POV shifts and the issues they create. If POV shifts are done incorrectly, they will stop the reader! This is what matters, not the contention of us misguided souls who work everyday in the industry.

If the reader doesn't know who is speaking, often the scene will need to be read again. If this occurs repeatedly in a story, it can cause a book to be set down for good. Even an occasional POV shift can destroy the flow of a narrative. I've cited this before, but Saul Bellow let a couple of unnerving POV slips occur in THE VICTIM. And while this proves that even the best writers can err in applying this element uniformly, a mistake by an iconic writer hardly justifies POV-shift acceptance.

Anything That Jars the Reader Is Not Good

Not a brilliant statement by any means, but this is what the POV issue is all about. Some writers can shift POV effortlessly, and to paraphrase what the famous writer E.M. Forster said, if it's effected seamlessly it doesn't matter at all. But when the reader notices the shift, then there is a problem.

When Is It Easiest to Shift POV?

Complete scene breaks and of course new chapters will lend themselves to POV shifts. I've also found that high-tension scenes are at times forgiving if handled deftly (this might seem an odd example to cite, but for whatever reason I believe it's valid). Some people write in an omniscient voice via third person and assume this always works. Unfortunately, it doesn't if the speaker is not clearly identified. So while omniscient third person enables wide latitude, it doesn't mean there aren't requirements.

No Final Word on POV Exists

Debate will always rage over POV. The best response I can provide follows closely with what I stated earlier, and this is to write whatever the reader finds acceptable. If a POV shift doesn't stop the flow of the narrative for the reader, it can be assumed the task was handled in a masterful fashion. The time to find out if a POV shift was unsuccessful, however, is not after the reader has put down the book because of becoming frustrated with it. And this is the crux of the entire subject.

Point of View – Techniques for Effective Shifts

The first question some people might ask is why any writer would need to learn techniques related to Point of View. Doesn't POV automatically synchronize with the character's thoughts as soon as these feelings are expressed by the writer? And isn't the POV of a scene easily identified by an attribute or obvious implication? It should be this simple.

Shifting POV Is Only a Problem When People Notice It

Some writers possess the skill to seamlessly shift from one person's thoughts to another. As readers, we won't give this the slightest concern—as long as we don't realize when it's occurring. But even some of the most well-respected novelists have at times jarred readers with ineffective POV shifts. So what is it that enables a POV change to be acceptable in one instance yet not in another?

A POV Shift Works When the Reader Finds It Desirable

Most writers make POV shifts in a traditional manner. They add a line space to signify another character's thoughts via a new scene or go so far as to start a new chapter altogether. But some writers will elect to show multiple characters' most intimate feelings—within the same scene—without the slightest hiccup. These adept authors are able to accomplish this for a reason.

POV shifts in the same scene are effective when we have become so involved in the characters that we want to know each of their innermost thoughts—immediately. Simply, the pacing and intensity of the storyline can eliminate what might otherwise create a problem for the reader.

So What's a Writer to Do?

There may indeed be that one instance in a novel, a hospital scene for example when an accident victim is bandaged like a mummy, and the following could occur:

John Wright blinked and could make out a doctor standing next to his bed, staring at him with a stethoscope dangling from his neck as if it were being held by two tentacles. John's thoughts turned to his wife and he trembled all over. With his lips quivering through thin slits of blood-soaked gauze, John tried to ask about her condition, but no words came out. The physician wanted to leave, but the anguish in his patient's eyes told him that he couldn't just walk away. He bent down to the broken man and said, "Mr. Wright, your wife—"

For consistent POV, the second-to-last sentence might have read: John sensed that the physician wanted to leave, but something told him he couldn't. The doctor bent down and said, "Mr. Wright, your wife—"

But is the scene as powerful if it's left entirely in John's POV? Or would the scene work better if the penultimate sentence began a new paragraph? I don't think so, but this is an individual decision that is highly subjective, and anyone would be justified in disparaging the illustration.

A Final Thought

Many learned people and grounded writers feel that POV is right next to "showing" instead of "telling" as an inviolable principal. And in most cases this is undeniably correct. But there might be that rare occurrence, such as in the example I offered, when a POV shift within a scene could even be preferable. And I'd hate to think that any writer would avoid providing the reader with insight into a character because of POV convention. There are a lot of techniques available to allow the telling of a story and the telling of it well. And it's obviously the choices that separate writers.

Political Correctness in a Novel

I remember being chastised by a submissions editor when I described certain characters in a novel of mine by country of origin and then provided their respective physical attributes. It never occurred to me that defining someone as a wiry Latino or fat Sicilian would be considered offensive in the context of a novel. When Shaffer's THE CASE OF THE OILY LEVANTINE became a hit, I assumed this set a reasonable standard for enabling a succinct reference to describe a character, even if it wasn't favorable.

Must an Attribute Be Assumed to Be Negative?

Should my Latino have been described as agile instead of wiry? And would it have been more appropriate if he were South American; hence, an agile South American? Would my Sicilian better serve readers if he were a well-fed Mediterranean? It does become ludicrous, to the extremes, when we are driven to write in bland or imprecise rhetoric in an attempt to create description that would not offend anyone, anywhere, for any reason.

Even Writing Inflections of One's Native Language Can Be Considered Offensive

I was even told to drop the accents I used for my characters, as they could be deemed to be condescending. My agile South American saying "Si," for example, was considered pejorative. And my well-fed Italian couldn't say, "Imma gonna tella you." I have heard many agile South Americans use the word "Si" as a medium for agreement, and I have a well-fed Italian barber who routinely says, "Imma gonna tella you." I wonder if he received the memo from Milano that his dialect shouldn't be replicated in print, lest one of his countrymen be offended?

There Is a Silver Lining

The one positive aspect of political correctness at all costs is that it requires a writer to show the individual traits that a character possesses rather than tell them. And this will almost always lead to better writing. For example, instead of a wiry Latino, Eduardo Ramirez—by his name—lets the reader know something about his native origin. Then if I write he is from Belize, we know for certain. Finally, if somewhere in the context of my characterization of him I reference how limber he happens to be, I've covered him in a way that will satisfy even the most sensitive reader. Perhaps like this:

Eduardo Ramirez was about to open the mailbox and drop in the letter he'd addressed to his mother in Belize. But just as he pulled the lid down, he had to jump several feet out of the way to avoid a teenager who had lost control of his speeding bicycle and was coming right toward him. When the lad finally maneuvered his bike to a stop after just missing hitting the mailbox head-on, he ran to Ramirez and asked in a nervous voice if the man was okay. Ramirez responded with a smile and an unruffled yes, not wanting to make a big deal out of what had just happened. Later, as he thought about his close call, he was happy he'd been paying attention, since he likely would've suffered a serious injury otherwise. And that afternoon he would not have been able to audition and win the role in the Broadway musical for which he was now famous.

What Is Right and What Is Wrong?

In the scene, we learn a lot more about Mr. Ramirez than he was a wiry Latino, so there is a great deal to be said for my being dressed down. I do, however, hope that society never gets to the point that plays like Shaffer's will require retitling. Every person from Latin America is certainly not wiry or a Columbian drug dealer, any more than everyone from Sicily is fat or a mobster. Connotations that promote judgmental attitudes are bad, but simple adumbration, in my opinion, should not be frowned upon. If the character is not of major significance or reoccurring in the narrative, my contention is that describing someone via a couple of words, such as "wiry Latino," is often advantageous to 150 words that are not essential to the plot.

Profanity in a Novel – What Works in Which Genres

Genre Trumps All Else

This would seem to be so obvious that it doesn't need to be mentioned, yet not understanding genre on the part of the author is a problem I find with a lot of material that's sent to me to edit.

Let's Start with Literature and Mainstream Fiction

Both genres cater to an essentially adult market, and constraints on profanity generally aren't an issue because of this demographic. But there can be serious concerns when a book crosses over. For example, if Holden Caulfield had said "F" this and "F" that in THE

CATCHER IN THE RYE, what sort of impact would that have had on the novel's sales (more than 60 million and still counting)?

Even material as stark as both STUDS LONIGAN and AN AMERICAN TRAGEDY were relatively profanity-free, and if an epithet was spoken, it was mild. And Henry Miller's material, while graphically sexual, contains little profanity of any sort. Even Cormac McCarthy's novels, which in my opinion are as visceral as narratives can get, are overwhelmingly sans profanity. The same can be said for Erskine Caldwell's works, as well as those of Faulkner and Steinbeck, both of whom often dealt with quite adult themes and circumstances.

Common Denominators for Profanity

If I'm reading jailhouse argot, or the conversation between two drunken sailors, every other sentence with an "MF" in it is perfectly acceptable. Likewise, to impress their peers, gang members are going to use all of the seven words that can't be spoken on TV as often as possible, and anyone writing dialogue centered in this environment has to lace it with profanity or the runs won't ring true with the reader.

But when writing dialogue in standard settings, one "F" word goes a long way, and unless it's part of a character's established profile, even a single utterance of the "F" word won't be acceptable to the reader. However, the "F" word used judiciously can indeed be a powerful tool. In no other book has the "F" word had more of an impact on me than in SO LONG, SEE YOU TOMORROW, by William Maxwell. And it appeared just once in the entire novel.

But Watch Out for YA

It's not so much what kids read, but what parents will let them buy or will purchase for them. The Internet makes just about any reading material available to anyone, but when considering a novel someone is paying for, regardless of who's remitting the funds, buyer demographics enter into the equation.

Even "hell" and "damn" can be a problem in a YA story especially if these words are spoken routinely by the story's protagonist without provocation. I always think of myself when I was 17 years old and meeting a girl's parents for the first time and cussing repeatedly in front of them for no reason, thinking it was cool. I was told in no uncertain terms by her father that my language wasn't acceptable in his household, and he escorted me to my car and made it clear that I was never to ask his daughter out again. This life's lesson applies to writing profanity as well.

Always Consider the Market for Your Story

Genre is market, and I'm concluding this article as it began by emphasizing the importance of identifying who will be reading your story. Will it be only older adults? Or will young adults make up your audience as well? Can profanity detract in any way from the image you're wanting your characters to portray, especially your protagonist? Does profanity fit the scene? And how do you want to use profanity–to shock or as part of a character's normal speech? Whatever the situation, think it out carefully and choose wisely.

Prologues and the Problems They Can Create for Early-Stage Writers

While I personally don't think there should be an issue with prologues, there apparently is, especially for the writer who is trying to find an agent or publisher for the first time.

Prologues Conjure Up All Sorts of Imaginary Demons

The unpublished writer has a lot of hoops to jump through that an author with a readership doesn't have to be concerned with, and this is why we see prologues preceding the work of some of our best-known scribes, and proudly so. Then what's the big deal about a manuscript from a new writer in which a prologue is part of the narrative?

As best I can figure out the thinking of certain agents, submissions editors, and publishers, it's that the prologue may give away too much of the story. It is therefore considered superior to place the information within the narrative, even as backstory, rather than to present it as stand-alone material that adumbrates in any way what is to come.

But There May Be a Real Demon Lurking in the Dark

Whatever anyone might feel about prologues, a legitimate argument can be made that they generally support "telling" instead of "showing" the action. And for this reason it would be better to place the prologue material at a later point in the narrative, as this new positioning might well foster a "showing" sequence.

I only offer this last sentence because as an editor I do see more "telling" within prologues. But this isn't always true, and certainly not an issue if a long-past event needs to be provided so a reader can retain something in the back of his or her mind to help solidify or flesh out a plotline.

It Seems as Though There's Little Choice But to Eschew Prologues—at Least for Now

If many of the people in the publishing industry who determine a manuscript's fate have developed a negative attitude toward prologues, budding novelists perhaps should decide if this bias is worth fighting. I can't tell anyone what to do, but I am looking doubly hard at anything I receive from a client in which a prologue is included, while at the same time gritting my teeth because of the seemingly burgeoning industry intolerance for this long-established medium for setting up a story.

Pronouns That Foster Incorrect Linkage

We see sentences such as these on this next page all the time:

* Everyone sat on the edge of his seat.
* Everyone sat on the edges of his seat.
* Everyone sat on the edges of his seats.
* Everyone sat on the edge of the seat.
* Everyone sat on the edges of the seat.
* Everyone sat on the edges of the seats.

Ignoring that some of the construction is abysmally awkward, the question is, which syntax is correct? But before even discussing this, my first argument would involve the use of "his" as an accepted complement to the antecedent "everyone." Yet "his" is accepted as a "given" in English, to represent "everybody" (read "anybody") when sex is unspecified, in a sentence designed in this manner. (I know, some of us have been marked down for using "his" in this syntax. What we definitely can't write is something such as "Everyone went their own way," as placing a plural pronoun with a singular one in this sort of context is a no-no without any wiggle room.)

For the answer, most people would select the first or fourth example, and perhaps the sixth. For a purist, the best choice is the first, since everything is singular.

Now let's take this one step further. If a plural noun is substituted for "everyone," as in these examples that follow, the problem becomes even more complex:

* People sat on the edges of their seats.
* People sat on the edges of their seat.
* People sat on the edge of their seat.
* People sat on the edge of their seats.

The simple answer is that the rhetoric in the first example is right, since "people" is plural and succeeded by the plural "their" and "seats," making for complete consistency. But is this correct? In reality, isn't this saying that a person, as a part of the multiple, is sitting on more than one seat, as indicated by both "edges" and the equally plural "seats?"

If you don't agree, and you have every reason not to, analyze the second example in the latter group. In this instance, "people," as plural, implies that more than one person sat, collectively, on the edges (as the plural indicates) of a single seat. Not a good prospect at all. In the third example, this same group is sitting on the edge of one seat, which implies a very large place to park a crowd, indeed. In the fourth and final example, people are sitting on the edge of their seats, sort of meaning that everyone is on an edge of many seats, which means the crowd has elastic behinds. What's the correct answer? Believe it or not, each is correct, in the sense that every example can be argued as acceptable grammar.

But here's where common sense has to enter the rhetorical equation. I've read the examples many times and found that the fourth sentence in the second list fits my eye best. However, I can think about it a while longer and feel better about the first construction. I've learned over the years it's best for me to go with my first choice in this sort of exercise, hence I'd choose "People sat on the edge of their seats." My reasoning is, though edge is singular, I'm going to argue that each seat has only one edge that a single person could sit on at a time. Conversely, since all the people wouldn't be sitting in one seat, this makes "seats" the right choice. Yes, this leaves me to once again contemplate "edge" and "edges," and I opted for the singular. However, the choice is up to individual taste.

Punctuation – A Parentheses Is One Form of Punctuation Never to Use in Fiction

I once wrote an article declaiming the use of the exclamation point in fiction, but mollified my fervor with the reluctant admission that there were indeed exceptions. And, in some instances, even an occasional benefit if the mark was used judiciously. But the employment of the parenthetical expression in fiction is not afforded the same luxury. And for three very good reasons:

The Action of a Parentheses Is Often the Opposite of Its Intended Function

The most problematic issue concerns the use of a parenthetical expression for emphasis, when the punctuation is designed as a means to express a derivative meaning or "aside." In the instance of a writer wanting to accentuate the narrative, a dash or dashes should be utilized. I remember a simple check-and-balance exercise for what to select in which circumstance: Consider a parentheses like two walls muting the text in between, while a dash, as in adding a dash of spice to a meal, heightens the flavor of the textual bill of fare. Perhaps a hokey explanation, but one I never forgot.

There Is Another Issue with Parentheses Use in Fiction That Is Even More Problematic

Once more, the evil "showing vs. telling" monster exposes its fangs, and long ones this time. This is because a parenthetical expression inherently "tells" of an action that could've, and often should've, been "shown." Simply, if the writer deemed the "aside" important enough to set off with specialty punctuation, wouldn't what fostered the exposition be worth detailing substantively for the reader? Ask again the critical question, "Was this rhetoric within the parentheses provided for modest purpose, such as clarity, or was it positioned within the punctuation to enhance the narrative?" If the answer is the latter, there's a distinct possibly that a valuable "showing" opportunity was missed.

Then There Is Patronizing the Reader

Many readers find nothing more grating than having situations or things explained to them via parenthetical supplements. If the reader can't figure out the narrative because it is so weak that it requires reinforcement, this is often an indication the section needs a serious rewrite, with a focus on "showing" and not "telling" the scene or scenes which are being cloaked within the parentheses.

Punctuation Concepts –
Ways to Effectively Use the Semicolon

When a Semicolon Doesn't Fit the Syntax

A writer friend of mine, who'd had four books published by major houses at the time we were speaking, critiqued something I wrote in which I had used a semicolon to set off a series in a section of comedy relief that read something like this: John wanted to own a farm, but without many common animals; namely, dogs, cats, cows, and horses. He suggested a colon for this sort of series, hence: John wanted to own a farm, but without many common animals: dogs, cats, cows, and horses. (We can argue the comma preceding the last item in both examples some other time). I wasn't sold on my friend's recommendation until I sat alone with the phrase and read it aloud both ways. Once I did this, from the perspective of fluency, it was obvious the colon was the better punctuation choice.

Is a Semicolon a Good Fit in Exposition in Fiction?

Many learned people say semicolons don't belong in fiction (especially commercial fiction). The contention is that a semicolon tends to stop the reader. Yet I recently read, in a book on contemporary fiction writing by a well-known author/agent, an eloquent if not passionate plea supporting the use of semicolons. But, to the first point, some feel that semicolons inhibit fluent prose and might even push many writers toward Faulknerian-length material; and, for this reason, semicolons should be eschewed at all costs. Consider the sentence you just read. Does it read better if broken into two sentences, or would the sentence be improved if the semicolon were converted to a comma and "for this reason" sans any punctuation? Could it be that the original construction is superior to either suggestion? You be the judge.

What About the Use of a Semicolon in Dialogue?

Even a short article such as this would be woefully incomplete if the semicolon and its potential integration into dialogue was not broached. Some astute literary experts would never consider setting a semicolon in a rift of dialogue. The suggestion would be to "write around" the speaker's words so the reader shouldn't be confronted with a semicolon. However, while people are not parsing what they hear for punctuation, is the reader of printed dialogue so quick to dismiss punctuation necessary to portray properly spoken syntax?

A multitude of semicolon naysayers would vilify a sentence written in which a character is saying to a friend as they are walking after someone in a crowd, "She looked back; no, I was wrong, she didn't." Is this spit of dialogue so horrible? If so, what is the more suitable element of punctuation to express the meter of the speaker's tongue in reaction to the moment? Does a period after "back," and a new sentence beginning with "No," convey the same degree of uncertainty? How would using all commas influence the flow? I think most might agree—not well.

What Is the Answer?

What is correct—and what is not—in many instances is a matter of style and not grammar. Semicolons are not evil. To the contrary, they often contribute great value. However, like any specialty punctuation, there can be a problem if overused. But not utilizing semicolons might be ignoring a marvelous tool for allowing a narrative to excel by providing a writer with a means to display greater proficiency in the art of crafting quality prose.

Punctuation Never to Use in Fiction – The Exclamation Point

"Never" Might Be Too Strong But "Seldom" Is Quite Correct

I've taken a little literary license with the title of this article, since to write that an exclamation point should never be used in a novel is preposterous. But to also state that this medium for emphasis should be used sparingly would not be out of line. Some experts feel that exclamation points are the sign of a lazy writer, or worse–an amateur. Whether the rationale for either opinion is sound or not, there are well-grounded reasons behind both.

An Exclamation Point Can Support Lazy "Telling" and Not Energetic "Showing"

To explore the first assumption, this forces considering the "showing versus telling" conundrum from yet another perspective. The terse line, John was shocked! eliminates what could amount to many pages (or at least a couple of lines) of exposition describing what had contributed to poor John's frenetic condition. Without adequate support for its selection, an exclamation point will often weaken–and at times dramatically–the very gravitas the writer is trying to impart. And what about when this sort of punctuation shortcut is taken with dialogue, such as when John turns to Mary and says, "I am shocked!" True, a lot could've happened that the reader is aware of which brought John to this horrific revelation. But it's when an exclamation point is not supported by antecedent material that serious writing deficiencies present themselves, and many experts agree that this applies equally to both exposition and dialogue.

Now for the Really Grisly Stuff

Nothing is more disappointing than reading otherwise good material that's besmirched with punctuation overuse. And seldom is anything more disconcerting than when a writer feels he or she can make every page stand out by overwhelming the reader with exclamation points. If anyone should be writing in this manner, please ask yourself, "If on the first page of my manuscript I have affixed four exclamation points, and continued my narrative in this vein and my work is 300 pages in length, is it conceivable that I've honestly created 1200 mind-rocking events? And of perhaps even greater significance, after the first three pages (and now 12 scintillating scenarios have occurred), can I expect the reader to withstand 1188 additional mind-blowing experiences before finishing my story? And how much impact can I expect exclamation point 1200 to have over what I wrote that elicited, say, exclamation point 662?"

There Is an Answer, and It's a Simple One

The example in the last paragraph was extreme, but I recently critiqued a manuscript that was very close to the exclamation point count I just described. And the author wondered why he'd never been published. There were other issues with the narrative, but it's unlikely any reputable agent or bona fide royalty publisher would've finished the first page after being inundated with so much "exclaimed" content.

Think One or Two Exclamation Points for an Entire Novel

A suggestion I've often heard, and agree with, is to parse the completed draft and count the number of exclamation points that were used overall. If more than one exclamation point per 25,000 words, then it's one too many. I've commonly gone back and analyzed fleshing out a scene rather than leaving an exclamation point to emphasize a story component. And I've found that adding to the narrative, and enabling this rhetoric to "show" the action—thus negating the exclamation point—to be the proper course of action in most instances. If you should discover your material infested with abundant "exclaiming," you might want to consider applying the same remedy.

Redemptive Characters in a Novel – Why This Element Is So Important to a Story

What Is a Redemptive Character?

In writing workshops I'm often asked what is meant by writing redemptive characters, and even by experienced writers, so it's not surprising when there's confusion about the meaning. In simple terms this implies writing a character(s) in a way that readers can find something about the person(s) to identify with or care about, and in best-case scenarios—root for. But this paints the explanation in rather simple strokes. I find there's much more to it, so let me spend the rest of this article providing some concrete ideas on how to apply this definition in a broader sense; but a little history first related to the traditional concept of the redemptive character.

Very Few Successful Novels Are Solely Plot Driven

I once asked an erudite workshop group to make a list of well-known novels with absolutely not one character who could be liked. After several months we'd parsed hundreds of books. There were a few honorable mentions (or dishonorable, if you so choose) such as ON THE ROAD and TROPIC OF CANCER. And I think THE SUN ALSO RISES and BREATHING LESSONS made the "almost list." But when we'd finally completed our task, and a dozen people had contributed to this study of what amounted to more than a thousand works, only STUDS LONIGAN and WUTHERING HEIGHTS made it to the top of the heap. So writing a book without a likeable character that will sustain a reader is not an easy chore.

Manuscripts Are Rejected Because Agents and Publishers Aren't Invested in the Characters

Not becoming invested in the characters is often because these figures weren't found to be redemptive. Another knockout factor is that the characters just weren't interesting. So this begs the question, "What is a way to make a character interesting?" One answer lies in writing a character who is genuinely likeable and therefore patently redemptive. Another technique is to make a character compelling, but with the reader's approval of the person's actions not necessarily entering into the equation.

A Character Doesn't Have to Be Paddy's Equal in THE THORN BIRDS to Qualify As Redemptive

This is one time when there is a magic bullet, and it's a Howitzer. But the answer is not always obvious. In THE GODFATHER, most of us pulled for Michael, along with the Don (and in separate eras). The majority of people cared about Clarice Starling in THE SILENCE OF THE LAMBS, but Hannibal held many people's interest even more so as an antihero.

Perhaps with the Don and Hannibal, readers (and moviegoers) respected their power, however disparate its source. Yet while many people had their vicarious sweet tooth satisfied by the earlier Don, they later sympathized with the older character, which is a tribute to Mr. Puzo's immense skill in character transitioning. With respect to Hannibal, a lot of people were enticed by Thomas Harris's brilliance to want to know why the good doctor had become a monster, and this was the plot focus of a later installment.

Writing Redemptive Characters Covers a lot of Ground, So There's Plenty of Room to Get Comfortable

Don Corleone and Hannibal Lector might not seem like sterling examples of my original definition of redemptive characters, but each in his own way is just that. Look at the recent vampire groundswell. The creatures are written in a manner that render people compassionate for their plight. A key to becoming published is to write characters who, regardless of their proclivity, are redemptive—for some compelling reason—in the eyes of the reader.

Redemptive Characters Redux – Why This Is So Important

I've had the privilege of recently reviewing and editing material for some superb writers, but I noticed in a couple of instances the tendency was to not "keep the protagonist redemptive" throughout the entirety of the narrative.

All this refers to is consistently presenting the protagonist in a way that readers will find appealing. To the converse side of this, some writers will lean too heavily on their heroes or heroines and the characters become Clark Kent or Diana Prince archetypes. However, once a balance between what a writer desires and what the reader will accept is met, then the task is to maintain consistency throughout the story.

Even a Rolled-Up Handkerchief Can Hinder Likeability

A character's "likeability quotient" is what redemptive character maintenance entails. When I first started writing, during the age when all of this was done on the side of a cave with charcoal, I sent a draft to my personal, very-first editor. I had designed a male protagonist I believed every reader would find easy to become fully engaged with and root for, as he was patently likeable (at least in my callow eyes).

One scene had him talking with a woman he was wooing, unaware that his shifting around in a chair had caused a handkerchief to ball up in his back pocket. This action seemed normal to me and demonstrated a legitimate level of anxiety for which I believed anyone under similar circumstances would feel empathy.

Don't Let Characters Have Warts Unless This Is a Purposeful Image

This editor, who has gone on to contract only with major imprints for their name writers, told me that my protagonist can't appear "clumsy" to the reader, which is the way he perceived I'd painted him in that scene. Some protagonists simply cannot have warts, at least not in the real sense.

While the character I'm going to be discussing next is not a protagonist by any stretch of the imagination, all a reader has to do is follow Paul, Frank Bascombe's son, in Richard Ford's INDEPENDENCE DAY. As if written exclusively to lend credence to my remark, Mr. Ford gave teenager Paul Bascombe a warty finger, and each time his text alludes to this the character becomes less attractive. While this is indeed an extreme example, anyone reading ID will soon realize the various ways Mr. Ford has made this boy unappealing, if not downright loathsome, with the wart creating an indelible metaphor.

Don't Create By Mistake What Richard Ford Wrote Deliberately

Readers don't want to be faced with the behaviors that all of us may deal with daily. For example, even though I've read of a character's bathroom habits, do people really want to read about this sort of thing? Likewise, in the realm of the undesirable, yet certainly not something everyone routinely has to contend with, do we find it appealing when some movie actress we admire tells the world she has contracted a sexually transmitted disease? Regardless of what some people might say to the contrary, is it out of line to feel that this actress's "star"—in the eyes of many—has been diminished forever?

Put Your Protagonist Under the Same Scrutiny

Celebrities, politicians, sports figures, and some other categories of "personalities" have never been able to recover from bad press. Yes, many do, but a lot don't. My point is that one's protagonist doesn't have the luxury of waiting for forgiveness, should it ever come. An average book requires ten hours to read, not three years to forgive and forget and then accept. And I'm quite serious about this.

A Writer Has to Consider What Constitutes a Good or a Bad Trait

As examples solely related to undesirable actions by protagonists, I've advised clients not to have their females sweat (let them perspire); not to have males "chomp" on food (even wolfing down a meal is a lot better than "chomping," as the latter connotes poor table manners); not to have the lead characters cleaning up after someone who's soiled a bed (avoid any reference, as the end-result of the voiding of an alimentary canal is not of interest—ever; did you enjoy reading about it via what I just wrote?); and not to have sex with someone who's taking medication (dead serious about this one, too, and it even includes an ED supplement unless this is meant as humor).

What Turns You Off Is What Should Be Avoided

I just mentioned some traits that readers find undesirable. So when reviewing a protagonist's relationship to a storyline, it's very important that this character, while not possessing non-normal characteristics, doesn't display the "normal" too blatantly either. This is a topic for another paper, but I mention it now because "normal" can be boring—and often excruciatingly so.

Effectively writing redemptive characters can be an enormously complex endeavor. So we should ask ourselves, while analyzing the way our protagonist comes across to readers, what are characteristics—if this were a real person—that we would find appealing? And what is there about our protagonist—again, if real— that we'd dislike? The task should then be to eliminate the latter if we want protagonists *whom readers will desire to identify with in some positive way*. I placed that last phrase in italics because it's the key to this entire article.

Redundancy Issues – Alliteration, Sibilance, and Repetitious Alphabet

It's All About Sound

Alliteration is often considered clever when used as hype by a newscaster such as Geraldo Rivera, but its horribly annoying to a lot of people when the novelty wears off or the technique is overused. Sibilant sounds are funny when spoken via a cartoon character such as Donald Duck, while not so humorous when part of someone's long-winded pontification at a school board meeting. And while writing numerous consecutive words beginning with or containing the letters "c" and "p" can be catchy in a commercial jingle, they might not be as well received when abundantly decorating a sentence of standard prose.

Sound Means Everything to Text, As It Facilitates Both Rhythm and Pitch

Strong words but true, since we hear what we read. Reason number 10,000 why it's critical to read out loud whatever we write before we consider posting it, mailing it, offering it, or publishing it. But reading out loud also means a lot of sometimes painstakingly slow work for the writer, and why this cardinal rule is often sidestepped. Yet listening for certain untoward sounds, and modifying the rhetoric that allows them, has as much to do with readability as any other factor.

Start with the Obvious and Work Toward Ferreting Out the Subtler Grating Performers

"S's" are the easiest culprits to recognize, since the hissing sound they engender is what sibilance refers to. And alliteration and sibilance combined are impossible for most readers to deal with. A phrase like, "She shifted seductively as she swayed towards his seat" is enough to turn off any reader. But what about subtle inflections such as "prepossessing smile," "successful city servant," and "seven consecutive series." There are indeed times when "smile" has to be modified to "allure," "servant" to "employee," and "consecutive" dropped and the phrase changed to "seven times in a row."

Too Many "C's" and "P's" Can Spoil the Soup

Soft "c's" were used in the earlier example, but a preponderance of hard "c's" can be annoying in their own right. "Accommodating change encourages actionable outcomes," is beyond a mouthful. And so is, "They appealed to the people in the principal opposition party." Consider how both phrases are sitting on your mind right now, and then read either phrase out loud and see if you don't come away with a sore jaw.

The Key is Balance

No writer sets out to aggravate the reader when the intent is to craft fluent prose. But the tendency for many writers is to be complacent and not look for the little tics that can sometimes evolve into major trouble spots. Reading material out loud, and listening closely to how it sounds, is the best advice anyone can give or receive. If it sounds bad, it reads bad. It's that simple. Again, it's all about sound.

Redundant Words and Phrases

Never is it truer that the human mind works in strange ways than when an author finds his or her draft littered with the same words or phrases. What makes this particularly galling is that proficient writers strive not to do this, yet quite often are unable to prevent syntax which is redundant—or reads as repetitive—from appearing on a page.

Words That Stand Out—Unfortunately

Oddly, it's the words that are most ordinary which can often cause the most grief. Words such as "because" or "become," should they be placed in consecutive sentences or paragraphs (even lengthy ones), can stick in the reader's mind as redundant. Along this line of commonality, too many appearances of "was" can gum up an otherwise good run of narrative. Word repetition can be as hard on the reader as the excessive use of specialty punctuation such as the semicolon or the exclamation point.

Some More of The Usual Suspects

Another chronic problem is the word "would," since the options for a suitable substitute generally are limited to "should" and "could," at best. Perhaps the greatest difficulty of all is what to use after the first "but." "However," "yet," and even "except," can often serve in a pinch, but—well, you see the problem.

The Fix for the Overuse of the Conjunction "But"

The best way to remedy repeating the conjunction "but" is to begin a new sentence as if it was an extended thought and not a contrary view. Example: John saw Mary in the park, but since he was scared of the guy she was with he kept walking. Rewrite as: John saw Mary in the park. He was scared of the guy she was with, so he kept walking.

Select Alternates for Prepositions

"Afterwards" can become "later," just as "under" can often be modified to "below" and not diminish the writer's intent. And while we are trained to use one word to take the place of many, it's sometimes prudent to write "at this time" instead of a redundant "now." Even a "presently" might need to be inserted instead of "now" to prevent duplication.

Homonyms Are Just As Problematic As Repeating Words

I recently read a draft with the following phrase: "The weather was going to determine whether or not they would be going out." This is an easy sentence to repair by substituting "if" for "whether," and dropping the "or not." But it's not always simple to spot a problem. In the following sentence, the syntax might be ignored: Every fall, John would haul wood. And even something more blatant might be missed. Consider: It was too much to bear, and I barely got out alive.

Complicated or Sophisticated Words Can Become a Major Issue

When a writer uses words such as "conflagration" or "beatification," these can be placed in a book just once. And I don't even like to see them in multiple works by the same author. The latter comment might seem a stretch, but when an author develops an unintended tic, this isn't good, since it makes the writing stale in the eyes of the loyal reader.

Phrases, Especially Clever One's, Cannot Be Repeated

A slick phrase will stay with the reader, and the ability to craft this sort of rhetoric is often why people lean toward certain authors. But it's important to keep in mind that the inherent nature of a unique rift of narrative is what will be remembered. A phrase like the following can only be written one time per lifetime: His face contorted, as if the result of an unpleasant musical note of his own making. And one contorted face per book, please, regardless of how it got that way.

But What If There Are Only So Many Ways Something Can be Written?

When I'm writing a Police Thriller, I often run into a problem with the word "policeman." After perhaps following it with "cop," and later "officer," then "patrolman" (if it fits), I'm forced to return to the first noun. There are indeed times when there are only so many options to identify a person by name or profession and still be accurate. In the "policeman" example, if the person's last name is Jones, creating Patrolman Jones, Officer Jones, or offering just plain Jones to the mix in a long scene might still not be enough, and there will be no other choice but to repeat a handle.

Yet when it's deemed necessary to restate a name in the same section, this should be an extremely rare occurrence and every attempt should be made to write around this sort of thing. And it's important to keep in mind that no matter how problematic the text might read when certain words continue to reappear, redundant phrases can leave an even more negative impression.

Restrictive and Nonrestrictive Clauses

Restrictive and Nonrestrictive Clauses

Certain books on grammar describe restrictive and nonrestrictive clauses as "necessary" or "unnecessary" clauses, and neither should be confused with "dependent" or "independent" clauses, which are also sometimes referred to as "main" or "subordinate" clauses.

Dependent and Independent Clauses

To the latter, take this sentence: "I can see the birds in the distance because I have excellent vision." "I can see the birds in the distance" is an independent clause, as it is a self-contained sentence that can stand by itself. However, "because I have excellent vision" is not able to stand by itself in this context, it is classified a "dependent" clause, since it depends on something else to make it part of a complete sentence (again, in this context).

Here's where it gets even more confusing: While commas don't always have to be used to separate dependent and independent clauses, they are mandatory to distinguish between restrictive and nonrestrictive clauses. Then to really confound the issue, it's the nonrestrictive (unnecessary) clauses that require commas and not the restrictive (necessary) clauses.

It's Good to Remember What Constitutes a Clause

To begin to weave through all of this, I've found it best to break it down in the simplest terms. And this begins with the definition of a "clause," which is a group of words with both a subject and a predicate.

Once we know this, in a sentence with multiple clauses, we have to ask if the one following the sentence's lead clause is necessary to the meaning of the sentence. Here are two examples: My brother, who gets all A's, is the star of the basketball team. Or: My brother who was a star player at his other school never made the team at his new one.

It's All a Matter of Degree

In the first sentence, the brother's academics don't have any relevance to his making the team, and for this reason the clause "who gets all A's" would be set off with commas. Conversely, the brother as a star player at one school and being cut at the other is pertinent to the message; hence, the clause doesn't require commas.

However, It's Not Always Cut and Dried

And this is the rub, as scholars have long debated clause relevancy in circumstances pertaining to an author's intent, and few decisions are as easy as the examples provided via my basketball player. So while I opened this article with the remark that all nonrestrictive clauses must receive commas, there is discretion regarding the designation of restrictive and nonrestrictive material. But the author can make the distinction and let others argue its validity, and for clauses that are clearly subjective, I'm of the opinion that it would be impossible to effectively disregard the writer's decision.

The Long Sentence Can Present Another Problem

Long sentences containing restrictive clauses can be very hard to read, since to be grammatically correct they will not contain commas separating the clauses. I don't remember in which Fitzgerald story I read the sentence, but he wrote one monstrosity that I had to read over and over to figure out the way it should've been punctuated. After the third of fourth time through it, I determined that he believed a particularly long clause was necessary to his sentence's meaning; hence, no commas.

I had to parse this sentence, as it was part of a project I was working on, but nonacademic readers won't routinely do this. And why should they? Frankly, if it wasn't a requirement I would've thought that the sentence was lacking punctuation and moved on. When text gets this cumbersome, my opinion is to revise the sentence. I'd hardly have advised Mr. Fitzgerald to take another stab at this particular patch of rhetoric, but most of the rest of us aren't quite as his level; so, in this sort of situation, I believe it's a good idea to consider an alternative sentence structure all the way around.

Showing vs. Telling Defined

"Showing vs. Telling"

What separates many writers is the ability to recognize when to utilize which technique. A suggestion is to always write the scene in a "show" format, knowing that you can always change to the "tell" medium if you wish to provide readers with a chance to catch their collective breaths.

The last statement should also explain the main flaw with "telling," as it can very often retard the pace of a scene. And while "showing vs. telling" is the normal syntax, for the purpose of demonstrating the difference in a way that I believe creates the greatest impression, I'm reversing the elements and beginning with "telling."

"Telling" the Action

Jack was having a tough time with life. Everything he was doing lately had seemed to turn out wrong. Even the simplest aspects of his daily activities had begun to take their toll. Look at what happened when he got out of bed in the morning. He had stumbled around, as if in a blue funk. He'd been hurt when he'd fallen against his dresser and pulled it over while he was trying to right himself. He didn't care who might have heard him throwing a drawer against the wall or the damage it might have caused. And after he made his way into the bathroom and began to prepare himself for another day, he wasn't sure if it was worth it.

"Showing" the Action

Like life itself, Jack could not find his balance. He fell against the chest of drawers and caught himself before stumbling backward and pulling the unit with him. A drawer flew open and hit him in the side, and he and it collapsed onto the bed like two clumsy lovers. He threw off a drawer and let it bang hard against the wall, cracking the plaster, unconcerned that the noise and vibration might have startled the newborn child in the apartment below. He weaved his way to the bathroom and stared in the mirror and ran the water, not caring if it was hot or cold, and took out his razor. He didn't lather his face, but kept glaring at what he saw—and wondered.

Not that these are spectacular examples, but they do identify the difference between "telling" and "showing." Which would you rather read?

Showing vs. Telling Further Defined

Sometimes "Telling" Is More Effective Than "Showing"

Francine Prose, an author and scholar for whom I have immense respect, added fuel to a long-simmering fire by stating in a book of hers on writing that too much is made out of "showing" instead of "telling." To paraphrase one of her points, she writes that the avoidance of "telling" leads to confusion which causes novice writers to think everything should be acted out. And to quote her: "There are many occasions in literature in which "telling" is far more effective than "showing."

Agents and Editors Are the Harshest of Critics

If everyone wrote as well as Ms. Prose (she has more two dozen titles to her credit), or the brilliant, mostly classical authors' works she cites in her book, who could argue? And that is the rub. Especially for someone trying to become published for the first time, and who is having his or her manuscript viewed by the harshest of critics–book agents and book publishers. People who are seemingly searching, as if with an electron microscope, for the most miniscule detail to warrant rejecting material.

Don't Wave a Red Flag–Avoid the Dreaded "Been"

In the real world of an author fighting tooth-and-nail for his or her manuscript to receive a fair hearing, the writer has to provide a narrative that does not wave a red flag–or even a yellow one. Nothing can kill a book quicker than if it is perceived to be written in a passive voice–as indicated by the constant use of "been"–which is a surefire disclosure that the scenes are "telling" rather than "showing" the action.

If a Choice, Overwrite "Show" Rather Than "Tell"

While 100-percent correct that many times it is advisable to "tell" instead of "show," for most authors pursuing a bona fide mainstream publisher, it is much better to have overwritten "show" than "tell." Let me put it this way: I've never heard of anyone being rejected for the former–but very often for the latter. So while the ongoing "show versus tell" debate might whet some appetites for eschewing the argument altogether, writers need to incorporate as many accepted elements as possible into their material, and "showing" (and the active voice it supports) is considered a component of quality prose writing, and superior to "telling" (in a passive voice) in the overwhelming number of instances.

Simile Use to Enhance a Narrative

Crafting Similes to Add Texture to a Story

A simile generally uses "like" or "as" to compare two dissimilar things to one another. I recently wrote an article citing Joseph Conrad as a terrific writer of metaphors, but more significant than even his skill with this element, I consider him the quintessential crafter of similes. Anyone skimming through LORD JIM will find more great similes than what are contained in the entire oeuvre of many prolific authors. Here are a few from LORD JIM as listed in Ariion Kathleen Brindley's "101 Best Similes in Literature":

"Only then did he find himself rolling head over heels like a shot rabbit."

"I would have given anything for the power to soothe her frail soul, tormenting itself in its invincible ignorance like a small bird beating about the cruel wires of a cage."

"All at once he sprang into jerky agitation, like one of those flat wooden figures that are worked by a string."

"The lumps of white coral shone round the dark mound like a chaplet of bleached skulls, and everything around was so quiet that when I stood still all sound and all movement in the world seemed to come to an end.'"

Fitzgerald Wrote One of My Favorite Similes

In the opening to TENDER IS THE NIGHT, Fitzgerald writes of the area around the old hotel on the French Riviera: "Now, many bungalows cluster near it, but when this story begins only the cupolas of a dozen old villas rotted like water lilies among the massed pines . . . ." Can a single line be more descriptive than this?

Fitzgerald's line communicates not only a scene but a mood for the entire story. I certainly can't write like Fitzgerald, and I wouldn't expect that of others either, but for a simile to be effective the comparison has to be pertinent. And the more poignant the better.

The Key Is for the Simile to Make Sense

Once, as a homework component of one of my creative writing workshops, I asked each participant to write two similes. Many of the participants were royalty-published writers, and one wrote for the local paper and another for a national magazine. Of the dozens of similes that were presented to me during the follow-up session, only two made any sense whatsoever.

Here's a Bad Simile

The comparison a simile illustrates, first and foremost, should be easily recognizable to the reader. "He hurried along like a turtle on hot pavement" is a clever line, but can anyone really associate speed with a turtle? Change "turtle" to "cat" or "lizard" or "barefoot child" and the writer might have something.

Here's a Good Simile

Actually, what follows is a great simile, and for years I've tried to remember who wrote it. I thought it was another of Conrad's but more than once I've parsed his books in my library and can't find the line, which goes something like this: "Like the plants under the water line, she weaved her way through life unaffected by the storm raging overhead." To me, that says a book's worth of words, and as with Fitzgerald's phenomenal opening to TENDER IS THE NIGHT, sets a mood that's spellbinding.

Simile Writing to Excess

In a recent article I extolled the virtues of crafting quality similes and the ways they can enhance the reading experience. But as I thought about this later, it occurred to me that I've often experienced cases when similes are used to excess, so I decided to address the issue of overuse.

First, One Simile Per Paragraph, Please

I've read material from famous authors in which two similes appear in a single paragraph, and even back to back. Honesty compels me to admit that I, too, committed this crime once or twice when I started out as a novelist.

The problem is that the second simile tends to diminish the impetus of the first one. For readers just getting through the initial simile, and what all writers hope will be a smile at the cleverness involved in its creation, a second following too closely does nothing but turn the text into a mental jigsaw puzzle in which the picture, once clear, is now jumbled. And the mind can stand only so much manipulation before it loses track of what's going on in the scene altogether.

Second, One or Two Similes Per Scene

And this scene might well extend throughout an entire chapter. In my earlier article I alluded to Joseph Conrad's enormous skill at writing similes. But I also remember what I felt was his overdoing it at times as well.

From a contemporary perspective, "heads in the crowd popping up and down like figures in a Bang-a-Troll game" is generally all the reader needs to know to get the full flavor of the author's characterization, and anything more will likely diminish the comparison.

Third, Everything Doesn't Require a Simile

Perhaps the most important statement of all is this subtitle. I've read many books by unpublished writers who believe that the more similes they write the better they will be respected as masters of the English language. One adeptly conceived simile that is pertinent to the theme of a scene is better than a dozen average offerings which do nothing to advance the characterization.

Quality Over Quantity Should Be a Writer's Mantra

I realize this applies to every aspect of prose writing, but an author's similes will be held to a high standard, and if they are not crafted at a consistent level of excellence, soon the technique will be viewed as overwriting—and a quick death for a work's chances at any level.

Simple Word Revisions That Can Dramatically Improve the Narrative of Any Story

Writers are always seeking ways to separate themselves from the pack. Today, elevating oneself is not only desirable but a necessity if an author is to have any hope of becoming published for the first time by a major house. The questions is, how?

Sometimes the Simplest Words and Phrases Can Make a Substantial Difference

A talented copyeditor who is an affiliate of mine worked through one of my client's novels recently and made several suggestions that I feel are worth repeating. These modifications provided the theme for this article, and involved "how" and "of," along with the need for consistency when using words such as "toward" and "among."

Determine the Instances When "The Way" Can Be Substituted for "How"

There are instances when two words are preferable to one, and this often applies when "the way" is substituted for "how." Here are two examples and their counterparts: Can you tell me how Mr. Jones was acting differently during the past two weeks? Can you tell me the way Mr. Jones was acting differently during the past two weeks? I liked how the thin lines along her mouth depicted anything but age. I liked the way the thin lines along her mouth depicted anything but age. In the second example in particular, "the way" adds allure to an otherwise bland run.

"Of" Can Be Problematic When It's Superfluous

The word "of" is being accepted almost to the point of idiom in sentences like this: "He spoke in as calm of a tone as he could." The correct syntax should read: "He spoke in as calm a tone as he could." Or this: "I never realized how good of a friend he had become," which should read: "I never realized how good a friend he had become."

"Toward" and "Among"

There are indeed times when "towards" sounds better than "toward" and "amongst" has a better ring to it than "among," but consistency is important. Thank goodness that checking for uniformity is now an easy task as a result of the "Find and Replace" button in all word-processing programs.

Then There Is "Over

Long ago I broke the habit of using "over" when "during" was correct, but I still find myself using "over" when "more than," "longer than," "greater than," etc., are better choices—if not proper grammar—in many instances. In defining periods of time, for example, it's desirable to write that something took more than an hour rather than something took over an hour. Likewise, longer than a month should be written instead of over a month, just as greater (or more) than a mile is correct and over a mile is not.

Don't Stop with These Examples

In this day and age, every possible opportunity must be exploited to gain an edge, and sometimes even the subtlest of nuances can illustrate accomplished writing and enable an author to take a major step in the right direction. And while there are indeed many examples of lazy rhetoric beyond what I mentioned in this article, paying attention to just the few words and phrases I've listed can make a major impression on an agent, publisher—and reader.

Sound in Writing

The most obvious idea that works for the majority of people is to read material aloud. Unfortunately, many writers get so close to their work that it's often difficult if not impossible to get a fair "hearing." Everything sounds good because of familiarity. And this is the real problem, not the purported inability to distinguish word tempo. If a writer—who claims imperceptibility to the nuances of his or her own work—reads somebody else's material, will the same issues persist? Probably not.

A Second Step Is to Listen As Someone Else Reads Your Material Out Loud

A lot of people can't sing a note but can readily distinguish the slightest miscue from a vocalist on stage. I've found that most writers can pick up flaws in their work when it's read to them. Personally, I pay attention to the slightest hesitation on the part of the speaker, because in almost every instance when this occurs it can be attributed to an inadequate word choice or a syntax issue on my part.

One Warning: Find Someone to Read the Work Who Is Not a Professional Speaker

I conducted a workshop series in which a woman who attended possessed a fabulous voice and was a public speaker by vocation. I think she could read the names and addresses from a telephone directory and spellbind an audience. Needless to say, when she read her own writing it sounded solid if not quite good at times. But without the benefit of her audio assist, when I parsed her material later, the writing was mediocre, at best. So, even if you know a Katie Couric- or Bob Costas-type, you're better off with Irene the secretary or Joe the salesman for this exercise, just as long as they're decent readers to begin with.

One Rule, and What a Writer Should Listen For

Once someone is willing to read material aloud for the writer who created it, I strongly suggest asking the reader not to preview any of the text; instead, to start right in with the narrative. The author should pay attention to any breaks that indicate obvious needs for a touch-up, but also to the ease or difficulty the reader is having pronouncing the words. Listen for repeating words or phrases that might have been ignored. Pay particular attention to repetitious sounds made by the letters "p" and "c," along with runs of sibilant sounds that make passages seem to be hissed rather than enunciated.

Make an Honest Evaluation

Did some of the sentences sound clipped? Were connectives utilized that enabled clauses to blend fluently with one another? Did the reader ever seem to be running out of breath? How well did the material transition from sentence to sentence, character to character, and scene to scene? As for the dialogue, did the words sound natural? And with respect to dialogue, was there adequate interior monologue to enable the reader to "relax" now and then? Was there variety in the construction of the overall narrative? And perhaps most important of all, did the reader seem to enjoy the material?

A Writer Will Have Answers

If a writer pays attention to the points I made in the previous paragraph, picking up the rhythm of the overall narrative will not be that difficult. And once the gremlins are eradicated, a revision will often produce a draft so superior to its predecessor that even the most challenged ear will appreciate the improved pitch.

Spelling and Word Meaning in the U.S. That Differ in the U.K.

U.S. Words That Differ in the U.K.

I was facilitating a writing workshop series some years back when a youthful participant commented that the British have some really weirdly spelled words. I good-naturedly told this lad that he needed to keep in mind that it was their language we've bastardized, not the other way around, and they probably don't like the way we spell many of their words. We all got a good laugh, and I thought this might be a fun topic for an article, which I never got around to until now.

Some Meanings Are Rather Straightforward

Everyone it seems is familiar with "bonnet" as a car's hood and "lift" for an "elevator." As for "bonnet," a dictionary definition includes "hood." Knowing this, it's not the slightest stretch to call a car's hood a bonnet. And "lift" means to "elevate," hence no further discussion is required. But do many know that in Great Britain a "chesterfield" is a "sofa"?

How About Phrases?

My favorite (or favourite if written in the U.K.) phrase harkens back to the travel site that was explaining how an "uneducated" tourist from the States could run into trouble without an experienced escort. An attractive young woman from America asked a desk clerk for a wake-up call at the countryside B&B in England where she was staying. The clerk promptly told her "He'd be glad to knock her up in the morning." Then he tells the television viewer how embarrassed he was and that his poor choice of words "Almost cost me me job."

A Common Word with a Powerful Added Meaning

I edit a substantial amount of material from the British Isles, and at times I find the writing more formal, but in a positive way. I recall being exposed to the word "purchase" to mean "advantage" by a British writer well before Nicholas Evans used it so well to his advantage in THE HORSE WHISPERER.

Spelling and a Couplet That Can Cause Trouble

I mentioned "favourite," and from my U.K. friends I see the "u" coupled with the "o" in a great many words. "Colour" is another common example of this. Then there's "programme" and "storey" (as in two-storey house, which I've always believed is the way this should be written in the States to differentiate it from a book's "story"). But "grey" might be the granddaddy of them all, as we are taught to write it as "gray" while at the same time we see the word "greyhound" correctly spelled at the dog tracks and on the sides of buses operated by the iconic firm of the same name. In many English words the "z" is an "s," although some of this is purely a French influence. There are a myriad of words that could be discussed, but the point is that the American way is not automatically the best. It's just ours.

When I was a youth, and all writing was done on the side of a cave, I wrote "different than" instead of "different from." I was marked down for this by my instructor, and I told this august bastion of the English word that I'd just read it in a book. I was informed that if I could produce the book with "different than" in it instead of "different from," my perfect score would be restored. I got so few perfect scores on tests in grammar school that I just had to find the passage, and of course I couldn't. As it ended up, years later I discovered a weather-beaten horse-racing tout form from Epsom Downs in a trunk, and there was the passage with "different than," and where I'd seen it written this way. Shows how my youth was spent. The point is that "different than" is considered perfectly good English in England.

A Peculiarity in Word Construction Often Delineates Greatness

I find it wonderful that I can sometimes read a single opening sentence and know where the writer hails from, and even a lone passage can often set the tone for an entire work. I'd hate to think that any person should want to conform, let alone be forced to fit someone else's idea of what is universal word construction. If this had been the case, I can only shiver at the thought of all the fabulous writers whose works I would never have read.

I surely would have skipped Jane Austen, George Eliot (Mary Ann Evans) and Rudyard Kipling, then Norway's Knut Hamsun, and even American writers such as Zora Neale Hurston and James Still. And more recently Charles Frazier. The English have every right to be proud of maintaining the language their ancestors created, and we in the States have every right to feel that we have improved the construction to suit our needs. But it always will be England's language first and ours second, since the provenance is one issue that is undeniably incontrovertible.

Starting the Story Sooner – What This Means and Why It's So Very Important

What Does It Mean When Told to Start the Story Sooner?

I attended a writer's symposium with a dais that included several well-known Mystery writers who fielded questions prepared by a skilled moderator. Each writer was asked what he or she felt was the single most significant issue for which anyone seeking publication should be concerned.

One of the program's participants, Jim Born, a successful local author I've gotten to know and whose writing I enjoy, said that beginning the story sooner was his best advice. It's mine, too, and I decided to devote this article to explain why.

Writing Without the Proper Regard for Movement

When I analyze a client's manuscript after reading it for the first time, I often have to make a determination as to when I think the story truly "begins." And when I submit my critique on the work to its author, at times this is confusing, since my notes, which I always include, might indicate the opening chapters were quite good or that the characters had been well developed—but that the story should've begun on page 31, or page 55, or page 100.

It's Not That the Early Narrative Isn't Good; It's That It Doesn't "Set Off" the Story

My all-time favorite example of this is THE RETURN OF THE NATIVE, a book I rescued from the trash can three times to discover a very good story for the most part. The first 50 pages, or so it seemed, were devoted to the description of Egdon Heath and its physical and social nuances. And while unquestionably of monumental importance to Thomas Hardy, I found this abundant early-stage minutiae to have nothing whatsoever to do with advancing the plot in what could remotely be considered a timely fashion.

Unfortunately, Some Writers Today Work As If in Hardy's Era

We have to grant Hardy obvious leeway related to the time when his book was published, since this was in 1878. However, today's writer has to be aware of the competition for the attention span of the contemporary reader. For this reason, as much as any, it is imperative to make an honest evaluation as to when the first compelling action in a story takes place. And it's critical to keep in mind that this is often not solely predicated by determining the first incidence of conflict.

But What About Authors Such As Jody Picoult or Tom Clancy Whose Narratives Are Intensively Descriptive?

It would be easy to look at either Ms. Picoult or Mr. Clancy and refer to genre to justify their writing styles, but this would be a gross miscarriage. Both employ their opening elements to set up their stories—and then they move on. And herein lies the major difference between their skill in this aspect of crafting exceptional prose and that of the average amateur writer trying to create quality material. Ms. Picoult and Mr. Clancy craft introductory material to propel their plotlines forward.

The Conflict Has to Be Advanced by the Ensuing Narrative, Not Supported by It

It is imperative to look at work and ask questions such as these: "Was it essential to write an entire chapter about walking through the graveyard?" "What about the laborious description of the house and the grounds before the fire?" "Was Jesse's attitude on the way to the funeral with Jim significant enough to write four pages about it?" Any of these seemingly stupendous story elements might not be that valuable if they are not a driving force behind the narrative that follows.

Sometimes it's nothing more than moving scenes from one location to another. But in other instances it's unfortunately necessary to hit the delete key–no matter how painful this may be–and begin the novel with only narrative that advances the plot in a concrete manner.

Tautology Defined

The first time I read the word "tautology," I thought because of the "-ology" suffix it referred to the study of something. However, in the realm of language, tautology isn't considered the study of anything but the analysis of an element of writing. Specifically, the needless repetition of a word. Not that I can improve on the definition of the three dictionaries I use for reference, yet I believe tautology is easier to understand if it's referred to as "modifying a word with a word that implies the same thing."

The All-Time Classic Is One Phrase We Hear Every Day

"It's the same exact thing," is the most obvious case of tautology we are exposed to on a routine basis. Can there be the slightest difference between "same" and "exact" in any context? Is there anything wrong with saying "It's the same thing" when discussing something that is identical? Yet those who write copy, for newscasters in particular, seem to relish telling us that something is "the same exact thing" at every opportunity. Or it's the "exact opposite," as if "exact" makes something *more* opposite.

Tautology Comes in Many Forms

In the drafts I'm sent to edit, many authors have written that a character has looked up at the sky or down at the floor. Unless someone is an astronaut, is it possible to look down at the sky? How about up at the floor? As with looking down at the sky, it's possible to create a scenario in which a person would look up at a floor, but it takes some work.

Tautology Creeps Into Our Rhetoric in Subtle Forms Too

An example I noticed in a dictionary was "widow woman." But what about the following examples: "hurtful injury," "unhappy frown," "mean sneer," "happy smile," "joyous glee," and "black darkness?"

However, if a connotation is desired that goes outside the accepted obvious implication for injury, frown, sneer, smile, glee and darkness, it's of course acceptable if not desirable to modify each noun. "Slight injury," "deep frown," "loud sneer," "brief smile, "tempered glee," and "eerie darkness" are each couplets with greater meaning because of the modifier.

Tautology Isn't Limited to Nouns

I read recently a line in which a photograph was "blown up larger." Could it be enlarged any other way? The same as "reduced smaller" or "fell down." Yes, someone can theoretically fall up the stairs, but this is certainly not common enough to be accepted as idiom. And it's what's acceptable to a language that in large measure determines tautology.

Ask Yourself, "Am I Saying the Same Thing?"

Variety keeps a narrative fresh, and it starts by making certain we're adding to the meaning of the nouns and verbs we modify. When a writer pays attention to tautology, I've generally found this author just as introspective when analyzing core thoughts and making certain these themes aren't overjustified by the text that follows.

And If It's Not Saying the Same Thing

One final remark, and it involves making certain something is indeed tautological. I was taken to task a while back for using the couplet "much more." An erudite chap mentioned that an instructor in his grammar school, no less, said this phrase was redundant and therefore superfluous. I respected his comment and complimented him for his good fortune at having a teacher who was so precise and willing to share such good advice with children that young. But I asked him, "Would you rather have more money in your next paycheck—or would you rather to have much more money?"

"That" —
Its Underuse, Overuse, and Misuse

Few words in our language cause as much trouble as "that." Not surprisingly, this is because "that" is a pronoun, adjective, adverb, and conjunction, and it also appears in a number of idiomatic phrases. And, should this not be enough, "that" is often substituted in casual conversation for "which."

Definitions, Definitions, and More Definitions

Defining "that" would consume this article. And the "that/which" explanation would cover another paper, and I indeed wrote on this very subject at length at another time. Hence, I want to focus on the subject of this article, which is the overuse, underuse, and misuse of "that."

One Self-Proclaimed Guru's Answer to "That"

Some years ago, when I had the time to participate in other folks' writing-related blogs, I remember being set back in my chair when a message-board "leader" informed his acolytes of his decision to omit "that" from every line in which it appeared in his latest literary wizardry.

I always wondered what happened when one of this fellow's characters should "realize the cherry" or "understand the toilet," instead of "He realized that the cherry had a pit in it only after he broke his tooth," or "He would understand that the toilet door needed a key after it was too late."

Then There's Too Much Clarity

At times I'll read something such as, "That is the thing that we need to be told that will make that clearer." The easiest fix for this is, "That is the thing we need to be told to make it clearer." When it is not impractical, I'm happy to recommend eliminating multiple uses of "that" in a sentence. Just not universally.

Substitute "Which" for the Second "That"

Many grammar experts don't agree with this, but I always like Dr. Jacques Barzun's contention, which states that "which," when substituted for the second instance of "that" if the latter occurs twice in a sentence (and it fits and makes grammatical sense), creates more fluent prose. But I always let the sound of the sentence dictate whether or not I substitute "which" for the second "that."

And in those instances when three "that's" occur, I'll generally place "which" between the first and last use of "that."

Misuse of "That"

"That" defines with specificity—and tautology if you write what I just wrote, ha ha—but I want to get my point across. It can't be substituted for "which" when the context is nonrestrictive any more than "which" can be substituted for "that" in restrictive text.

The Best Determinant for "That"

I obviously disagree with the guy who decided "that" was a bad word and it should be banished forever. Strict grammarians might even say I needed a "that" before "that" in the previous sentence. It's easy to find a place for "that," as it has abundant uses; however, I do believe the word is overused.

The old rule of thumb is to read the sentence with and without "that" and decide what makes sense, applying the method I used with the cherry and the toilet. Both examples indicate a clear-cut need for "that," but when it's not absolute, my advice is to omit "that" and read the sentence aloud (and the next day if possible) to determine if the decision was a sound one.

The "Chase" in a Story

Many years ago I was playing golf with my literary agent, and we were discussing a new novel of mine that he'd agreed to represent. He'd just finished reading a substantial revision he had urged me to make, and I was anticipating a positive response to what had taken a great deal of effort on my part to make happen. But when I asked him what he thought, his reply stumped me, because all he said was that my story needed more of a "chase."

Writers Must be Alert to What They're Told by Agents, Editors, and Publishers

The agent and I had become good friends over the course of a three-year period. So when I heard his remark I wasn't uncomfortable telling him what I thought of it. I remember even saying, after I topped a ball into the lake, that I was not going to revise the story any further. Instead of snapping back at me, he laughed and told me that no writer can ever say "never" to revising. Then he explained his meaning of "The Chase" to me.

Conflict and Peril

A writer must heed what his or her agent is saying—no matter how much it might hurt to hear the truth, and the conflict surrounding a story's protagonist, especially since this has so much to do with a story's pacing, is an element a seasoned agent will understand intimately. My agent's contention was that I hadn't placed my protagonist in enough consistent peril for my Thriller to work in a mass-market environment.

More Honest Words Were Probably Never Spoken

I'm convinced that book was never published because I failed to take my agent's advice and create a more structured plotline that constantly focused on the jeopardy my protagonist was facing. The agent even told me exactly how to do this, but I was too immature as a writer to understand what he was suggesting. Today, I'm five novels beyond that one, but I've looked back at the book on several occasions and chuckled at my indifference to what I recognize now as such an obvious deficiency.

A "Chase" Means One Thing

All writers must have this goal for their stories, and this is to make it hard (read, "impossible") for readers to put down their books. This is what writing a strong chase is all about. And it applies to all genres.

Can Ma and Pa Ingalls make a new life on the prairie for Laura and the rest of their family? Is Buck ever going to be reunited with his owner in Alaska? What is going to happen to Billy Budd while he is being tried for a crime he didn't commit? Will Scarlett ever marry Rhett? Can Agent Starling capture Dr. Lector? Will Harry survive the trials and tribulations foisted on him by his detractors at Hogwarts?

The "chase" gets down to maintaining a level of anxiety that keeps the reader engrossed in the protagonist's predicament, and it's undeniably one of the most critical elements in any story.

The "Reveal" in a Story

In writing, the "reveal" is the key element that explains "what it was in the narrative that held the reader's interest beyond anything else," and a component that is generally retained until the last possible moment. Many a book is judged by how well this is handled. If the work is strong, commonly this is because the finale contains a riveting "reveal," yet it doesn't always mean this occurs at the very end of the story. More on this later.

Certain Genres Lend Themselves to Great "Reveals"

By their very nature, Mysteries and Thrillers are the most obvious genres for which scintillating "reveals" would seem best suited. But Romance, Fantasy, YA, and every other genre demand a "reveal." If not, a story's premise would never be accepted by the reader. And material falls short when the narrative doesn't finish with a powerful enough "reveal." Simply, the ending doesn't live up to the plot elements. And nothing is more frustrating for a reader than to be left unfulfilled because a feasible "answer" didn't materialize.

At Times It Works Best to Write the Ending First

I often suggest to authors who habitually have struggled with endings to write them first. In this way, they can craft material to meet the standards their respective "reveals" require, and not the other way around. It's sort of like writing a joke, since commonly the punch line is created initially and the material leading up to it is figured out later.

The "Reveal" and the Denouement Can Be the Same, But Not Always

It's easy to slip into the mold of thinking that a "reveal" and a denouement are always interchangeable, but this isn't the case. In THE HUNCHBACK OF NOTRE DAME, while Quasimodo's bones turning to dust at the very end is indeed startling, the booties being Esmeralda's is the "reveal" the reader has been waiting for, and this occurs earlier in the story.

Examples of Books with Great "Reveals"

What makes a work memorable–and often remarkable–is a "reveal" that provides for the reconciliation of an "open" plot element and answers an unexpected twist set up by an earlier plot point which carried throughout the entire narrative.

Some of my favorite examples of "reveals" are provided via the classics, with THE AGE OF INNOCENCE perhaps illustrating the quintessential example of a "reveal." In the more contemporary market, I liked the way Amy Tan finished THE JOY LUCK CLUB, E.L. Doctorow's treatment of BILLY BATHGATE, and Ken Follett's "reveal" in THE EYE OF THE NEEDLE.

Threads in a Story and Methods for Tying Up Plot Elements Effectively

Story Threads Can Be a Huge Problem If Not Resolved, and Even Some of the Best Writers Are Not Sacrosanct

A thread is a plot element, nothing more, nothing less, but a problem for authors if they do not reconcile their threads for the reader. The obvious rationale for an exception is to purposely leave the plot point unresolved to engender interest in reading a sequel to the story. But when the aforementioned is not relevant, the problem can be excruciating for the reader. And some of the most respected writers in literary history have been derelict by not tying up their threads acceptably.

One of the Most Flagrant Examples of Not Tying Up a Thread Is in INDEPENDENCE DAY

In Richard Ford's INDEPENDENCE DAY, for which he won a Pulitzer Prize in 1996, he provides great detail in describing the circumstances surrounding the brutal murder of a real estate agent. Then, later in the novel, he brings up her death often, heightening the reader's enthusiasm for an answer to who did it. But the thread is never developed, and as a result the culprit remains unknown throughout the entirety of the narrative. The murder therefore has no relevance to the story, and an awkward hole is left in the plot, although apparently not egregious enough for the Pulitzer committee to find fault.

WAR AND PEACE and THE RETURN OF THE NATIVE Were Also Not Immune to Threads Left Dangling

I call this lack of resolution a dangling thread, and a wonderful bad example (ugh, I know) can be read in the two novels cited in this subtitle.

Anatol is a profound early character in WAR AND PEACE (he's the guy who ties Pierre to the bear, should anyone have forgotten). Tolstoy relates much later in the tale that Anatol lost a leg in battle, but there is not a single mention of him in any other section of the book.

In THE RETURN OF THE NATIVE, Captain Vye is a fabulous character for whom great fabric is knitted by Hardy. But after Eustacia meets her end, there is no further reference to Vye—and his feelings regarding Eustacia's demise are not expressed in any way—thus leaving the story and the reader with a huge void.

Can There Be a Happy Medium?

Perhaps an expedient way to view threads is via Dos Passos's USA. Eventually he had to leave some threads to their own devices or he'd have been writing ad infinitum because of the type of historical chronicle the story happened to be. However, USA demonstrates in abundant terms how threads can be continued to reach a satisfactory conclusion in the mind of the reader—yet sans "finality" in each and every scenario.

Shouldn't the Writer Be Cut Some Slack?

Some can argue that it's not a literary transgression to defer providing a detailed chronology for the life of every character in a book the size of WAR AND PEACE. This is certainly not disputable, but in my opinion it does beg reconciliation by the author when a character is prominent enough to drive a significant segment of the story. This is my contention in the Tolstoy example, and for me it's even more acute in Hardy's work because Captain Vye is such a visible character in so much of the narrative.

It could be nothing more than an issue of degree, but if readers were to parse the stories they didn't enjoy, there might be a legitimate question as to how often their disappointment was due to dangling threads.

"Tic" Definition and Examples

Most people associate a "tic" with the spelling "tick" and think of it as the little parasite that sucks the hemoglobin from someone's pooch. Then it becomes not so little anymore as it morphs into a giant sac of blood in a host that's hard to kill even when squished. I find it appropriate to apply this gross analogy to a tic in writing.

A Tic By Any Other Name Is Still a Tic

By definition, a tic in writing parlance is "a frequent quirk in the narrative." The operative word is "frequent." And what isn't added to the description is that tics, like their animal counterparts, can be so annoying to their recipients that they also become downright painful.

"You Know?" Can and Does Apply to Writing

Everybody has a friend or acquaintance who asks "You know?" in every sentence. In speech, this sort of tic is easy to pick up. However, in a narrative there are other forms of tics that are more difficult to spot—until it's too late.

"Chuckling," "Laughing," and "Looking" Lead the List

I read a raw draft recently that was quite good except that the writer's characters had a penchant for chuckling. And often for no apparent reason. I had another work in which everyone was constantly laughing, apparently finding things more humorous—at all times in their lives—than their less jovial counterparts who only grinned. I remember that one of my own early drafts contained characters who were constantly looking up, down, around, over, under, through, and into things. Way too much "looking" was taking place.

The overworked actions I just mentioned can be sought out and corrected, as a search via the "find" function will immediately display the number of times a common word such as "look" shows up in a narrative. But some tics are subtle, and this is where it can get sticky.

Too Many Characters Can Have the Same Attributes

This doesn't mean that their dialogue is identical, or their personalities, or their appearances, although each of these characteristics could be considered a tic. In the world of "ticdom," to make the grade each character can simply react to something in the identical manner, numerous times throughout the story. I read an otherwise brilliant novel recently that had multiple characters tossing out clever one-liners, from the grocer to the plumber to the pediatrician. Only a single comedian per novel, please.

Search for Repetition

When a writer starts out, it's easy to have several characters saying and doing similar things. But as authors mature, it's important to delineate syntax so tics don't occur unless they're a component of the storyline. And it's valuable to recognize that if a character is repeating the actions of another, this is no different from a dialogue oddity that becomes nettlesome to the reader. Again, a tic is still a tic.

Time and Distance in a Narrative

During a creative writing workshop of mine a while back, a man who had served on the first nuclear-powered aircraft carrier read me a scene from a war story he'd written. The prose was fine, but the flow of his material was disrupted by constant references to military time, as if he were providing a report to his superior officer, on a rigid schedule.

Constant Time References Retard Pacing

Nothing can slow the pacing of a story quicker than constantly referencing time. The reason is that time references inherently draw attention to gaps, and the reader tends to wonder what happened during the periods that were not accounted for. The problem be-comes especially acute when the reader's attention is drawn to long spans of "missing" time. The assumption is "What did I skip?" even though nothing was omitted from the story.

"Soon" and "Later" Are Great Levelers of the Playing Field

Timeline issues are exacerbated when the reader is focused on them. If something starts at midnight and nothing else is discussed until 11:30 the following evening, readers are going to wonder what hap-pened for almost a full day. To remedy drawing attention to gaps, words that express time in the abstract, such as "soon" and "later," can be used to fill "open space" in a narrative.

Avoid Specificity with Time and Distance

Not long ago I remember reading in someone's early draft that it was about 2:27 p.m. First, 27 minutes is as exact as it can get unless the book is about Greenwich Mean Time or some event that requires split-second action. Just write "at 2:27" and continue the thought. And if something happened at 2:27, there had better be a very good reason. Otherwise, round the number to the nearest half-hour, as most readers hate having to pause to consider exact time.

However, for purposes of pitch or tone, a writer might use "about" or "around" to modify time. The same with phrases such as "shortly before" or "just after" a specific time reference, such as noon or midnight. But the decision to write time in this manner should be made with care—and applied with an ear toward the rhythm of the run.

Distance Has Its Own Set of Preferences

Walking "about" a mile, or something was "approximately" a half-mile away, is a waste of two good adverbs. "Walking a mile" or "It was a half-mile away" is much easier on the reader. "About 6 feet tall" is certainly acceptable in some circumstances, but writing "6 feet tall" without the modifier is almost always better. Likewise, "He weighed about 200 pounds" is not superior to "He weighed 200 pounds." Does anyone really care about "about," even if a careful reader somewhere might wonder how the writer knew the exact weight of somebody of something.

Here's an Easy Exercise Regarding Approximations

Would someone write that his shoe was almost a size 10 ½? or that his cap size was approximately 7 ¾ inches? Most people would write that he wore an average-size shoe and a medium-size hat. Even though these examples pertain to size, if we think in those terms it makes it much easier to express time and distance in a way readers can quickly assimilate.

Timeline Gaps – How They Negatively Affect a Story's Continuity

When writing a novel it's easy to assume that as long as time is accounted for in some manner, all will be well. Nothing, however, can be further from the truth. In reality, the explanation can often be more damaging than the omission.

What Happened During the Time Readers Aren't Told About?

Consider this passage: John and Mary are having a torrid extramarital relationship that her spouse has suspected for some time. He's known for being hot-headed, and when his suspicions are confirmed he's blind with rage and immediately seeks ways to retaliate against both of them. Three months later, John and Mary are confronted in a parking garage by her husband, who, wild-eyed, is brandishing a machete and screaming epithets at both of them.

Huh? I'm certain anyone reading the preceding paragraph would find it downright ridiculous that 90 days passed before this caliber of firebrand did something drastic, yet I read these unexplained–and therefore undesirable–gaps all the time.

Imminent Actions Require Equally Imminent Timelines

Could readers be expected to accept that a character with a short temper–and now blinded by rage–would put off doing something drastic for even 90 minutes? On a softer but no less important note, if a writer wrote 90 days of inactivity into an action story, is it practical to expect readers not wanting to know what was transpiring during that interim?

In the case of the example, what was Mary's husband doing during those three months? Was he planning the ultimate reprisal, and did it require this much time to adequately prepare each aspect of his scheme? Or was he more concerned about not having evidence of his actions point in his direction, and therefore everything had to be just right? Or did it require that much time to plan the perfect escape?

Sometimes Even a Solid Explanation Isn't Enough

In Mary's husband's situation, no amount of explanation could likely justify 90 days of inactivity in the storyline. And this is the problem with so much of what I'm sent when writers are more concerned about adhering to their "datelines" than providing continuity for the movement of their plots. Authors should never be criticized for their concern for accuracy, but this can never trump movement. Because once the reader stops to consider a gap in time, everything in the story at that moment comes to a screeching halt.

Omission Is a Technique, But It's Far from Foolproof

Omitting time references is a method to avoid hindering a plot's natural movement. But these exclusions can be just as detrimental if the reader wonders what had occurred during those times for which there was no accounting.

The only way to guarantee continuity is to determine the crucial plot timelines and eschew referencing those that fall outside that category. Once the critical time references of the story are isolated, a writer can then decide how often and where to integrate them into the narrative.

A Gap Is a Gap

With the rarest of exceptions, tight timelines are mandatory to hold a reader's attention. Long or unexplained gaps will confuse people, and once a timeline seems improbable, the reader will put down the book. A good way to look at this is from the perspective of timelines as a pacing medium. If something seems to take a long time to develop, is the scene's energy level–and therefore its pacing–generally going to be fast or slow?

Title for a Book – Coming Up With An Excellent Name for a Story

When I was recently asked to write an article on how to come up with a great title for a book, it would have been easy to suggest that someone should craft a great story first. But GONE WITH THE WIND, THE SUN ALSO RISES, THE SOUND AND THE FURY, and THE POWER AND THE GLORY would've been exceptional books regardless of their titles. So would THE MAGIC MOUNTAIN, AN AMERICAN TRAGEDY, SHIP OF FOOLS, and ATLAS SHRUGGED. But in both groups, only SHIP OF FOOLS would've been a certain match for someone browsing the shelves of a library for something to read, since the story did indeed take place on a ship on which a lot of foolish people had embarked.

An Author's First Responsibility Should Be to Identify the Story's Most Significant Element

Just as many writers have difficulty recognizing the genre in which their story is written, authors are often perplexed at how to present their material in terms that clearly and succinctly relate its unique characteristics. If a writer works on this skill, and anyone who has any hope of becoming published by a mainstream royalty publisher must do this, channel this presentation into a ten-second elevator pitch, since you'll need to perfect one of these too. In these ten seconds you'll likely have spoken 15 to 20 words. Assuming you've toiled long and hard to craft your short presentation, what is the message?

Use the Most Powerful Point in the Elevator Pitch to Create Your Title

Since you've now broken down your story to its most definitive level, something in the narrative has motivated you to come up with a powerful spit of rhetoric that says it all. Your story is brilliantly conceived and Fitzgerald should only have written as well. Now remember your favorite novels and think about their storylines and their titles. Look at your manuscript in the same way and imagine what would best encapsulate the words you wrote.

KANSAS FLASH might not be about University of Kansas and Chicago Bears football great Gayle Sayers, but the life of a county fair huckster who became a phony tent evangelist and then really turned to God (a modern-day Beckett); THE CRUMBLED HEART, instead of Romance or Horror could be a story of the inability of a child prodigy to attain expected greatness; THE BITTER TASTE OF SWEET SUCCESS might tell the tale of a character like Harry Angstrom in the RABBIT series.

Keep in Mind That Your Publisher Will Have the Final Say

At the time I wrote this article (June of '09) I checked Amazon for each of the three titles I just made up, and none of them were listed. I suggest doing the same (and with your local library) with whatever you create. This is especially important if your title matches or impinges on another author's in the same genre in which you are writing. This happened to me twice in 15 years, so this is one subject I can relate to from personal experience and wish I couldn't. And remember that no matter how good you think your title might be, the publisher may suggest or even require something altogether different.

Transitioning Narrative Effectively

As a writer advances through the process of creating what he or she hopes will be a novel people will pay to read, one of the most daunting challenges is to meet the requirements for effectively transitioning material. For many writers, transitional elements can be difficult to comprehend, let alone achieve.

Transitioning Is Necessary from Both a Micro and Macro Perspective

To understand transitioning, it is necessary to have a solid grasp of what this involves at "the single word within the sentence level" first.

One word, such as a strategically placed "before" or "now," can impact the meaning of a huge volume of text and provide the perfect link to the next plot point.

Other times, a short clause such as "over the next few months" or "never again" can provide the ideal bridge. The right clause lets the reader seamlessly take in one story element and comfortably move onto the next without a break in the action. Conversely, inadequate transitioning often prevents a manuscript from being read, let alone considered for publication.

An Entire Paragraph Is Commonly Used to Transition Material

A paragraph is the most logical choice in many if not most instances, since this provides the easiest medium to achieve the desired result. However, it often requires several paragraphs to bring about the proper effect.

A Complete Scene Dedicated to the Transition Is the Next Choice

We are now to the macro level, although some might say this was achieved when the paragraph was broached as an option—and certainly when multiple paragraphs were suggested. Whatever one's feelings, an entire scene dedicated to a transition point is second only to an entire chapter's being utilized as a transition element.

We Must Not Forget About Dialogue As a Transitioning Medium

When writing about effective transitioning, it's easy to think that it primarily involves exposition and not dialogue. And while exposition could certainly be considered the prime facilitator, the use of dialogue to transition material cannot be underestimated. This is why it's so critical to analyze dialogue to determine how well it transitions plot elements, not only for the narrative that preceded it— but for what is to follow.

Villains in a Story –
How Bad Can They Be?

At first pass, asking how bad a villain can be seems like a fun topic to write about. The most horrible characters in literary history have commonly revealed themselves via their thoughts or actions in ways that readers found appealing. Evildoers such as Hannibal Lector and Annie Wilkes and certainly Dracula have elicited some sort of positive reaction from much of the public at one time or another.

For Many Villains, It's the Bright Side and Not the Dark Side That Makes Them Appealing

Thomas Harris enabled Lector fans to learn about the doctor's youth in plausible terms that explained why he became a monster. Annie Wilkes was simply deranged, but she displayed eerie justification for her actions that made her creepiness, while certainly not acceptable, remotely understandable. And Drac had all these years of never enjoying peace until a bevy of contemporary writers gave him a reason to live. I'm stretching all of this, but each of these villains is acceptable to the reader, and that's what matters.

Here's Where the Fun Part Ends

The difficulty with writing villains becomes problematic when it relates to whom and how they choose to do-in they prey. An antagonist who kills children or the mentally challenged can present a huge issue for a writer. Mainstream publishers also shy away from stories about pedophilia, incestuous relationships (unless subtly referenced, such as in A THOUSAND ACRES), and criminals who attack the defenseless.

Here Are Some Antagonists to Avoid

I receive many novels each year that I refuse to edit because I know in their present character configurations these stories would have no chance with a major royalty publisher. One recent plot involved a returning GI who began a sordid relationship with his 10-year-old daughter. Another story started with the dismemberment of a young boy and the central character's lust for murdering children seeking a father-figure (I see a lot of this sort of material of late for some reason). A recent story depicted a grotesquely unattractive man who bought retarded children and raised them as sex slaves. As sickening as what I just related happens to be, there is some stuff I've been sent that's even worse, but I hope what I presented clearly expresses where I draw the line.

It's Not Censoring, It's What a Publisher Thinks the Public Will Read

In the Thriller and Mystery genres, major royalty publishers aren't going to present a book solely for its shock value. However, there might very well be a market for each of the storylines I just mentioned if placed in the hands of a Gore Vidal- or Normal Mailer- or James Dickey-type. At these exalted skill levels, even the most disgusting topic could be made palatable in a novel (or if someone wanted to write a nonfiction book that deals with any of the subjects). But in the realm of pure commercial fiction by an unknown author, I give this sort of material no chance whatsoever.

Writers Must Consider Their Audiences

The purpose of this article is not to tell anyone what to write but to explain markets. According to many polls, women buy more books than men, and people over 65 buy three/fifth's of all Mysteries and Thrillers. Is it reasonable to think that these demographics want to read about pedophilia, incest, and the dismemberment of children? The avid older readers I know won't touch books that contain any of these plotlines.

If there is no interest in becoming signed by a major royalty publisher, then there is no reason to pay attention to anything I offered by way of explanation. However, if becoming signed by a respected imprint is what's desired, one of the first things the editor will consider is the platform for the story, and it behooves authors to be aware of what would be deemed acceptable–and that which isn't.

Voice – Active vs. Passive

I recently read the unpublished draft of a manuscript that reminded me of something which hadn't come up in some time. And this was the problem with material written in a passive voice. It's easy to assume this is simple to understand via the well-touted converse implications of "Mary was playing the piano" and "The piano was being played by Mary," but it's often difficult for some writers to fully comprehend the unintended baggage passive voice brings with it.

Past Tense Shouldn't Be Confused with Passive Voice

As everyone knows, "John walks in the park" is present tense in an obvious active voice. We all learned in grammar school that "John walked in the park" is past tense, and also in an active voice. And that "John was walking in the park" is past progressive tense, but again in an active voice. We were also taught that "John has walked in the park" is present perfect tense in an active voice, and "John had walked in the park" is past perfect active tense. For anyone who has an understanding of the rudiments of English, this is about as basic as it gets, so what's the problem?

Passive Voice Creates a Different Meaning

"Been" seems to creep into amateur writing with ever-increasing frequency. Phrases tend to crop up like, "John had been walking through the park when he spied Ellen strolling down the sidewalk." The sentence would be fine, except it indicates that John was doing his walking in the past, and this is likely not what the author wanted to convey.

An Effective Fix That Is Not Always a Simple One

One way to avoid passive voice is to find substitutions for "had" and "have." It's not always easy, and all action-verb writing can become annoying to the reader, but judicious alternatives for "had" and "have" will provide a summary remedy. A mess like "Loud rain had been falling on the roof" could be converted to "Rain pummeled the roof." In the second phrase, the decibel level is obvious by the word "pummeled," and the single-word verb, while taking the place of the three-word "had been falling," conveniently places this scene in an active voice.

What About Too Many Instances of "Was" in a Perfectly Good Sentence?

This sentence is a no-brainer: While John was walking through the park, he was thinking about what was bothering him of late. The last "was" of course could be changed to "had been," as a passive phrase is perfectly acceptable in this context. This next sentence poses a fix that's not so easy: John was walking through the park, worried about what was happening in his life, and he was particularly concerned about what was occurring with his marriage. Even though everything is active in John's mind, would not a "had been" placed in front of "happening" help the flow?

Let Your Ear Guide You, But Stick to Active Voice As Much As Possible

So while there are times when it's advisable to interject a passive element, let this be predicated in large measure by how the sentence sounds when it's read out loud. Just keep in mind that it's far and away best to write in an active voice whenever possible.

Voice – What Does It Mean?

Everyone Seems to Have a Different Definition for Voice in Writing

Much of the confusion seems to come from the way critics often extol the virtues of a newly published author. We'll read something like, "John Doe, a striking new voice on the scene," or "Mary Jones, the richest and most vibrant voice to hit commercial fiction in a long time." Nice words indeed, but do they really say anything about what makes either voice special?

Voice Is Each Writer

I've long stated that voice is "you," and I firmly believe this. If someone is told he or she displays a striking voice, I'd like to think there is something genuinely scintillating about that writer's particular style. Likewise, if someone is claimed to possess a rich and vibrant voice, I'd expect to read a work with well-developed characters and expansive characterizations. But there is no way to be certain this will be the case, since the term "voice" is anything but definitive.

A Voice Can Be Something Specific

My least favorite phrase is when someone says a writer has a strong voice. Why not just state that the author's prose is intelligently written? Or that the content will make the reader think? Or that the plot is complex with well-conceived threads that are expressed in an exciting and realistic manner?

Voice Is Genuinely Often Quite Distinctive

Perhaps one of the ways to illustrate voice is to look at four of the most famous American writers of all time: Faulkner, Steinbeck, Hemingway, and Fitzgerald.

Faulkner is known for intricate sentence structure that he utilized to present extraordinary characterizations; Steinbeck wrote in an easier-to-read style, but with a comparable depth to his storylines; Hemingway on the other hand crafted brilliant characterizations via a terse, sharp style that required perfect word selection; while Fitzgerald infused his narratives with characterizations so rich with imagery that they created a mood for his stories which the reader could "feel" on every page. Each of these writers achieved a like result, but with unique, unmistakable voices evidenced by the mastery of a particular writing technique.

While It Can Indeed Be Difficult to Define, Voice Is Always Present

Voice is whatever any of us want to make it. It is a word that has few limits, since it can describe quintessential material just as well as something quite pedestrian. Yet owning a voice to be complimented is what all writers should strive for, regardless of how feeble the attempt might be to explain exactly what was recognized for its excellence.

Voice and Tone – The Difference Between the Two

For many, tone and voice seem synonymous, and it is easy to see why people might feel this way; however, the terms are decidedly different. But before either can be properly differentiated, it is important to take a close look at writers who mastered voice.

Thomas Mann's Short Stories Showcase Voice

One of the best ways to understand something is to provide different treatments of the subject. Thomas Mann's eight stories in the popular Vintage imprint with DEATH IN VENICE as the lead title is ideal to work from since each story is written in a different voice. Yet Mann's masterpiece, THE MAGIC MOUNTAIN, depicts his voice as a seprate entity unto its own—and one could say that it was his true voice, although this could be heatedly argued.

While the short stories in the DEATH IN VENICE grouping enable a relatively quick study of the range voice can take, this is far from conclusive. The reason is because voice is without boundaries. This open architecture, in and of itself, leads to much of the confusion about voice. And this is the first distinction between voice and tone, since tone can generally be identified without too much of an argument.

So What Is Voice

When someone hears that "a new voice has exploded upon the literary scene," does one automatically expect to read the next Marcel Proust, Virginia Woolf, Ayn Rand, Ralph Ellison, William Faulkner, or Erskine Caldwell; or should we seek writers from our current era such as Pat Conroy, Elmore Leonard, E.L. Doctorow, Tom Clancy, or Barbara Kingsolver for reference?

Each of these writers possesses a distinctive voice, but what do we say about authors who create work in the same genre and are similar in style? Does each writer still have a separate voice? Of course he or she does. Just as one singer can sound like another but not possess the identical range in every key.

An Attorney Letter and Family Correspondence on the Same Subject Illustrate the Difference

One of the best ways I can come up with to express voice is to parse an invitation for the reading of a will from an attorney and compare this with the same request from a close relative.

The first might read something like this: Dear Mr. David C. Howson: Please be advised that your attendance is requested on Thursday, January 11, 2009, at 1:00 p.m., in the offices of John Carlton Jones, Esquire, Attorney at Law, 201 West Michigan Avenue, Chicago,

Illinois, 60601, for the reading of the Last Will and Testament of Horatio Clark Howson.

Conversely, here is an invitation from a close relative: Dear Davey, your uncle's will is going to be read next week at our attorney's office, and we look forward to seeing you there. Jo Ann will call you with the details. Love, Aunt Mary.

Style Establishes Voice, but There's a Lot More to It

Same message about the dearly departed, and although both are conveyed in what is considered a soft tone in relative terms, they are written in decidedly different voices. So while it is obvious that style creates voice, what about an academic paper written in an authoritative tone? Isn't this the same as an authoritative voice? Certainly, except it would probably be easier for definition purposes to claim the voice as authoritative and the tone as strong.

Tone Has Three Basic Mediums

All sorts of elaborate academic definitions are available, some consuming as much text as this entire book, but for my purposes, tone is either soft, moderate, or strong. These areas of course can have any number of gradients, from very soft to aggressively strong, but the three delineations provide the basis for comparison. This is still speculative, because what one person considers moderate another might feel is strong (and of course vice versa). But it's much easier to come to a consensus on a specific tone than to devise a chart that categorizes voice.

So, Again, What Is Voice?

Voice is you. Should you and another person write a book about the identical topic, your story will depict your way of telling the tale via words and syntax that differ from what the other person will create. So when you write a book, and the critics proclaim a fantastic new voice has roared onto the scene, these pundits are talking specifically about you, because you are the voice of your writing. And a unique voice indeed.

Word Consistency in a Manuscript

One of the elements an editor looks at is the consistency of word usage in a narrative. Certain words seem to come to the forefront, and this article will identify some of the main culprits so writers can be on the lookout for them. And if ever there was one fantastic feature in word-processing software, it's the Find and Replace function.

"Towards" and "Amongst" Are at the Forefront

In my own drafts I often find instances in which I think "toward" sounds fine in one sentence and "towards" better in another. The same with "among" and "amongst." However, "toward" is the preferred spelling, as is "among." But the most important issue is to be consistent throughout the narrative, regardless of which spelling for either word is initially used.

"Backward and "Backwards" Can Have Different Meanings

These words are tougher, because both can be used as either adjectives or adverbs, and in some instances the two words aren't interchangeable. For example, someone might say that Joe was a little backward, but not that Joe was backwards, unless of course Joe was facing in what at the time was an opposite direction.

"Afterward" and "Afterwards" Can Also Cause Problems

I have never been comfortable with "afterwards" instead of "afterward," yet the former is accepted as correct. Whichever spelling is used, again, make certain it's applied uniformly throughout the draft.

"Too" and "Also" Are Exceptions

A writer recently asked me about "too" and "also." As if the subject of this article isn't already difficult enough to keep straight, these words are a horse of a different color. "Too" and "also" can be interchanged throughout a manuscript without raising any red flags. Frankly, it's a good idea to mix them to provide variety. The reason is because we aren't dealing with "too" and "toos" and "also" and "alsos."

The problem occurs when words, such as the others I mentioned, have the same meaning with or without the "s" at the end. Then, as I've indicated, it's important to stay with the first usage and make certain the entire draft is consistent.

Words and Phrases
That Are Used Incorrectly

In grammar school, everyone is exposed to the common bugbears in English, then as we become more educated we learn that the rules aren't universal, nor are they applied uniformly. This article deals with some elements of our language that seem to have become more confused over time.

"Less" and "Fewer" Lead the Pack

Let's start with "less" and "fewer." We all know that less is used for things that can't be counted and fewer for things that can be quantified. And everyone has read the rebukes leveled at super-markets when the sign for the express checkout line reads "ten items or less" but should read "ten items or fewer." After all, counting ten items certainly means the number can be quantified. But what about writing a comment in 50 words or fewer? Has anyone ever seen that? Both 10 items or less and 50 words or less are idioms that are overlooked because they are used so often that even some experts accept them. Now it's all clear, right? Maybe not. Use less with plural nouns that refer to time and money, but not people: Less than 100 years ago, less than one hundred dollars; but, fewer than 50 people. Now how easy are less and fewer?

"Among" and "Between"

These words seem quite simple to apply correctly. "Among" is used with three or more of something, while "between" implies an occurrence that involves two. A snap, right? However, when something can be physically divided, this also requires "between." Hence, the turkey was divided between our family, relatives, and neighbors. And "between" is also used when there is a commonality of entities, such as, "The negotiations took place between Russia, China, and Japan." Yuck, this was supposed to be a breeze.

How About "If I Were" or "If I Was?"

During my youth, I remember thinking that when "if" introduced material it always required "were." ("Were" is referred to by grammarians as the subjunctive mood.) But then I learned that when "if" applies to something that's not contrary to fact or hypothetical, "was" is correct. ("Was" is referred to as the indicative mood; meaning, it could happen.) Here are examples of each: 1) If I were a bird, I'd fly to Chicago. Subjunctive mood "were"; couldn't happen: 2) If I was able to make that flight, I wouldn't be talking to you on the phone right now. Indicative mood "was"; real scenario.

I've noticed some well-regarded writers foul up the use of "if," and many educators are lobbying to do away with the subjunctive mood altogether. But while it's still with us, careful writers will have to address it accordingly and pay attention to its nuances.

"Series" Can Be Singular, and "Blonde" Is Never an Adjective

The word "series" is singular when used as in these first two examples: "The hit series is set to open in September." "That series of events is bothering everyone I know. But, "several series of events are about to take place," is correct because there is more than one series as determined by the adjective. "Blond" is used for all males and whenever it's used as an adjective, regardless of the gender it's modifying. Hence, when "blond" is used as an adjective it's always without the "e," even when modifying a female. Only when a female is referred to as a "blonde" is this correct. Hence, a female cannot have blonde hair, only blond hair. I believe a lot of people can win money betting on who knows how to apply this rule correctly. And, yes, the advertising for some of the most popular hair-care products is written with flawed syntax.

My Favorites Are "Assure" and "Ensure"

When someone's safety is guaranteed, "ensure" is routinely used. Yet this is often the third or fourth meaning in a dictionary, and some eschew this definition altogether. "Assure" is the better word in the vast majority of contexts in which it's used. "Ensure" has become such a catch-all, however, McDonald's now "ensures" my meals if I check my receipt. The company is not going to guarantee I get the food I ordered, but the firm is committed to making certain the welfare of my burger and fries is protected.

English Is Tough Enough and Shouldn't Be Made More Difficult

This article shows just how recondite some aspects of our language can be, even for those of us who work with it every day. And in defense of everyone who tries to write as well as possible but doesn't always succeed, many physicians study for 15 or more years and then don't always make correct diagnoses. Attorneys who teach in the best universities provide consultations that blow cases. And Wall Street economists disagree diametrically about topics each has spent a lifetime studying. So if someone's nonagenarian great-aunt should write something such as "Amongst you, me, and that there hound dog I own, if I was a young filly I'd buy a blonde wig to be ensured to look just like Dolly Pardon," don't be too tough on her.

Words That Cannot Be Modified

Adhering closely to the creative writing syllabuses I wrote for an adult series, I mentored a group of gifted middle-grade children at a very fine school in my community. At a session I brought up the topic of words that are unable to accept a modifier, and the youngsters supplied some suggestions to add to a list I provided. Here's a brief compilation of the biggest culprits we came up with.

Unique Is at the Top of the List

I don't know how often I've heard someone say that something was somewhat unique, or very unique, or even quite unique. I even remember reading an ad for items in an antique shop that were unique and unusual. Can something be unique and not be unusual? I mentioned to those at the workshop that I was asked to write an ad once for jewelry that was rare and unusual, which is just as bad as unique and unusual; however, "rare" and "unusual," when apart, can be modified.

No One Can Be More or Less Flabbergasted

I remember reading about a character who was completely flabbergasted (a million years ago I even wrote this once; horrors). This is like being really dead. Flabbergasted covers the experience just like dead covers those not breathing anymore. In this realm of the absolute, words such as "confused" and "forgot" also lurk. And while in the loosest of circumstances it might be allowed that a person could be somewhat confused, is this really possible? Likewise, when a person says I totally forgot about it, or I completely forgot about it, is either adverb modifier appropriate? Could someone partially forget something?

Some Words Do Provide for Partial Treatment

One of the young adults in the workshop offered the word "awkward." I considered that a person could be somewhat awkward, the same as there could be a quite awkward moment or a really awkward set of circumstances. But are any of these modifiers enhancing the meaning? Doesn't "awkward" without an embellishment continue to make the identical statement? Then there is "absolutely worthless" as an expression of the most abject level of something lacking value. However, doesn't "worthless" by itself say it all?

This Doesn't Mean Throwing Out the Baby with the Bath Water

We can look at many words with –less or –ful as suffixes and make an argument against their relative values. Yet it shouldn't be assumed that all modification is of little or no significance. Or that every modifier should be challenged, even in the slightest. The way modifiers are used is what makes for the richness of our language. It's the phrases rife with tautology that should be avoided, not text that adds to the fabric of the writer's craft.

When I lived in a suburb of Atlanta, a vibrant, elderly fellow frequented town hall meetings that I also attended. He was historically against anything the community leaders wanted to do. To scare people into not supporting a proposal, he'd always bring up the point that once something got started it couldn't be stopped, saying, "It's like being a little bit pregnant," which from my recollection is one of the few intelligent things this chap ever said. And I strongly suggest that writers embrace this man's remark when determining if a word can benefit from a modifier, because if a word is definitive in its own right, nothing added to it can advance or stifle its implication.

Words That Define in Absolute Terms and Those That Don't

Amateur writing is full of misused modifiers and other syntax culprits that foul a narrative, but nothing might be more glaring than the improper use of some of the rudiments of rhetoric such as "a" and "the" or "will not" and "would not."

Tex Must Have Entered a Bar on the Verge of Foreclosure

The words "a" and "the" are often interchanged without the writer understanding the implication. "The cowboy sauntered up to the bar and pulled out the stool," says to the reader that there was just one lone bar stool in the place, since the article "the" implies there is only one of something. Hence, Tex should've sauntered up to the bar and pulled out "a" stool.

Chronology Also Impacts Correctness

If it's established for the reader that Tex had pulled out a stool at an earlier point in the scene, then it would be perfectly acceptable for our cowboy to pull out "the" bar stool he'd sat on previously, since in the world of rhetoric he had taken possession of the object via his prior action. Likewise, if the author had written that there was only one open bar stool, or that there was indeed only one stool in the entire bar, then it would be correct for Tex to saunter up to the bar and pull out "the" bar stool, since there would be no other stool in the saloon for him to grab.

Won't and Wouldn't Are Not Synonymous

I read a message on a blog by a fellow who didn't understand the difference between "won't" and "would not," but who was published by a small indie. I'm glad he got it right if he used the words in his story, or certainly his publisher would've called him on it. "Won't," as the contracted form of "will not" is definitive; conversely, "would not" is imprecise. I "wouldn't" do something means that you don't want to do whatever it might be, but it's not a certainty. It's the little bit of wiggle room that "would not" provides which distinguishes its meaning from "won't."

Don't Forget "That" and "Which"

It's easy to lose sight of "that" and "which" as defining modifiers, but they are. It took me the longest time to understand an example I read years ago that differentiated "that" and "which." The two sentences went something like this: The lawnmower that is in the garage is red. The lawnmower, which is in the garage, is red.

The "that" example implies there is more than one lawnmower, but that the specific lawnmower in the garage is red. The "which" phrase means there is only one lawnmower, and it's in the garage and it (the lawnmower) happens to be red.

If any of you are like me, this at first will make no sense. If anything, it might even seem the opposite should apply. But if you think about it long and hard, at some point the meanings of "that" and "which" in these examples will become clear. And once this is understood, a writer is one step closer to crafting prose with modifiers that accurately define the intended meaning.

Parse a Manuscript for Places In Which Words Are Placed in the Incorrect Context

It's easy to make mistakes with any of the words I discussed in this article, but it's incumbent on the author to make certain each is applied correctly. So getting back to our cowboy, did Tex really pull out the only bar stool in the Long Branch Saloon? What do you think?

Words That Stand Out But Shouldn't

Simple Words Can Be the Greatest Culprit

If anyone guessed the word "actually" would be atop the list, that person would be right. It's one of those words that has no place in a book, any more than the phrase "as a matter of fact." Yet, I would be lying if I implied I hadn't used either the word or the phrase at one time or another. But I shouldn't have, and you would be wise to avoid the word and the phrase, as well.

Another disastrous word is "really." I mean, really, when would any author really write "really" into a sentence in a story unless it was really being utilized to really illustrate the dialogue of a valley girl from the 1980s? Ignoring my feeble attempt at humor, "really" is a word that's easy to slip into a narrative. Don't let it.

Adverbs Can Become a Nightmare for an Otherwise Quality Draft

When I review a manuscript, I'm not as big a stickler in the arena of adverbs as many editors. Of course it depends on the genre, but for commercial fiction an occasional "easily" or "slowly" is not going to give me the willies. But some adverbs are abominable when used without consideration for the subject or scenario they're modifying.

My least favorite is "suddenly," because very few things in life don't take place in a sudden manner. "Mary suddenly jumped up from her seat when the bee stung her." How else would she do it? Would she announce while in pain that she was going to leap from her chair in a couple of minutes? Here are two more lollapaloozas: "The young boy accidentally got lost." How else would someone get lost? On purpose? "The soldier carefully walked through the mine field." Does anyone think he'd do this any other way?

Then There Are Those Words That Can Only be Used Once Per Story

I read a raw draft recently that was quite well-written except for the author's penchant for giving a thesaurus a workout. This person used words like flabbergasted, mastication, serendipitous, lascivious, and a host of others of the same ilk. The words were fine in the context in which they were placed but repeated in the course of the narrative. I remember reading about four people who were flabbergasted at what they'd witnessed, two men having mastication problems while dining, two serendipitous meetings, one at sea and another in a department store, and three lascivious comments made at a sorority dance, a movie, and a wedding rehearsal, respectively. Some words, like mastication, are good only once per story—and perhaps just a single time during any writer's long career.

A Tic by Any Other Name Is Still a Tic

When a word becomes annoying to a reader, this is just like being bitten by a live tic. If we read "actually" a half-dozen times, don't we "actually" often want to put down the book for good. "Carefully" closing the door so the baby won't wake up sometimes makes me want to throw the book against the wall out of sheer frustration—so the author wakes up. If my character is flabbergasted on page 3, I hope he will not be that distraught again on page 293. And if the neighbor's maid in the story is undressing seductively on page 11, I hope she is not seductively doing anything on pages 27, 67, 107, 256, 299, and 343.

Tics Can Be Just As Hard to Remove from a Book As They Are from a Pet

Most writers have a difficult time seeing redundancies in their personal work. This is only natural because we tend to write what sounds good to us, and we might, for example, say "actually" in our normal speech. I employed a salesman once who couldn't speak a sentence it seemed without the word "basically" in it. And he wrote the same way. When I jokingly pointed it out to him, he was stunned that he'd fallen into this rhetorical malaise. An odd aspect of this scenario was the ease in which he remedied this once he thought about his overuse of the word.

There's a Time to Ask for a Little Help

Some authors might catch most of the words that stand out when they read their work out loud. But others, who are on a never-ending quest for the perfect sentence and constantly revising their material, often have a draft that reaches a point when it's impossible to recognize flaws such as tics and words which are memorable due to their rarity or flamboyance. When a manuscript reaches the point of "I can't see it anymore," it's likely the time to ask someone to read the draft who has a legitimate understanding of what to look for.

On Publishing

Bestseller Lists for Fiction – Why So Many Novels on Them Are Lousy

During a writing workshop of mine, I was asked by one of the participants the very question that is the title of this article. At the time I was discussing the merits of Proust, and I guess this is what triggered the thunderous applause that followed. I quickly cited a few examples of florid writing from SWANN'S WAY that I felt were incontrovertible and moved on. Later, it dawned on me that anyone writing in earnest and hoping to be published deserves an honest answer to the question, "Why are so many novels on the bestseller lists lousy?"

How Well-Known Is the Fiction Author?

This is a huge issue. Publishers want books that can sell. A well-known author will have a guaranteed sale of "x" number of books, regardless of the quality of the work. This is why we can pick up a book written by a heretofore quality author that reads as though it had never come across a line-editor's desk. And, if the truth be known, the novel might not have.

Do All Prolific Authors Write Their Own Work All the Time?

No. Is it realistic to think that a person can write an 80,000-word novel each and every month? Yet a hugely successful Romance writer puts out work at this very pace. And I've been told by a writer friend of hers that she is a workaholic who writes every line. I respect the author who told me this as believing it to be true, but I don't. Famous writers have admitted to employing a dozen or more full-time people, not to provide ideas—but to write the material we see in airport gift shops and bookstores. That I do believe, and James Patterson is example number one, and he now lists his various "co-authors" on his covers.

Bestseller Lists Can Be Skewed, Very Skewed

I recently attended a popular fiction writer's presentation of his latest offering. He told the group his agent had informed him earlier in the day that the novel was going to open at number 12 on the New York Times Bestseller List. How is this possible when the first copy has not been sold? If a publisher arranges enough presale commitments from bookstores, libraries, etc., a lofty position on a bestseller list is not a difficult chore. Especially if one keeps in mind that 20,000 copies sold will land a book on the NYT list.

What Is the Answer?

If books are not always written by the person who is listed as the author, material is not edited, and presales cannot be representative of actual sales, what is a the public to do? My best answer is to be certain that the store where the book was purchased will accept a return. It is the only prudent course of action I can recommend. Publishers are in the most demanding positions of their collective corporate lives. They want to go with what brung 'um. If an author of theirs has sold well, he or she will be provided with the opportunity to sell well again, unfortunately many times to the detriment of the consumer. This is why so many novels on the bestseller lists are lousy, and it's as simple as that.

Blockbuster Novels – What Makes a Book a Mega Hit

What Really Made FIFTY SHADES OF GREY, HARRY POTTER, and THE DA VINCI CODE Mega Blockbusters

I've read many books, articles, and reports by writers, agents, publishers, and lay readers as to what made a book a big hit. Along with my reading, I've attended workshops and symposiums and listened to other writers explain their rationale for success.

Some Say a Book Needs a Healthy Dose of Sex

GREY certainly proved that to be true. But HARRY because of the genre, couldn't suggest even the slightest carnality. And DA VINCI's one scene with the elderly folks my age was more laughably spooky than sensual.

Al Zuckerman Had the Answer

Mr. Zuckerman, who founded and then ran the top-caliber literary agency Writer's House for more than 35 years, in my opinion, had it right. In his book, WRITING THE BLOCKBUSTER NOVEL, he said it was "family" more than any other factor. But how did "family" play into what have become the largest-selling book franchises of all time?

"Family" Means More Than the Word Implies

Yes, a little word tap dancing is being done, as I took "family" to mean something globally, even though Mr. Zuckerman often cites THE GODFATHER in his book as the model for his thesis. And it's hard to argue that the Corleone troupe's close bonds didn't sell the story, but I view "family" from a broader sense, and this is why I believe this perspective applies equally to each of the other narratives I cited that have captured the minds and hearts of such a large segment of the reading public.

First, There's GREY

While sitting at a bar in an upscale restaurant, I listened to three separate sets of women discussing the E.L. James book. As the titillating issues wore themselves out, one woman said she hated the story but would buy the next book in the series to see what happened to Ana. Another lady said the writing was abysmal but she couldn't put down the book because of Ana and the way she played into the story. The remainder of the lengthy dialogue followed Ana, as these women in one way or another identified with her character, hence my definition of "family."

POTTER Contained the Same Sort of Empathy

While it might have seemed so peripheral to the story that it could have been omitted, Harry's abuse by his hateful relatives was brilliant in that it planted a seed in the reader's (or viewer's) mind that could never be removed. Kids identify with cruelty, whether it be from a relative or a bully at school. We've all had to deal with some aspect of this—and we didn't like it. Hence, we wanted to see Harry succeed. And we were part of his "family."

DA VINCI Takes Family to Another Level

What has greater gravitas than the combination of family and religion? Relating DA VINCI to family in the context of this paper might seem like a stretch to many, and on its mere face value my own copyeditor didn't accept my contention. But family, from a global perspective, was the premise behind the story, as Robert Langdon's quest "proved" that Sophie was a descendent of Jesus. Each person reading this article can decide if this is or is not a "fair" family issue.

Argue the Point, Not the Reality

I find a relationship to these family-related implications indisputable. People care about Ana, Harry, and Sophie. Their trials and tribulations rival concerns readers have about like circumstances in their personal family settings, whether directly related or peripheral. It's my opinion that GREY, HARRY, and DA VINCI's relationship to some aspect of family is what a mass of humanity identifies with and what motivates people to maintain not just an interest but a rabid enthusiasm for the subject matter. And this is why I chose this form of syllogism, however arguable it might be.

Copyrighted Material –
How to Gain Permission to Use It

I'm often asked by both clients and those who attend my creative writing workshops about using another author's copyrighted material, whether this pertains to citing a title or reprinting an entire passage. Citing a title of a work is not a problem, unless it could be construed in a negative way as it relates to the text in which it shows up, but I always give the same advice, and this is to be certain to gain permission if material in a passage is going to be used, no matter how limited.

All Mainstream Publishers Have a Permissions Desk

The desk or department grants rights for quotations, excerpts, photos, illustrations, charts, etc. Each publisher has essentially the same requirements. But there can be variations, so it's important to understand that no one size fits all. For reasonable guidelines to follow, here are the requirements from the Penguin Group:

- The title and author of the Penguin Group (USA) book from which you wish to use material.
- The description of the exact material you wish to use.
- The title of the story or poem. The page number(s) on which the illustration(s), chart(s), graph(s), etc., appear.
- The name of the publisher who will be publishing your material.
- The title and author of the book (or other publication) in which you wish to use the Penguin Group (USA) material.

You will need to provide your publishing details:

- The publication date.
- The size of the first printing or circulation.
- The format (hardcover, paperback, CD, e-book, etc.)
- The list price.
- The total number of pages for each edition of the book (or other publication).

If a magazine, the circulation and frequency of the publication in which you wish to use the Penguin Group (USA) material is also required.

Photocopying material has another set of guidelines.

Permission Is Not Necessary Until the Material Is Definitely Going to Be Published

Many times a writer will ask when permission should be sought, and the answer is not what most people think. The Permissions Desk is a very busy place, and the personnel do not want to be involved with being required to perform their due diligence until it's determined that a manuscript is definitely going to be published. Yes, this means an author should have a "backup" in case the request is refused—or be prepared to delete the reference—but it also behooves a writer not to get hung up on receiving a release until the correct time in the process.

The Overall Chronology Must Also Be Clearly Understood

Permissions departments commonly work with a six-to-eight-week window related to lead time. But, again, this can vary by house. Also, permission requests are generally placed in a queue in the order in which they are received, so unless a writer is a big-time author or knows a staffer owing a favor, most people can plan on a couple of months before getting a response.

A Final Thought

Writers get excited about wanting to cite known material, feeling this will enhance their credibility. No doubt in some instances this is correct. But, overwhelmingly, the reference to another work, song lyric, etc., has nothing to do with the quality of the narrative. And to one other important point, no release is necessary if work is in the public domain, regardless of who is publishing the material.

Critique Groups – Are They of Value? The Pros and Cons

For many years I've facilitated creative writing workshops in either public or private settings. These programs attract participants from 9 to 90 years of age who are from a wide variety of economic, educational, and cultural backgrounds. My workshops have always been structured, and by this I mean I follow a syllabus I write. And during all the time I've conducted developmental, intermediate, and advanced creative writing workshops, I have never allowed the reading of individual work unless it was directly related to a group assignment. As this article moves along I'll explain why. But first some more setup.

At the Early Stages, It's Definitely Important to Create Confidence

I think it's fair to state that the vast majority of unpublished writers at every level need reinforcement. For this reason, a group of friendly folks sitting around a table and providing encouraging words is a good if not noble idea. But once a writer's confidence-quota is reached, this budding author in my opinion would be better off taking courses at a college, such as a refresher in English 101, or English Lit 201, or Composition 301. I suggest supplementing this coursework by reading books on writing by experts such as Jacques Barzun, William Zinsser, and Theodore Bernstein, along with material that pertains to the respective genre in which the person is writing—and leave the critique groups to other amateurs.

In My Opinion, Amateurs Critiquing Other Amateurs Is a Waste of Time

And this isn't just my opinion. Every A-grade agent, editor, submissions editor, and publisher I know says the same thing. And many don't just say it, they yell it. I offer this: Would a person with chest pains sit around and discuss his or her condition with a group of friends who have all experienced a heart attack—rather than immediately rush to a doctor? The answer is so obvious it makes the question absurd, yet these heart-attack victims are more capable of diagnosing their friend's illness than amateurs who give advice to other writers via critique groups. Please think carefully about what I just wrote before considering me a snit for offering this analogy.

Again, I Support Critique Groups, But at the Early Stages of Writing Only

A few years ago, at my request, one of my workshop participants who holds a Ph.D. in English took over an established critique group at the library where I was conducting my programs, and reading and critiquing individual material was a component of this person's format. I would never have asked this woman to mentor the sessions if I didn't feel the experience would be of value to her CV and to aspiring writers with respect to the confidence they would gain. Still, I've found critique groups to be a springboard at best, and I feel it's important to sever the cord as soon as possible.

There Is an Exception

If a critique group is led by someone who is involved with the major royalty publishing industry as a published author, working editor, or established agent, this changes the playing field. Then the group will likely receive competent advice. Yet even in this sort of setting, it's my contention that individual critiquing by the members of the group, other than passing comments, is not advisable or desirable for the reasons I've already mentioned. While respecting the opinions of amateurs, let professionals do what they're trained to do—and be certain not to lose track of who's who.

Something Else to be Aware of

Another issue to consider is that just because someone is published this doesn't automatically mean the person would be a good editor. On the opposite side of the coin, a quality editor, while possessing developmental ability and/or line-editing or copyediting skills, might not be a particularly good writer. This representation applies to all fields. Some highly regarded law professors are not the most adept attorneys in the courtroom or for certain sorts of trials. Not in any way excusing Mike Tyson's abhorrent behavior, but ask him if he'd hire Alan Dershowitz again.

E-Book Price Points for Mainstream-Published and Self-Published Fiction Authors

Can an Unknown Writer Compete at a Higher Price Point Than a Franchise Author?

The question posed by the subtitle is too absurd to even consider, yet it happens all the time. My favorite story involves a fellow who thought so much of his skill that he priced his e-book at $16. After a year of vigorous promotion he complained he'd sold only four copies, and one his wife bought for a relative. If e-books by major authors are priced in the $10 range, shouldn't this have told the writer something about pricing his work?

Success Stories Abound for the $.99 e-Book

All anyone has to do is look at Amanda Hocking's success and the way she priced her material. If I remember correctly, she even gave away some of her work to "grease the wheel." Many authors, who often possess more marketing savvy than writing skill, have given away three-fourths of their books and offered the respective endings to their stories for a buck or so. And some of these books have sold in the tens of thousands of copies—and in a few instances even more.

It Seems Like $2.99 Is the Far Outside

I attended a seminar not long ago at which a successful e-book pioneer discussed pricing. This person had experimented with all sorts of price points and determined that $2.99 was the absolute outer limit for an e-book that was not previously released by a mainstream print publisher. His position was that $2.99 is the stretching point an e-book can withstand that's not of the Stieg Larsson ilk, and anyone even remotely attune to the publishing industry knows how seldom a phenomenon like that occurs. It might be worth noting that the first e-book concerning Bin Laden's death was released at the same time as the print version, and the e-book price tag was $1.99! (I'm discussing fiction in this article, but the Bin Laden book is a prime example of desiring to sell many copies at a low price rather than much less at a higher price point.)

So It Appears That $.99 to $2.99 Is the Comfort Zone

At the recent BEA conference, the CEO of one of the major publishing firms explained what everyone already knows, and this is that no one in the print business has yet learned how to market e-books. He went on to say that all of the distributing mediums which currently exist are quite good for hunters (of material) but not very good for what he called gatherers. With this in mind, it's paramount for e-book writers to understand that unless a marketing plan is in place to drive a reader to a particular work, even a free book won't be read— because no one will know it exists.

Editing and the Various Services Editors Provide

I recently read something that leads to me to believe that the field of professional developmental book editing needs to be covered in detail.

Editors in the U.S. Have a Poor Reputation Abroad. Really?

I happened upon an Internet message board for writers on which someone was asking if hiring an editor to critique a novel was a good idea. When I read a little further, I noticed the person was specifically asking about me and my company. This was certainly okay, as I always strongly recommend scrutinizing any potential editor, agent, or publisher. But what really piqued my interest was a reply from a person from Great Britain who said that editors were respected in his country but that their contemporaries in the U.S. did not enjoy the same standing. This was certainly news to me—and I imagine a few other editors in America if they'd read the same remark.

Rationale That Defies Logic

There were no comments one way or the other in response to the man's query regarding me or my services, but it was mentioned that book editors had been the source of a number of recent threads, so I decided to venture further into the site. Two hours later I pushed back from the computer, aghast at what I'd read. With few exceptions (very few), there were dozens upon dozens of posts vociferously denouncing editors. One of the site's apparent gurus firmly stated that it would be of no value to hire an editor, because if a publisher sent a manuscript back to an author for correction, if an editor had been used, what would the writer do, since this person, independently, would be incapable of properly making the requested modifications.

If Professional Editors Are Such a Bad Idea, Why Do So Many Best-Selling Authors Praise Their Work?

Logic like what I'd just reported doesn't deserve the compliment of rationale opposition, to quote Jane Austen, but let me at least provide a little help for those who universally defamed professional editing. As one lone brave contrarian who responded to the thread stated, "If editors are such a horrible idea, why do so many best-selling authors, in their respective Acknowledgments, extol the value of those who edit for them?" To step farther onto this cold deck, I'd like to see a list of best-selling authors who say they don't use an editor. I even noticed a piece the other day from a man who has edited for both Stephen King and John Grisham. Both those authors must surely have needed counseling for employing this fellow at some point in their futile careers.

There Is a Time When Amateurs Critiquing Other Amateurs Doesn't Work

I used to facilitate writing workshops sponsored by a large community library system in South Florida, and at times I encouraged program participants to critique each other's work based on a project I assigned. But I also made it crystal clear, if a writer was serious about having material considered by a legitimate royalty publisher, at some point the material would require a professional review.

Here Is What Editors Do

Professional editing is not about correcting grammatical errors, punctuation, and syntax issues, even though certainly anything a writer might have missed will be identified. Editing at a professional level entails considering a work related to its publishability in the current literary market; and specifically what it will require to polish a draft so it will be accepted for review by a bona fide royalty publisher. Depth of characterization, quality of the characters, character arcing, transitioning of the exposition and dialogue, dialogue quality, dialogue rhythm, story pacing, the pitch of the scenes, lack of contrivance, point-of-view consistency, redundant words and phrases (this is a bigger deal than most amateurs think), the strength of the story, and the overall readability of the narrative, are just some of the issues an editor must address.

An Amateur Can't Know What the Industry Is Looking for

For many experienced writers, this is the number-one reason to employ a professional editor, since this person will possess the expertise to know what is working in the business at a given point in time—and what isn't. The professional editor will also know where and with whom agents are placing work. This is particularly important because there are often esoteric happenings in the publishing industry that are weakly disseminated or aren't provided to the public, at all.

A Professional Editor Can Save a Writer a Lot of Money, Time, and Aggravation

It doesn't cost a lot of money to have a professional editor read a manuscript and provide a critique. Isn't it a lot better to find out if a work has a chance, rather than to send out queries and submission packages with no idea of the true caliber of the material? I've read an inordinate number of drafts from writers who have spent years promoting work that has no chance of being published in the condition in which I received it. And what unfortunately happens to an often-rejected writer who doesn't understand a work's deficiencies is that he or she becomes disillusioned and at times even bitter.

Having a Work Professionally Edited Is a Means to an End

For the overwhelming number of writers who are with major royalty publishers, professional editing is not only a means to reach a satisfactory result, but the only way. For anyone who wishes to question this remark, I only ask this person to seek out any wildly successful author and ask if a professional editor has helped that writer become published—and remain that way.

Editing – When Is the Right Time to Hire a Book Editor?

I don't know when, on the writing curve, Stephen King or Nelson DeMille might seek editorial advice, only that it is documented that they do. So it begs the question, for the writer trying to break into the business with a major royalty publisher—and who accepts that a professional editor looking at the manuscript might not be a bad idea—when is the right time to hire a book editor?

Generally There Are Two Issues

For most people, it's a matter of time and money. Let's look at the time element first. A common practice is for a writer to send a manuscript to an editor for a critique after it is felt that the material is in A-grade condition and ready for market—except for perhaps the slightest touch-up. But if it's determined there are plot or character elements that cannot be remedied by modifying, deleting, or inserting a few sentences here or there—which is overwhelmingly the case—then the entire piece will often require a wholesale revision.

How Much Time Does a Writer Have?

If an author should seek an editor to review a story concept and its setup from an early point in the creative process, steps can be taken to keep the plot elements in focus. And the time saved can be substantial, since a revision can often require months. From a time standpoint, isn't it better to catch any problems early—and rectify them—rather than spend considerable time on a draft that will have no prospects in its current condition? If a writer has the discipline to work with an editor during a manuscript's developmental stage, this initiative can be a valuable time-saving practice.

How Much Money Does a Writer Want to Spend?

No one likes to pay a second time for a process that failed initially. This is the most salient reason I can think of to justify bringing an editor into the fold at the start. The early-stage placement of a manuscript with a professional editor is almost always the most economical way for a writer to work, and usually substantially so.

Does Anybody Really Do It This Way?

Unfortunately, many unpublished writers will consider an editor only after a series of rejections from agents or publishers who accept unagented submissions. This article is not going to change the modus operandi of a great many writers who are already ensnared well within the publishing labyrinth. But I hope these contentions might motivate some others who read this piece to consider contacting a professional editor toward the beginning stages of the first draft and not after it's completed.

Editors Are Becoming More Flexible

As with most everything facing a writer who is hoping to become published for the first time, there is no one size that fits all. And while I hate to close an article with a disclaimer, it is important to report that some well-respected editors continue to accept completed manuscripts only. Yet it seems that a sizable body of highly regarded editors are acceding to this article's primary premise, which is to encourage authors to present early-stage material for review.

Editing – When Not to Hire a Book Editor

Not long ago I received a request to review an author's query letter. It was awful. The letter was written in a structure that would make a seventh-grade English teacher cringe. And as is commonly the case with writers who are unfamiliar with the nuances of the publishing industry, the genre definition for the novel was incorrect, as well.

A Monumental Mistake Compounded

While discussing how to improve the letter, one question led to another, when the author informed me that over time he had used SIX editors on his novel (and he was dead serious). This floored me. How does a writer find a half-dozen editors on this planet who don't understand the genre of the work they are editing? This ineptness by both parties (I'm lumping the editors together as one entity) brings up several issues that I feel a responsibility to address.

Anyone Can Claim to Be an Editor

First, sadly, anybody can claim to be an editor. There is no formal credentialing. I know of people who cannot write but claim in their advertising to have helped dozens of writers get their novels into print, only to learn that every one of these works was self-published. I have had people attend my creative writing workshops who do not understand writing at anywhere near a professional level, but have "Editor" printed after their name on a business card. History is littered with editors making all sorts of outlandish assertions, such as guaranteeing a writer a contract with a major royalty publisher (which landed the principle of one editorial outfit in jail a few years ago).

The Problem With a Manuscript Can Generally Be Attributed to One of Two Factors

I've found that working with clients is about honest relationships as much as writing. If a writer has found a competent editor, and nothing has happened in a positive way with respect to the manuscript after exhausting all of the available avenues, there is likely something wrong with the concept for the market in which the work is intended—or the writing is not up to the demands of the industry. This last statement does not imply that the editor was less than scrupulous in supporting the manuscript, only that there is only so much anyone can do with a project. And my experience is that hiring another editor will not help.

Respected Editors Will Not Compromise Their Relationships With Top Agents

Another thought to bear in mind is that most industry-respected editors have long-standing relationships with A-grade agents. One reason for writers to employ highly regarded editors is the desire to have their manuscripts presented to those agents with whom these editors have a fellowship. This is particularly important today, because an ever-increasing percentage of top agents are not accepting unsolicited material, with the bulk of their referrals coming solely from editors. And no editor I know of wants to harm his or her reputation by suggesting material that is not thought to be publishable. I can't state this more emphatically.

The Best Advice Anyone Can Receive

Now back to the fellow whose experience with six editors fostered this article. I have to assume he was either quite naive or very unlucky, as somewhere along the way one of the editors had to have told him the truth about his writing. Or he didn't want to listen and kept burning through editors in hope of finding someone who would like his work. There is no value in dragging along a corpse. Related to his fiasco, from my personal experience as a writer and not as an editor, the advice someone gave me decades ago is in my opinion still the best recommendation anyone can receive about a manuscript that is not going anywhere—and this suggestion was to write something else.

Two Critical Issues to Understand and Accept

I want to offer a final remark on query letters and another on editors editing manuscripts: For an unpublished writer, the greatest query letter ever written is not going to enable a deficient manuscript to become accepted by a bona fide royalty publisher. And neither can a host of the best editors in the industry, short of one of them ghosting the entire piece, save writing that is flawed.

Editing Manuscripts –
Do Agents and Publishers Edit Material?

A short while ago a young scribe wrote over a post of mine that writers did not need to have their manuscripts edited prior to submitting them to an agent or publisher. His rationale was that agents and/or publishers would provide the service, and therefore the writer could and should avoid the independent editor's fee. I tried to explain the fallacy of this person's thinking, of course to no avail, but later I decided to take a closer look at why this sort of misunderstanding might occur. My findings are the purpose behind this article.

Editors Do Still Edit

Although I lead the topic line of this article with agents, I want to discuss editors first, and state without qualification that editors at the publisher level do still edit. But this is far from universal, and there is widespread disparity as to who does what for whom. A franchise writer with a major house will have all the stops pulled out to see that his or her material is polished in every way, should the author allow any "tampering." The executive editor who works with the writer may even personally edit this author's manuscript if there is some last-minute tweaking to be done. But more often than not, if a draft requires attention after it's submitted by an established writer, this manuscript will be sent outside to an independent editor for fine tuning. And, yes, the cost would be absorbed by the publisher.

What I just wrote applies to large publishing companies. However, I've also noticed a substantial number of boutique publishers who've sprung up during the past few years who legitimately provide developmental editing as well as line-editing for material they accept. The downside is that the editor is usually the publisher, and often he or she is one of only a couple of people involved in the entire operation. Hence, with the backlog any start-up royalty publisher will generally have to contend with, lead times can soon run amuck. And if a writer does some research into these sites, my comment will be borne out. The most common lament I've read is that the specialty publisher could not meet the promised release date—or anything close to it.

What If a Writer Isn't at the Franchise Level or Interested in a Start-up Indie?

In the middle is everyone else, meaning 99.99 percent of all writers. On the very day I was defending independent editing as a discipline, I received an e-mail from someone who was working to have an editing prospect of mine represented by an agent. I didn't feel this man's work was ready, but this liaison presented the draft to a major publisher and a high-powered agent. Both summarily dismissed the manuscript, with the agent saying, "In today's market, a manuscript has to be perfect in every way to stand a chance." For me, that's the end of story. But there's confusion because of what some agents do offer, as well as the way manuscripts are treated in other countries.

Some Agents Also Edit

In the scenario I just alluded to, this agent was not in a position to edit this writer's draft. I can assure anyone reading this article that most don't have the time or the staff. But there are exceptions. A well-respected agency states on its Web site that it works with its authors from a developmental perspective and will also line-edit their work. I've never submitted to this agency, nor do I know anyone personally who is signed by this firm, so I won't provide the company's name, but they are legitimate in every respect and certainly do not charge fees for reading or editing. But I think someone will have to search long and hard to find a second such firm. However, I do know of independent agents who work with their clients' drafts, so others of a similar persuasion do exist. They just aren't standing on every street corner advertising for clients.

So, in Truth, What Can a Writer Expect?

It's pretty clear: For a writer's material to receive in-house editing, it depends on who the author happens to be, as well as the agent or publisher. I think I'm being accurate in stating that the overwhelming number of agents do not edit material for their clients. From the perspective of an unpublished author's material, if the manuscript doesn't look relatively clean to an agent or publisher, it's rejected. But if a spotty draft somehow passes muster with an agent, what are the odds a publisher will accept it? I can't answer that. However, when a work reaches an exalted point in the evaluation process, especially at the publisher level, I believe any writer would be prudent to make certain the manuscript is in as good of shape as possible, and this means having it professionally edited beforehand.

Editing to Excess

Perhaps a better title for this article might be "Editors Gone Wild," because it seems lately that I'm hearing about this way or that way to write something—and it's now the only way to design text.

Spacing Started This Some Time Ago

A few years back, the book reviewer with The Palm Beach Post, Scott Eyman, graciously agreed to judge some short stories I had a workshop group of mine prepare as the capstone to one of my creative writing series. So Scott would have drafts with the same formatting, I provided guidelines, which included double-spacing after periods.

During an early evaluation session of mine, one workshop participant presented me with a draft that contained a single space after each period. Not a major event by any means, but I asked why she had done this and was informed that an editor she knew told her that two spaces after a period was "old school."

All I could do was laugh, as what "old school" was she referring to? There is no rule. Never was one. The idea behind two spaces was to provide editors, in years gone by, with more room to manually make annotations. And it's the reason I prefer two spaces, as it enables me more area to draw symbols and lines and make notes, etc. There is a forest in the trees, and sometimes this has everything to do with where the seeds were originally planted.

Dialogue Tag Placement

A respected writer wrote a piece, and others copied it, which said that interior monologue should always be placed after the run of dialogue. Quite often this is a great idea, but it's far from absolute. The pitch of the dialogue exchange should always be the deciding factor, and this far outweighs someone's self-righteous idea of perfect structure.

I've made the mistake in my own writing of leaving too much exposition between exchanges. Most often writers do this because they've moved text around and never caught the problem during rereads. Editors are paid to correct this, and they should. But if we read inarguably some of the greatest dialogue writers of all time such as Forster and Steinbeck, or more contemporary dialogue geniuses the likes of DeMille and Leonard, notice how often "tags" are placed in front of dialogue. It's all about pitch.

Attribute Placement

While I'm on dialogue, I used to always prefer a speaker attribute "to follow" a series of short-to moderate-length sentences. But I've become more comfortable during the past few years with seeing an attribute break up the opening spit of dialogue. Regardless of my or any other editor's predisposition, the "urgency" of speaker identification should always be the determining factor influencing attribute placement. Nothing else.

To take this one step further, a wonderful writer of Westerns, Elmer Kelton, who I'm sad to say passed away, had more than 50 titles published during his illustrious career. Mr. Kelton precedes almost all of his dialogue with an attribute (whenever he deemed one necessary, of course). The style would be eschewed by many editors, but it works beautifully in that no reader has to pause for even a millisecond to consider who is speaking. Pick up one of his books and see how well this technique plays out. And as a by-product of this exercise you'll also enjoy a dandy story.

"Telling" Instead of "Showing"

A good friend of mine gave me READING LIKE A WRITER by the enormously gifted writer and educator Francine Prose. Of the many sound comments she made, the one that resonated the most with me was her remark that it isn't always better to "show" and not "tell" a scene, and to paraphrase her, way too much is made out of "showing" everything.

Nothing makes Ms. Prose's credentials any more valuable than those of any other fine author/academic, but this does illustrate that even "showing versus telling" is not without an occasional detractor who possesses an outstanding reputation.

Passive vs. Active Voice

I had a book I'd written eons ago reviewed by an editor friend of mine, and I was criticized for writing a line in passive voice. Well, if I wrote it a thousand times within the context of the run I'd designed, it would remain in passive voice. Should writers try to write in active voice? Certainly. All the time? Hardly. Pitch and clarity should always dictate what is written and its location in the text.

In Closing

In the realm of prose writing, claiming something as absolute in my opinion is like what was referred to in the '70s as the "Dianetics mentality." Someone would refer to someone, who no one had ever heard of, as an expert. Another person would agree with that person's assessment, and all of a sudden this first "who is this person?" was an authority in the field.

In writing, there is no such thing as absolute authority. Yes, there are rules, and some are as inviolable as a brick wall, but even the sturdiest of structures can be breached. My position is that the most important element any writer should pay attention to is readability. If a writer will concentrate on providing material that's easy on the eye, a lot of ills can be cured.

Fair Use and Copyright Infringement – A loose Translation of Rights

A couple of years ago I was asked to write a paper on the "Fair Use" section of the U.S. Copyright Law. I begged off the project, explaining that I didn't feel remotely qualified. In all honesty, I don't feel much better equipped today to address this issue, which I find enormously complicated. But so much of late has come about that deals with what I perceive as an abuse of authors' rights, I feel compelled to offer a loose translation of "Fair Use" from a writer's perspective and not that of a jurist.

The Four "Fair Use" Factors Plus One

The "Fair Use" of a copyrighted work is constructed around four principles as defined in Section 107 of U.S. Copyright Act, with a fifth, unofficial metric thrown in for good measure.

The preamble states that the reproduction of copyrighted material is considered "fair" if this copy is used as criticism, comment, news, teaching, scholarship, or research. The four factors used to legally consider if the particular use of something is "fair" are:

* The purpose and character of the use, including whether such use is of commercial nature or is for nonprofit educational purpose.

* The nature of the copyrighted work.
* The amount and substantiality of the portion used in relation the copyrighted work as a whole.
* The effect of the use upon the potential market for, or value of the copyrighted work.

"Fair Use" Is a Muddle of Confusion

"Fair Use" doctrine provides no specificity whatsoever as to the number of words that can be used; nor the number of lines; nor even the amount of notes that may be taken without permission. And to address perhaps the only issue that's clear in any of this, citing the author of a passage, as we all did with footnotes in school, is not a substitute for gaining the permission of the copyright's owner.

Any Writer Can Sue If It's Felt the Reproduction Wasn't Flattering

This is factor number five, and as silly as this might seem, plaintiffs have been awarded judgments based on having their feelings hurt. With such abstract guidelines, is there any doubt why "Fair Use" leaves people who routinely deal with it scratching their heads? "Fair Use" probably gives credence to the Cory Doctorows of the world who believe that everything should be public domain once it's published. But what happens to that thinking when applying the Supreme Court ruling in 2012 that paved the way for works in the public domain to be copyrighted. Yes, the insanity surrounding "Fair Use" goes full circle.

What I Tell My Clients

As an editor, I have always strongly advised all of my clients to acquire written permission for anything they might use that is not their own. If not, the only thing certain about "Fair Use" is that they could be litigants in a protracted lawsuit that might cost them some martini time and a whole lot of money.

Formatting a Manuscript
For Agents and Publishers –
8 Hints for an Acceptable Layout

A writer can start with THE CHICAGO MANUAL OF STYLE and move from it to any number of academic works on what a manuscript layout should look like. But adhering to the following eight suggestions will assure an acceptable format for almost all fiction.

Hint Number One–Your Name, Page Number and Book Title in the Top Left Corner of Each Page

In the top, left corner of the page, many editors prefer your last name followed by a hyphen and the page number, and one single space below this, the title of your book. Then three single spaces below this (if you're not beginning a new chapter, which I'll cover later) begin your narrative.

Hint Number Two–Double Line Space the Narrative

No one I know will accept a single line-spaced manuscript, and there is good reason. In the days of the covered wagon, when everything was edited with a pencil, the suggested corrections were made between the lines. Many of us still prefer to work this way, and the format is paramount when line-editing material manually. Plus, most people find double line-spaced copy on an 8 1/2" x 11" sheet of paper much easier to read and therefore more comfortable to work with.

Hint Number Three–Double Space After a Period

Double spacing after a period enables room to manually annotate punctuation changes and draw lines to move sentences around. I am aware that some people are saying this is "old school" and therefore the double space after the period is no longer necessary. But every editor I know prefers two spaces after a period, as do I, even though for the purposes of this published piece the text is provided with a single space after each period. Finished copy and submission material are two different animals.

Hint Number Four—Indent Paragraphs 1"

Most word processing programs seem to use a 1" indention as standard, but I often receive manuscripts with erratic or inconsistent paragraph indentions. If you always indent 1", then your text's appearance will be consistent and this will also enable you to "fudge" when you want your text to look its best from an aesthetic standpoint.

Hint Number Five—Never Justify Text

Under no circumstances should a manuscript be submitted with justified text. This makes copyediting a nightmare (read "impossible"), since extra spaces between words are something a copy-editor flags. The spacing in this paragraph is a prime example of the problem justified text can create.

Hint Number Six—Locate the Chapter and Its Number in the Center of the Page

As with unusual or inconsistent indentation, I receive a wide variety of chapter setups. My suggestion is to type out the word Chapter with a capital C and follow this with the number 1, 2, 3, etc., one space after the word; i.e., Chapter 1. This isn't as Mickey Mouse as it seems, because this differentiates a Chapter 1 from Part 1, for example. The chapter designation is a location in which centered text is not only acceptable but desirable.

Space the chapter identification down however far you desire, with an equal number of lines below it before your begin the narrative. Five single spaces from the book title in the top, left corner to the centered chapter identification, then five single spaces to the beginning of the narrative, is a good template.

This again provides room to "fudge" if need be during later revisions and not require a writer to have to repaginate an entire chapter—or even the entire book. With our more sophisticated word-processing software, this isn't the big deal it was 20 years ago, but there are times when it's desirable to have material appear in a certain way on a specific page, and this is why I continue to suggest allowing extra room to maneuver text.

Hint Number Seven—Use a 12 Point Times New Roman or Courier Font

Many in the publishing industry seem to recommend these fonts. Also, if a writer sticks with either Times New Roman or Courier, this could save having to manually go through an entire manuscript to clean it up should it have to be changed to either of these font styles later. Because, even with all of the word-processing genius that's out there, different fonts don't often wrap in the desired manner when the entire text is converted from one font style to another.

Hint Number Eight—Leave an Extra Double-Spaced Line at the End of Each Page

If you choose to ignore everything I've written, please leave an extra line or even two at the end of each page, especially during the early drafts of your work. Meaning, instead of typing to the last line, which will generally be line 24 of double-spaced copy, type only to theoretical line 23 or line 22. This has nothing to do with editing but will enable you to revise and often not have to repaginate work, irespective of the sophistication of your word-processing software.

If you follow the suggestions outlined in this article, you won't have any difficulty with 99 percent of the editors, agents, and publishers out there.

Genres –
The Importance of Understanding Genre
When Querying Agents

Genres Can be More Than a Little Confusing

There is perhaps nothing more perplexing in all of writing than trying to understand genre. While preparing this paper, I ran across the following subgenres for Romance: Suspense, Paranormal, Fantasy, Time-Travel, Futuristic, Licensed Theme, Medical, Regency, Medieval, Highland, War, Gothic, Western, and Mail-Order Bride. And these are by no means all that fall into the Romance bailiwick. There were a couple of dozen more.

In the Mystery category we have the Cozy, Police Procedural, Forensic Hard-Boiled Crime, Serial Killer, Suspense, Thriller, Legal Thriller, Medical Thriller, Technical Thriller; and other extended Mystery subdivisions that include Science Fiction, Gay, Military, Political, Paranormal, and so many more that the separation is beyond blurred. To confuse anyone to the point of no return, if that's not the case already, take a look at the Writer's Digest genre listing. And it's not all-inclusive.

What Makes Genre Even More Complex Is That It's Often Not Specific to a Particular Publisher

Long ago, the editor-in-chief with a major publisher indicated to me that one of my novels was rejected because it did not fit into the firm's definition of a Thriller, since its titles are exclusively "gruesome murders by a serial killer tracked down by a cop who is in turn threatened." Traditional Thrillers involve international intrigue and a life-and-death struggle to save the planet (or close to it), which is the way my story was written.

An Author Must Determine the Genre and Relevant Subgenre in Which the Novel Is Written

The point is obvious. A writer must determine the genre and sub-genre in which his or her work is written, and then tailor the presentation to the agent and/or publisher to whom the material is being presented. This requires parsing books on the agent's or publisher's list to make certain the submitted novel is indeed complementary. An author who makes this effort can eliminate the major hurdle that a submission is "not a solid match," since the writer will know beforehand that this could not possibly be the case.

Genres and Mixing Them – The Problems This Can Create

I never realized the problem with writing a novel that fit in with many genres until I received a rejection many years ago from a publisher who had at one time been my editor. She told my agent that my Thriller fit medical, military, and political genres, and her imprint's guidelines were too restrictive to support a book such as mine. Of course I was crushed and couldn't understand such lunacy.

Readers of Certain Imprints Have Specific Expectations

It required many years before I finally accepted what I'd been told, and I believe what I eventually understood is worth passing on. First and foremost, people require an imprint to provide a consistent product. As an example, a person reading an Avon book expects a Romance, and a particular sort of story with a specific set of characters. Likewise, readers of Pinnacle Thrillers anticipate a mass murderer, killing victims in a gruesome manner "on stage," while pursued by a cop who will have the tables turned on him or her, and this person's lover also being brought into the fray.

Platforms Have Little or No Wiggle Room

As the latter example indicates, a single murder wouldn't work, nor would a potential catastrophe of cataclysmic proportions. For a book to be accepted by Pinnacle, there must be a heinous mass-murderer on the loose, and the story needs to contain a traditional law enforcement element pursuing the evildoer. So, no pandemic can be about to be unleashed. Or there can't be an imminent nuclear threat along with some prefabricated agency's personnel trying to save the day, such as with the TV show 24.

If a Genre Is Not Specific to the Story, a Myriad of Problems Can Develop

I'm often faced with having to explain to my clients that their books not only fit into multiple subgenres, but that the narratives also cross the lines of major genres, as well. I find this particularly common when someone is writing YA material that begins as a Mystery and then turns into pure Fantasy. Or YA material that suddenly depicts a murder or a sex scene in somewhat graphic terms, making the work unsuitable for young adults yet overall too soft for commercial fiction. Another problem area is a contemporary Thriller that becomes Sci Fi/Adventure later in the narrative. If you bought what you thought was a James Bond type of story that morphed into Dr. Who, how would you feel about your purchase?

Distinct Boundaries Exist

I hope this is now starting to make sense for readers of this article much quicker than it did for me many years ago. There are specific guidelines that publishers expect their stories and therefore their authors to follow. And with all the current subgenres, these parameters are more restrictive than ever. So when I suggest that writers approach only those agents or publishers who work with material in the genre and subgenre in which their particular stories are written, there's a definite method to my madness.

ISBN Coding System Explained in Detail

One of the most confusing issues in all of publishing involves ISBN codes. How does a writer get an ISBN for a book? How much does one cost? What does the number mean? Does a book require a new ISBN if it's reprinted? Are the numbers different in countries outside the States? The list goes on, but unfortunately seldom if ever are the most important questions asked. The purpose of this article is to explain how the ISBN works. I'll also be providing several links along the way for verification and clarification purposes, but it's important to explain the basics of the ISBN first.

The ISBN Is One of Many Codes

ISBN stands for International Standard Book Number. The definition of the ISBN is provided by isbn.org, but a simple explanation is: The ISBN code is a unique identifier for books that are intended to be sold commercially. The system was created in the U.K. in 1966 by W. H. Smith and called SBN or Standard Book Numbering. It was adopted in 1970 as the international standard ISO 2108. Another number, the ISSN, or International Standard Serial Number, is used for periodicals such as magazines.

Be Aware That Different Codes Are in Use in Countries Outside the U.S.

The first issue to keep in mind is that many countries use their own ISBN system. For example, Canada uses the CISN format, which means Canadian ISBN Service System. Also, Amazon uses its own identifier, which the firm calls ASIN (however, the number follows the ISBN code). The second issue to be aware of is that the ISBN has no relationship whatsoever to the Library of Congress Control Number (which is free, by the way). I think anyone serious about becoming published in any medium would be prudent to click the Library of Congress link and spend the 15 or so minutes it will take to read through the FAQs.

Instances in Which a Writer Doesn't Need an ISBN

It's important to understand that if a writer has no intention of selling his or her book via a commercial setting, handing it off to a wholesaler or distributor, or is not planning on placing the book in a public library, there is no need to apply for an ISBN. But, if the author plans to sell the book through an outlet(s) of some sort, to answer the first question I posed, the ISBN may be purchased from only one official source provided by the U.S. government, and this is publisher R. R. Bowker, 630 Central Ave., New Providence, NJ 07974-1154. The company's toll free phone number is 877-310-7333.

Yes, R. R. Bowker Is the Only Official Government-Authorized Purveyor for ISBNs in the Entire United States

Now that I've clearly established Bowker as the originator of ISBNs, what about the inordinate number of firms and individuals who resell the numbers? Here is where it really gets sticky, but let me begin with cost first. The cost of a single ISBN from Bowker is currently $125, while ten ISBNs are sold to the public for $295 or $29.50 each (these fees are from 2015). The first question is, why would anyone need more than one number? And the answer is, the person wouldn't– unless the writer plans on having a book published in multiple mediums.

If the latter is the case, each format, such as an e-book, hardback, softcover, trade paperback (which is different in size from mass market softcover), etc., requires a different ISBN to identify the particular medium for the book. Simply, one number applies to the hardback and another to the softcover, etc. But as long as nothing changes in a book in the original medium in which it is published, it can be reprinted ad infinitum under the same ISBN. But change any wording in the narrative, or the medium in which the book was originally published, and a new ISBN is required. Not rocket science, but we're not even close to being finished with this topic.

A Barcode Is Necessary for All Books Sold Commercially or Placed in a Library

The next issue is the need for a unique barcode number, and this must also be purchased from Bowker (I know, how convenient). A unique barcode number is necessary so the bookseller can identify the price point at which you want to sell your book. So the first rule is not to purchase a barcode until you determine at what price you want your book to sell. And since you might have an e-book at one price point and a softcover release at another, you would need a separate barcode for each; hence, again, the need for more than one identifier.

Barcodes don't have the dramatic price drops that are commensurate with ISBN codes (more on this to come). A barcode is $25 each from 1 to 5, $23 if purchased in lots of 6 to 10, and $21 in any spread from 11 to 100 (again, 2015 numbers). Again, since they involve price points, you will have to tell Bowker your retail pricing for each style book so everything can be keyed-in accordingly. While we're still a long way from quantum physics, what comes next is a black hole that can reshape a writer's universe—all the wrong way.

The Following Section May Be the Most Important Information a Writer Seeking Publication Will Ever Read

A great many publishers and individuals resell the ISBNs, and it certainly appears advantageous for a writer to buy a single number for say $40 in lieu of $125. The problem is, who owns the legal right to the title the ISBN identifies if the author has not received a release from the company or person who sold the number? According to the staff at Bowker, and I pressed them on this issue several times to make certain of the consistency of what they were telling me, each year they are contacted by a multitude of writers who are justifiably distraught after they learn the rights to their respective books are really owned by the person or company that resold the ISBN to them!

I would think this is also a double-edged sword for the individual (or company) that is retaining the rights, since if the work is plagiarized, the person (or company) will be sued right along with the thief. So, unless the staff at Bowker is lying to me to protect their interests (which I highly doubt), I think it would behoove any writer to make certain an ironclad release is signed before acquiring an ISBN from anyone outside of Bowker. By the way, 100 ISBNs are only $575 (according to what Mrs. Milsey taught me in the 4th grade, that's $5.75 each), and 1000 are just $1000! It's easy to see why buying in bulk and reselling the numbers at a 20- to 40-times markup has substantial street appeal.

The ISBN and Barcode Can Be Combined on One Format

If you should be interested in how the barcode is determined, since it also has a book's category and other information embedded, Barcode Graphics Web site explains the process in detail and this is why I chose to highlight the firm in this section. Included in their definitions is the tidbit that the Bookland EAN symbol is the barcode of choice in the book industry throughout the world because it allows for the encodation of an ISBN with the barcode on a single label.

This company's price for 1000 of a single label with both codes in a standard configuration is $27.75. So once a writer has the ISBN, and a price point, a single label can be ordered. Just be aware that there are a gargantuan number of graphics outfits that can print labels, so it would behoove a writer to shop around, but I imagine $27.75 for 1000 labels is a pretty strong baseline.

To recap, if you're going to sell your book outside your individual efforts, you will have to acquire an ISBN and a barcode number that can be affixed to each book (unless of course the publisher prints the Bookland EAN combined-label somewhere on the book). And, again, as with changes or different formats that will require a separate ISBN, you will need a unique barcode for any price points that aren't the same.

The Release Should Be Issue Number-One

Regardless of from whom anyone acquires an ISBN outside of Bowker, the single most important issue is for the writer to have a release signed by someone who has the authority to do so (which is another subject, and a monster in its own right). My opinion, if anyone wants it, is that it's probably better to go ahead with Bowker, buy ten ISBNs, get the exact number of barcodes that are needed initially, and be done with it (other than having the labels printed in some manner if your work is not exclusively an e-book). And if someone accepts my quantity suggestions for each component, the total for everything for one e-book and one printed book that can be sold by a wholesaler, distributor, retailer, or placed in a library, looks like a price tag of around $400 (this as of January 2015).

It would be easy to load up on Bowker because of the company's obvious monopoly status, but in fairness, would it be conceivable to have a hundred different authorized outlets dispensing numbers? This seems like perhaps the only instance I can think of in which our government could've handled something internally—such as via a Library of Congress affiliate agency of some sort, especially since this is already being done with periodicals—and made money rather than turning it over to a private concern. But, as many have said before me and many more will say after, who knows?

Listing a Manuscript with Ingram, Baker & Taylor, and Amazon – What This Really Means

It's Important to Recognize That a List Is Just That—and Nothing More

Over the years, I can't begin to count the number of times writers have contacted me, bubbling with enthusiasm, to let me know that a book of theirs was now listed with the major distributing venues, and they are now "on their way." I always hated to tell them that the only thing they are on the way to is disappointment, should they believe the lists are sales vehicles that will move even one book for them.

Don't Get Excited by Placement with Ingram or Baker & Taylor

Today, almost any title can be placed on either of these lists. And it's easy to believe that Ingram's distribution lock with bookstores and B&T's with libraries would constitute an immediate path to sales. After all, there are still more than 10,000 retail bookstores in the U.S., along with almost 125,000 libraries if the educational system in the U.S. is added to the mix. Let's see, if those libraries buy just a single book from Baker & Taylor, the world is mine oyster. If only this was the way it worked.

The Function of Ingram and Baker & Taylor

These firms, which I believe it's fair to imply have attained monopoly status, since they distribute books to retail bookstores and libraries respectively with really only a single other company of any size infringing on either's turf, have one thing in common: each is a distributor, not a sales entity.

Distribution Means One Thing, Sales Another

Neither firm sells the first book via its respective list (Ingram now publishes through its own company, Lightning Source, but it still does not sell books via the medium; however, marketing programs are offered, which is a topic all unto itself). It bears repeating, neither Ingram nor Baker & Taylor employs a sales force to sell books. They fill orders for books that are <u>presold</u> by sales teams from the various publishers. And that is all!

An Unknown Author on a List Is Like a Drop of Water in the Atlantic

All sorts of statistics are published as to the number of titles on Ingram or Baker & Taylor's list at any given time, but 70,000 is commonly bandied about. Without publicity, how easy would it be for a reader to find a title amidst 70,000–when the search is not author or title specific?

Amazon Has Its Own Issues

Placement with Amazon might seem like the final step to sales, celebrity, and perhaps salvation. But the same issues exist as with Ingram and B & T. Yes, with Amazon, there's a lot of "help" available, but the title count in this case is exponentially greater, and therefore the chances for success governed by the multiplier. One of Amazon's high-ranking executives revealed not long ago that some books on its list don't sell a single copy.

Back to Understanding What Placement on a List Really Means

For a book to have a realistic chance for a writer, it's imperative to be listed with Ingram, Baker & Taylor, and Amazon. But this is a starting point and not the top to what is a very tall mountain–that except under the rarest of circumstances must be climbed one slow step at a time.

Literary Agency Sales Numbers and How to Find the Right Agent

If querying literary agents isn't difficult enough, how is a writer who is attempting to break into the business supposed to decipher the sales figures that are posted by major agents when individual statistics during a 12-month period might indicate the placement of more than 100 titles by a single person?

Sales Numbers Can Reflect the Entire Agency and Not the Individual Agent

Keep in mind that an agent such as Richard Curtis, who one agent-tracking Web site credits with 159 titles sold during a recent 12-month period, is stating the figures for his entire agency. Prolific producers such as Richard Curtis, Sterling Lord, Al Zuckerman, and Jane Dystel are historically providing numbers generated by their respective agency imprimaturs and not their individual sales, although they certainly might play some role in each transaction.

Query the Right Agent for Your Material

If you check their individual Web sites, you will notice that some of these high-production agencies are mammoth, employing a couple of dozen agents and numerous subordinate staff members, such as readers. This is why it's imperative to find out which representative at an agency is the right choice for a particular work. And why it does not behoove a writer to send material to the lead agent when another person is better suited.

Be Careful of the Agent on the Marquee

The reason for this admonition is because many agencies don't pass material from agent to agent to see who might like it from a genre perspective. So in instances in which a Cozy Mystery might be ideal for Jane Jones, it might not be suitable for Hard-Boiled Police Mystery-guru John Jones. And if John Jones is the agency founder—and the person queried—his personal attaché may look for material that will fit his eye only. And no agency I am aware of enables a writer to submit to multiple agents within the same firm, as this seems to be universally disparaged.

There Is an Exception to Be Aware of

There is, however, one disclaimer that must be made, since there are indeed some agencies for which all queries are reviewed by a submissions coordinator, regardless of to whom the letter is addressed. This person screens queries and passes those that are deemed worthy to the agent who is thought to be the best fit for the project. But I don't think anyone would consider it bad advice to suggest that a writer find the right person to query, from the outset.

Proactive Things a Writer Can Do That Will Work

Nothing about locating the right agents to query is easy, but with the last sentence in the preceding paragraph in mind, a serious writer can save a lot of time and aggravation by making the effort to do these four things:

1)   Closely follow Publishers Marketplace to learn which agents are selling what and to whom.
2)   Become knowledgeable of the content of the recent book(s) an agent of interest has placed so something can be referenced in the query, especially if there is plot or thematic similarity.
3)   Utilize the Agent Query Web site at agentquery.com to verify the agent's title, address, etc.
4)   While on the Agent Query site, access the agent's personal information (the URL is often shown; if not, go to the agency Web site and search for the particular agent you want to query). This is important because the submission criteria listed for the agent is often more detailed and current (read "different") from what is provided in the short bio provided on Agent Query.

A writer making the effort to complete these four tasks will be ahead of 95 percent of the querying competition—which is an immense advantage when considering the overall numbers.

Literature Defined As a Genre

In the strangest of ways, attempting to define Literature brings to mind the judge who said he couldn't describe pornography but knew what it was when he saw it. And I'll state up front that I don't have a concrete answer for what constitutes Literature. But I have some ideas.

Defining Literature Is a Personal Matter

Literature seems quite often to be in the eye of the beholder. For light reading, I happen to enjoy Nelson DeMille, yet I teach UP COUNTRY as Literature because I believe the work illustrates exceptional dimension. Cormac McCarthy's NO COUNTRY FOR OLD MEN is a flat-out Thriller, yet who refers to it as that, or to him as a Thriller writer, since he is considered a major artist in the craft of Literature? I think Jody Picoult has written Literature, since I've found some of her material just as profound as work by Barbara Kingsolver or Jane Smiley or Colleen McCullough. But I don't believe any of her novels, as least those of hers that I've read, are ever sold as Literature.

Literature, as I see it, is defined by the substance written into a story that makes the reader think rather than just read. Of course people can say that Romance novels make them think, just as well as Science Fiction or any other genre for that matter. But Literature has that special quality of making the reader dig deeper into his or her thought processes, and this in my view is what separates it from commercial fiction.

Literature Is More Plot-Driven Than Character-Driven?

That's a contention which makes me laugh, and I've read this thesis often. If this is the case, how many works can anyone name that are famous and solely plot-driven? After STUDS LONIGAN, WUTHERING HEIGHTS, and perhaps BREATHING LESSONS on a contemporary basis, what's left?

Character-driven material leads the Literature genre by such a wide margin that it's incomprehensible for me to see how anyone might feel that plot-driven novels are emblematic of the classification. All of Shakespeare's comedies have one theme: love conquers all. And some (okay, many) of the plays indeed have identical story elements, yet are any of the key characters the same?

Characters Matter—A Lot

I watched THE MERRY WIVES OF WINDSOR at The Old Vic some years ago, and it was presented as occurring in the 1920s. Very clever, and the lines held up, which surprised me. But to my way of thinking, the key character in the play has always been Falstaff. And, while admirably portrayed in the milieu of the 1920s, he couldn't be reconstituted in that time frame and made remotely as funny as I found him in the era in which he was originally cast. Someone could say this points to plot and contradicts my position, but I'm not so sure about that. The strength of the characterization was diminished by the setting, not by the character itself.

Is the Seriousness of the Work the Primary Determinant?

Returning to novels, maybe it's poignancy itself that's the deciding factor in determining the definition of Literature, regardless of whether or not the story is plot-driven or character-driven. And Literature generally involves an adult theme, although this isn't always the case. After writing this article, I know just one thing, and this is what I stated at the beginning: Literature is impossible for me to define with any degree of accuracy. But I hope I've provided some idea of what motivates me to think of a work as Literature—and that I've given others who have struggled with the concept some fodder to establish their own criteria for a subject I find most interesting.

Manuscript Evaluations – The Use of Interns and Subordinates to Read Material for Agents and Publishers

The same as a secretary or administrative assistant to any executive, interns or subordinates are often used to screen manuscripts to make certain that the agent or publisher isn't inundated with substandard material. And considering the volume of submissions agents and publishers must sift through, now multiplied many times because of the Internet, without good gatekeepers the process would be overwhelming.

So What Is a "Reader" Looking For?

It's not so much what they're looking for as what they're looking at. And whether anyone wants to agree or disagree with many of the contentions proffered by respected agent and author Noah Lukeman in his book THE FIRST FIVE PAGES, A WRITER'S GUIDE TO STAYING OUT OF THE REJECTION PILE, I firmly believe he's spot-on when he says that "readers" look for reasons to reject a work. And they look hard. Real hard.

Exactly What Aides Evaluate

To effectively answer this, ask yourself what you would look at first. Wouldn't it be grammar? Forget for a moment about how fast the "hook" was established, or some spectacular characterizations, or how rapidly you were engaged in the protagonist, or any of the other "gripping" issues we who write live by. Isn't grammar the first element you notice when beginning reading any text?

It's very basic, but if the sentence construction is flawed, most people will put down a book from an unestablished author. Yes, well-known writers, or highly publicized material, go by a different set of rules, but we mere mortals have to deal with the throes of what Ms. Milsey taught us in 4th grade and what other indomitable spirits worked so hard to drill into us from that point forward.

A Clean Draft Is the Single Most Important Issue for Writers To Contend With

This is so important, I'm going to elaborate on what I wrote in the previous section. How do you react when you pick up a book and you're immediately exposed to sentences with improper subject and verb agreement, pronouns not related to the correct antecedents, unacceptable comma placement, runs of exposition that stop you because of misplaced modifiers, superfluous wording, elliptical expressions, or any of the other rhetorical bugbears?

In this respect, a staffer employed by an agent or publisher to evaluate material is no different from any of the rest of us when we're reading for enjoyment. Enjoyment is not having to revise the story in our minds while we're reading it.

If a Draft Survives the "First Cut," Publishers' Assistants Then Go for the Jugular

If material is patently readable, then the real work begins for "readers," as they look for whatever they can find to have the draft rejected. Here are several considerations that can deal a death blow to a manuscript:

* High on the list are POV shifts, an element that even the most skilled authors sometime find difficult to reconcile.
* Passages written in passive voice are often cited as negatives, even though there's absolutely nothing wrong with injecting text with occasional passive runs, as it's often impossible not to use passive elements and retain content fluency.
* "Telling" and not "showing" is an easy way out for aides who are eager to dis material, as there's always rhetoric that can "show" the action in more vivid detail. This element is important but often grossly overstated as to its significance, as many scenes need to move along and not be bogged down with capillary-level introspection.
* The overuse of adverbs and adjectives. Old as the hills, but still a killer.
* Dialogue pacing is another element that's a high priority and something many writers never consider.
* Some aids are taught in college, or have read or been told, that an "expert" has determined interior monologue should always follow a spit of dialogue. These "readers," and many are not

early-stage interns, won't bend this rule, ignoring the pitch of the entire scene to ferret out a single "offending" exchange.

Quirks and Still More Quirks

An inordinate number of issues can destroy a manuscript's chances, and this article touches on just a few of the more potentially contentious elements. It's important to always remember that agents and publishers have preferences, just the same as we all do. And they, like the rest of us, hire aides who will pay strict attention to their likes and dislikes. Hence, if a subordinate sees something unappealing about a draft, it's sent to the slush pile to wallow forever, in all but the rarest of cases.

Manuscript Evaluations – What Publishers Consider

Overwhelmingly, publishers are an honorable lot. And I firmly believe that the very first consideration for most is the literary value of any work they're considering for publication. Yet even though I'm confident this is an accurate assessment, would any publishing house refuse TWILIGHT or FIFTY SHADES OF GREY once either's readership was established?

What's the Norm?

For the sake of the integrity of this article's topic, let's assume we aren't discussing what surrounds one mega blockbuster that comes out every three years or so and controls the bottom line of a major publisher. Instead, we're looking at the industry based on a manuscript presented by a writer who's trying to gain a foothold.

The Market for the Story Will Be High on the Agenda.

If the draft appears patently readable (this isn't a joke), the initial consideration often gets down to market. This isn't always from a dollar-driven perspective but relates to the specific market to which the imprint's sales team sells its books. The key to this is the word "specific," since each publishing group's marketing operation has generally spent years (read "decades") branding its various imprints.

I've mentioned Pinnacle before, and since I've tried to write for the firm a couple of times and missed the mark for one reason or another, I can discuss what I experienced firsthand. Pinnacle wants a Thriller with the murders described as they occur and in gruesome detail. The killer must also go after the story's protagonist, and the latter must have a love interest that's clear to the reader from the outset. Fail to deliver on any of this and the manuscript will be rejected. Almost every imprint has a set of guidelines that are inviolable.

A Publisher's Comfort Zone Has To Be Recognized

Ask yourself, would a story sell to the New York market if written about an Amish buggy maker from Yoder, Kansas, who trades in his leather punch for a pair of handcuffs and travels the 30 miles to battle crime on the mean streets of Wichita every night? As silly as this might seem, I've experienced difficulty getting traction for a soon-to-retire criminal investigator from Florida who happens upon a serial murderer in rural Indiana. If the historical aspect of the story wasn't absolutely paramount to the plot, I'd have moved this narrative's setting to Long Island or outside of Philadelphia. Really! Geography is a legitimate consideration.

It's Crucial To Examine Exactly What an Imprint Publishes

If a publisher is strong with Historical Romances, for example, it's hard to get a Mystery accepted by the company even if the house might've published one or two in its oeuvre. And it's particularly problematic if the Mystery is written in a minimalist style, such as THE POSTMAN ALWAYS RINGS TWICE or THE MALTESE FALCON. I know from experience that any Thriller submitted to a publisher with definite Historical Romance underpinnings had better be strong on

physical scene description, deep into introspective characterizations, and committed to layers of character dimension. Of course
it's hard for most writers to pace a Thriller adequately while providing service to each of the elements I just outlined, but a publisher's comfort zone cannot be overestimated, and a writer must
adhere to what I'll refer to as the "house rules" or his or her time will
be wasted.

Once More, Will It Sell?

I read years ago that certain publishers would accept noncommercial
material to enhance their prestige, and I don't doubt this was true
then and remains a noble position that many industry executives
continue to hold in high station. Yet the "Will it sell?" mantra–now
more than ever–seems to trump everything else. So if a book is not
considered highly marketable, it's doubtful in today's crowded,
corporately controlled environment that many works with limited
commercial prospects will stand much of a chance. And this is even
true when a previously published author has not achieved success
with a most-recent work. The sad realities are what they are, at least
as I know them, and this is why many established writers have
chosen, or are exploring, alternatives to mainstream publishing.

Print on Demand (POD) Publishing and the Self-Publishing Industry

The first obvious issue for any reader of this article is the title, since
it strays dramatically from the norm of using "versus" to separate the
two mediums. The reason for my word choice is because technology
now enables anyone to self-publish an e-book for very little out-of-
pocket expense.

This still doesn't imply that self-publishing is not loathed by the major
print publishers and upscale indies, along with the agents who
support them via their submissions, but the rising presence of the
electronic medium seems to have created a degree of acquiescence

for the digital aspect of self-publishing. I want to reiterate that this newfound tolerance should not be considered akin to support, since the stigma assigned by the mainstream industry to self-publishing remains as strong as ever, and the purpose of this article is solely to try to provide a degree of clarity.

[This article was originally published by me in 2010, but the material continues to be relevant in 2015 except that a softcover can be acquired for around $5, and it must be noted that the mainstream publishing houses; meaning the mega-major royalty publishers and quality independent presses, are all involved with trying to gain e-book market share. For this reason, the bias against self-publishing, in large measure because of the widespread acceptance of digital, is no longer near as pronounced as it was in 2010.]

POD Is Not Self-Publishing

Print On Demand is confusing to the people who assume this to connote self-publishing. POD has nothing to do with self-publishing, except that it enables a self-published book to be converted into a hard copy—and at a heretofore unavailable low cost. A single copy in a paperback book, including cover artwork from a template, can be printed for as little as $35, with the entire process taking less than five minutes (the present technology consists of a sophisticated printer with a couple of other components, which combined have a price tag of around $100,000. Read on, however.)

A run of a few hundred copies of a book by a traditional printer, depending on the purveyor, can reduce the cost of a 90,000-word book to approximately $5 per unit. According to industry figures, the average self-published book (average in this instance refers to the mode or most common number), sells 41 copies. For someone bent on seeing his or her name in print, I think most folks would agree that a single shopping bag with a couple of dozen books in it at a total expense of a few hundred dollars is indeed preferential to a garage loaded to the ceiling with paperbacks and a hole in a bank account of several thousand dollars.

Major Royalty Publishers Are Utilizing POD

Because of the high cost of distribution and warehousing of non-bestsellers, especially since gross retail sales for a particular title are usually far from a sure thing, it only makes sense that major royalty publishers have embraced the POD model. Publishers can produce (or have produced, as the case may be) an exact replica of a soft cover–on demand–and not have to keep the book in inventory awaiting a consumer buying decision that might never come.

From a business standpoint, the POD model for a soft cover (and probably hard cover in the not too distant future) makes all the sense in the world. This might mean that the remaining major stand-alone bookstores will be reduced to kiosks in the mall, and considering the high cost of maintaining large retail space, this dramatic change could occur sooner rather than later. [I've predicted this for some time, and I'm currently seeing this happen with unnerving frequency, as for the most part leases on brick-and-mortar bookstores aren't being renewed.]

So What about Self-Publishing?

Self-publishing is changing too. Authors are now being solicited (okay, badgered), via a constant barrage of POD options presented by the self-publishing houses, to buy the books the writers themselves wrote. Rather than once again creating a new business model, it's much easier for a self-publishing company to access the convenience of POD and not view it as a competitive medium. Unfortunately, self-published writers unwittingly fall for their respective publisher's constant solicitations and still end up with a trunk full of unsold books (which I guess is advantageous to a garage full).

Self-Publishing Is Still Self-Publishing

Like leopards not changing their spots, self-publishing is what it is. And my advice is still the same for any writer who has run out of patience and tossed in the towel: self-publish as inexpensively as possible. If a print copy is desired, as I mentioned earlier, POD technology, with Createspace for example, makes a single copy softcover, in a trade paperback size with cover, available for less than $5 (in 2015), and the company provides the ISBN at no charge. [The author is responsible for the cover design and layout of the text, but when finished, the cost for a book such as what you are reading now is around $4.50, and it's 88,000 words.]

Before Self-Publishing, Consider the Regional Independent Publishers

The advance from a major royalty publisher (the mega houses plus Kensington) for a heretofore unpublished author for a work of fiction is generally in the neighborhood of $20,000 (but of late can be as low as $5,000, and I've even heard of one instance of $1,500 being offered to a previously published fiction writer whose last work hadn't sold particularly well). There are, however, some very well-respected independent presses that are worth looking into after the big guys have sent out their rejection slips. In most instances the advances will be less than what the majors offer, and a writer might have to do considerable grassroots marketing (although the majors are requiring this, too, and more so than ever), but I continue to suggest giving the independents a shot rather than immediately turning to self-publishing.

Publishers Marketplace Is the "Old Reliable"

Publishers Marketplace, via its daily Publishers Lunch Newsletter, shows which agents are placing what and with whom, and a writer can learn which indies to ply for a specific genre by checking the respective links. A writer can also Google the words "Independent Publishers" and create a list. The problem with this, however, is sifting through the vanity presses that disguise themselves as legitimate royalty houses. This is why I suggest Publishers Marketplace as the first and in my opinion best resource for accurate, concurrent information.

But if sourcing the bona fide royalty publishers fails, to take one more precaution against ending up with the garage full of books I always warn against, I also recommend that authors make a visit to the "Preditors and Editors" Web site ("Preditors" is spelled this way, and I have no idea why), as this medium has historically done a good job of singling out the bad guys. This will be time well spent and enable one more snapshot of what can be lurking in the bushes, which might be something with the body of a lamb but with a head that immediately morphs into a hydra the moment the contract is signed.

A Final Few Thoughts on Self-Publishing and POD

In fairness to self-publishing history, there are indeed accurate tales about people who have self-published and been wildly successful. But to my knowledge, all had one of two things in common: phenomenal marketing created via a gargantuan Internet presence or a highly successful advertising or media career. In the nonfiction market, those who made it were also the undisputed experts in their respective niches. Most of us mere mortals aren't fortunate enough to fit any of these categories, and this is why I keep stressing to self-publish the absolute cheapest way possible, should this be perceived as the only option still available. And if print is desired, use a POD medium and make the least number of copies that will satisfy immediate needs, even if the cost per copy might not allow for a profit on the early sales. If the book sells, then move into larger print runs that will reduce the cost per copy so a viable sales model can be developed. I promise I'm giving good advice on this.

Proofreading By Nonprofessionals and the Problems This Can Create

No one likes spending money to hire an editor. I certainly don't, and I am an editor. But it is a necessary evil, should a writer view it this way, and there are specific reasons why proofreading by an untrained person is a recipe for problems if not disaster.

The Secretary

Several distinct categories of amateur proofreaders exist that I've found writers gravitate toward, and at the top of the list is the personal secretary. I've been blessed with a number of extraordinary secretaries in the5 years I worked primarily on the business side of the healthcare field. And each one was able to spot my typos, missing words, and punctuation miscues, and I had a couple who routinely provided better ways for me to phrase something. But better ways to present my position? Never! If that had been the case, I should have been doing their jobs and they mine. And I'm dead serious about this.

A secretary who can clean up a boss's hurried or sloppy writing is an immeasurable asset, but having the skill sets to understand the nuances of copyediting is like implying that a bookkeeper is also an accountant. These aren't the same jobs any more than secretarial responsibilities can translate to understanding what is or isn't a restrictive clause and if commas are or aren't required. Sure, some secretaries can accomplish all of what any editor can provide. Look at J.K. Rowling. But how many Ms. Rowlings are out there, and do we know that she never used an editor?

The Spouse

Has anyone had a significant other provide golf lessons? Shouldn't that answer using a spouse as an editor? To take this full circle, I don't know of any editor who hasn't at one time or another had a client's spouse question the editorial decisions. I had to drop a good writer because his wife decided she could edit better than I and my copyeditor. She made wholesale changes to a draft I'd spent more than 200 hours on and effectively drove the material to perdition with no hope of absolution. This can apply to any relative, but I've found the spouse to be the primary culprit in the realm of bad-decision number two.

The Friend

The third worst offender is the friend. Usually this person is considered really smart and often incredibly well read, having consumed thousands of books in his or her lifetime. However, it must be understood that reading for enjoyment is not going to make a person a competent proofreader any more than looking at fine art will assure a person proficiency as an artist. Reading or looking at art obviously helps on the appreciation side of things, but has little if any relevance to practical application, as easy reading is the by-product of very hard writing, something that's been cited quite often recently by a wide array of noted authors.

Proofreading Is a Specialty

I estimate that I catch 95 percent of the copy errors a writer makes, while the remaining 5 percent would take me another lifetime to fully comprehend. Simple things like writing height and weight or the length of a room or the width of a board are missed by almost everyone who is untrained.

Pronouns such as "their" being used with singular antecedents can foul up the best writers. Using "different than" when it should be "different from" (unless you're in the U.K.) is easy to miss. Applying "him" when "his" should be used to indicate the possessive is often overlooked. Past progressive tense when past tense is correct is a common error.

Proofreading Requires Enormous Knowledge and Extensive Training

The list of anomalies that apply to the English language is in the thousands, not hundreds, and no wonderful secretary, loving spouse, or uber-intelligent friend can be expected to demonstrate proficiency in a science that has a tome of guidelines and which requires a precise level of learned and practiced expertise to apply correctly. It's just the way it is. And I wish it were different myself.

Publishers – Large vs. Small
and What to Expect from Each

I believe it's fair to state that the size of the publisher is probably the last thing on the mind of most writers who receive a contract in the mail. But there are issues to consider, especially with the ground-swell of consolidation at the high end of the publishing industry and the proliferation of publishing options at the entry level, with small presses in the middle.

Big Means Big

The good part of being signed by a mainstream publisher is that this can never be taken away. And how much, peripheral to money, is this worth? If it's like the job market, a survey was done years ago that indicated the majority of people would take a pay cut to receive a more prestigious title. No joke.

Big Means More Advertising Dollars Are Available

The question is, how much of that advertising money will be spent on your book, especially if you're a relative unknown? And if your book doesn't "take off" right away, how long will the major house stay with you before saying "sayonara"? A small house might be inclined to be substantially more patient with a book, since each work it publishes will have a stronger impact, by percentage, on the bottom line than one title "placed" within the larger number published by a major imprint.

A Number Rather Than a Person

Then there's always the problem of getting "swallowed up" in a large organization, no different from the workplace, a school, a church, or whatever. Once the handshaking is over at a major publisher, unless the book is a blockbuster, phone time will likely be at a premium. And at a smaller publisher, a writer might be more able to sit down and discuss marketing options face-to-face rather than via the vapidity of an e-mail. I'm not implying that personal contact isn't available with a major imprint, but I believe it's fair to say that the opportunities for one-on-one meetings will be few and far between unless the writer is a star.

Small Can Mean Small Budget

The opposite of Random House, D&W Publishing (a name I've made up for this illustration) will almost certainly have a small marketing budget, so a writer can forget about a full-page ad costing six figures in the NYT. And a small publisher might expect more individual marketing by its writers, and at each author's expense. However, to that point, it seems all publishers are urging if not demanding that their writers hit the bricks now more than ever.

Smaller Budgets, However, Can Have Advantages

In line with what I wrote earlier, a small press will almost always provide its authors with a closer sense of family, and many writers find this of great value. And while a smaller publisher will most often "stay with" a book longer, I've been told by authors who have signed with firms of both sizes that the smaller presses were easier to work with all the way around. However, I've had others tell me there was no difference, and if the big press paid a larger advance it made the lack of "homeyness" a nonissue.

Time Enters into the Equation

If an author has spent years trying to land an agent, then more years pursuing a major royalty publisher, all to no avail, there can be huge satisfaction working with a small press. Some of these smaller publishers are renowned for their high-quality work and for the care their editors provide writers, and many "indie's" can be approached without an agent's assistance.

And, Yes, the Money

For many years, the major houses seemed to have a "standard" advance for new fiction novels, which was $20,000. During this same period, the smaller independent publishers' advances were in the $5,000 range for new work. Today, I've heard of major publishers' imprints paying $5,000 to debut authors, and one purportedly offered as little as a $1,500 advance to a previously published client. And I know of several quality upstart independent publishers that sign work on consignment; meaning, the author is paid royalties on sales, with no advance.

Publishing Issue – Why Can't I Get My Perfect Novel Published?

Abundant bear traps exist in the current literary marketplace that even writers who are old hands at accepting the vagaries of the publishing industry are having difficulty navigating. Here are several issues–some old, some new–to consider.

Pitching a Book to the Wrong Agent or Publisher

Genre specificity plagues a lot of authors. It's important to recognize that a Hard-Boiled Detective Mystery with a lot of torrid love scenes is not classified as Romance. If a writer is having difficulty pinning down the genre for a specific work, a friendly library staff member might be a wonderful resource (just please don't expect this person to read your entire draft). Only after the genre is identified can a writer adequately source the query sites for suitable agents or publishers.

Agent or Publisher Bias Can Knock a Work Out of the Saddle

Years ago I presented material to a well-known independent publisher, only to be told that the firm did not handle anything dealing with Russians or the Mafia, something that was not mentioned in the already abundant submission guidelines. As luck would have it, a significant character in my narrative was a member of the Russian Mafia.

Of course this could be modified, but the point is that any writer can be blindsided by a bias against anything from Lithuanian folk dancers to fly fishermen from Montana. It's important to keep in mind that this is a quirky business. And it seems that once something is found to be deficient in a manuscript, the agent or publisher tends to turn up the power of an already very intense microscope.

A Manuscript Can Suffer from the New Rock Band Syndrome

A manuscript can be deemed to be too close to other material. Or too far removed so that it doesn't fit with anything else. Related to the way musical groups sound, I'm told these are standard rebukes in the recording industry. My personal experience is that it would be easier to climb Mt. Everest naked than to persuade an agent or publisher to accept material for which either has a predisposition toward rejecting for one of the reasons I just mentioned.

What if You Write the Perfect Manuscript, But It's Really Not So Perfect After All?

Many writers contact a professional for assistance well after sourcing scores of agents and numerous publishers. It's important to keep in mind that only so many agents and publishers work with each genre. And, unfortunately, agents and publishers inherently do not want to see work they've previously rejected. For these reasons, it's critical to have a manuscript polished to a very high sheen (read "show-car level") before submitting it.

Publishing Issue—Reasons Why Some Lesser Quality Novels Are Published

Everybody Has a Story Worth Telling

There's a good possibility you have either been told this, heard this, or feel this way for your own reason(s). And while it may not be irrational to believe that each of us has a story worth publishing, doing so in a manner that's palatable to a market that extends beyond our family and closest friends is indeed what separates writers.

It's Often Not a Matter of Ability

I don't think it would be out of line to state that we've all read a novel, for which we've paid our hard-earned money, and later shaken our collective heads in wonder and disgust at how the book ever got published. We might have even said to ourselves (and often) that we've written material that's much better than what we just read, yet our stories were rejected. So why did a writer's inferior material attract a publisher when our superior work hadn't? Maybe our material wasn't so perfect after all.

Specific Manuscript Faults That Can Cause Rejection

Assuming that basic grammar and punctuation were not an issue, several factors can determine why a manuscript was never considered publishable. In no particular order, here are some of those reasons. And please note that all of these shortcomings are the result of inadequate editing.

* Certain plot elements seemed contrived
* The characters were not interesting

* The scenes were not fully developed
* There was not adequate conflict
* The dialogue was not realistic
* The pacing was slow
* The text was difficult to read
* The premise was poor
* The story design was wrong for the genre
* Paragraphs and/or chapters were too long

These are some of the common reasons for rejection, yet we may have just read material published by a major imprint that contained some if not many of the very flaws that are listed. How is this so? Read on.

The Not So Obvious Reasons Poor Material Is Published

It is important to understand that today's publisher is interested in readership potential more than ever, and an established author with a guaranteed market is key. The penchant to print books that will assure a certain number of sales encourages the following:

* Books are written too fast, and this results in diminished quality
* Books are poorly edited, since many publishers do very little of this today
* Some of the most successful authors do not write some of the material under their names
* Some of the most successful authors do not write any of the material under their names

The list is much longer, but the point is obvious. And this is why a plan is critical for an unpublished author, or an already difficult task can soon become insurmountable.

Before Committing the First Word to Paper, Formulate a Plan and Force Yourself to Follow It

For those writers who have the foresight to create a plan and the discipline to follow it, here are a few suggestions that will at least give each of you a fighting chance to have your novel considered by a quality agent and/or a bona fide royalty publisher:

1) Determine the genre and subgenre of your book. If you should be having difficulty with this, go to the free "agentquery.com" Web site for current definitions and a listing of agents who work in your category.

2) Review current novels in your genre and subgenre to determine the authors who are being published and by whom. Make a list of these authors' agents (they are generally referenced on any novel's Acknowledgments page). This will provide you with a group of agents to query, and you'll likely find that some if not many will accept unsolicited material.

3) It is imperative that your novel is an exact fit for the publisher's definition of the genre–not your definition of it.

4) Pay attention to word count, paragraph length, chapter length, and general layout. Avoid long runs of italics and all parentheses if your material is fiction (the latter is a personal hang-up of mine).

5) You can certainly take advantage of critique groups, writing workshops, and friends and relatives. But have a professional editor–one you have thoroughly checked out–at least read your manuscript before sending it off. And if you do take my advice on this, find an editor who has experience with royalty publishers in your manuscript's genre.

6) You will not get a second chance with an agent or publisher. And the list of good ones who are still accepting unsolicited material is dwindling. So make your manuscript as perfect as possible in every way prior to submitting it for consideration.

Put the Cart in Front of the Horse and Create Your Liner Notes First

For anyone still in the planning stages, this is the time to put two paragraphs of your dreams for your novel on paper. Design before-hand what your liner notes (and ultimately your query letter) should

look like when your manuscript is finished. Do this and your characters will never be shallow and your scenes will never be weak. Now
follow your dreams.

Query Letter Writing –
Finding the Perfect Agent for Your Novel

More Agents Than Ever Do Not Accept Unsolicited Manuscripts

In the fiction area of the book-agenting arena, other than most
agents/agencies now requesting or requiring submissions via e-mail,
the rules for presenting preliminary material have not changed
appreciably in the past 20 years. What has changed is the number of
agents who no longer accept unsolicited material. Hence, they will
only consider a project referred by someone with whom they have a
business relationship, such as a respected colleague, well-known
writer, or editor.

Understand an Agent's Submission Guidelines and Follow Them

As stated in the opening paragraph of this paper, during the past two
decades submission guidelines are still relatively unchanged, depending on the agent: one-page query; query with three pages;
query with five pages, query with first chapter; query, synopsis, five
pages; query, synopsis, first three chapters, etc. The primary difference, as I also mentioned earlier, is that many agents now accept
only e-queries/submissions.

Identify the Genre and Subgenre in Which Your Manuscript Is Written

Once the criteria for querying a particular agent is understood, a
writer can save a great deal of time and aggravation by creating and
following a plan.

First, it is critical to recognize the genre and exact subgenre in which a work fits. For example, depending on who you talk to, there are now more than two-dozen subsets in the Suspense genre alone. The Association of Authors' Representatives, Inc., @ aaronline.org is a great place to start an agent search, and another excellent free site is agentquery.com.

Query Agents Who Represent Authors Your Style Most Closely Emulates

A second option, if your story is written in the style of a popular author, is to check the Acknowledgments page of a book by that writer, for his or her agent. Query this agent—even if the person professes not to accept unsolicited material. The worst that can happen is a rejection. But you could receive a request to see a portion of your novel, and there is a solid reason why.

Agents Work in Genres in Which They Are Successful

People are generally most comfortable with what they know. Agents are no different. Familiarity, in this instance, is most often an asset and not a liability. Agents want books they believe they can sell—and they will gravitate toward genres in which they have a positive history.

Query Letter Writing –
The Process Dissected

I've written many articles during the past few years on the art of composing query letters, and these have consistently ranked among the most popular of anything I've published. But even after explaining what an agent is looking for, and that a query must read like liner notes and not a synopsis, I continue to receive questions from writers. So I thought it might be a good idea to dissect a query down to what I call its capillaries.

Successful Queries Consist of Four Distinct Parts

The four parts of a query letter are as follows: the hook, the layout, the reason the book will appeal to a wide market, and the writer's credentials.

The Opening Paragraph

The opening paragraph must contain a hook that differentiates the story from all others. It also must encapsulate the primary focus of the novel. Then it has to tell the agent that what follows is genuinely scintillating material which will be indicative of a story that is going to be a blockbuster, since all agents and publishers want only the next big book. This is not a joke or hype, even though some agents might indicate otherwise, especially when they are in a professorial mood. I do, however, know some agents who absolutely value quality over any other factor, but they too must put food on the table, thus the marketability of the book is not a minor consideration even for them.

Here's What Not to Write for an Opening to a Query, As It's a Synopsis

My 85,000-word historical novel opens with Ma and Pa leaving Virginia in 1872 with plans for settling in Missouri. Uncle Dirk goes with the family and is arrested for killing a man in a bar fight. Pa tries to spring him from jail, but shoots the sheriff and gets himself arrested too. Ma goes on by herself with the family and meets a man in Missouri who is more to her liking than Pa. Especially since Pa probably won't get out of jail for many years, if ever. Ma has a baby by this man, a boy who when he grows up runs for public office. Pa is eventually released from jail and tells Ma she done him wrong and is going to let everyone know what kind of woman she really is, and that her son is illegitimate. She decides to shoot herself rather than face her shame.

Here's the Same Opening for a Query That's Not in Synopsis Form

A VOW NOT TAKEN, my 85,000-word work of commercial fiction, is the story of a young woman whose husband is sent to prison in 1872 for trying to spring his brother from jail and shooting the sheriff during the botched escape. Emily Davis must brave the frontier to find a new life for herself and her family, and she discovers love and happiness with a man after she settles in Missouri. Her life is everything she could hope for, until her husband shows up 20 years later and threatens to expose her as a bigamist; and her son, who is now running for public office, as a bastard.

Now that the agent is excited, what more can the author offer? The woman has decided to shoot herself rather than face her shame. Is this by itself enough to build on? Let's see.

The Second Paragraph Has to Elevate the Query to the "I Have to Read This Book" Level

Emily contemplates taking the easy way out. One shot from the pistol and she is free. But as she places the gun to her temple, her life flashes in front of her and she uncocks the hammer. If only her husband had listened to her and left his brother in jail. She never told him what Dirk had done to her. Getting free of him was a blessing, and after Dirk was jailed, why wouldn't her husband leave as she had asked? Why wasn't he stronger—and why wasn't she?

The Third Paragraph Cinches the Deal

A VOW NOT TAKEN is a story of a woman in conflict, yet Emily's methods for defeating adversity will give readers a window into their own hearts and a different perspective on the difficult decisions that form people's lives. Emily shows that clarity is a matter of conviction solidified by time, and readers will be gratified when she is rewarded for maintaining her dignity while in the throes of intense peer pressure and public scorn.

A Little About Yourself and a Request

A VOW NOT TAKEN is my first novel. I have an English degree from CCNY, and I finished first-runner-up in statewide creative-writing contest sponsored by the local library system where I live. I maintain an active blog on which I offer chapters of my novel for review, and I am encouraged by what has become a substantial following. I am writing to ask if you would be interested in considering A VOW NOT TAKEN for representation. I am most appreciative of your time, and I look forward to hearing from you.

The Key Is to Write a Comprehensive Opening Paragraph and Break It Down

Everything in this query for this pretend story, other than what I wrote at the end, came from the opening paragraph. Look for the parts in your story that set it apart. Is there love, hate, joy, fear, anxiety, jealousy? What is the story's strongest element? That should be the lead.

In the make-believe novel I invented for this exercise, a woman is left to carry on by herself because of a husband who did not exercise good judgment. But can he be faulted for his brotherly love? And was he completely ignorant of his brother's violation of Emily? I chose not to focus on the latter issue in this query, but in your treatment it might be the compelling element.

Once it's established what makes the story tick, the entire can be designed around this. It's solely a matter of filling in the blanks. Just be certain not to "tell" the story in the query. Instead, "show" what makes the narrative work.

Query Letter Writing
and What Not To Include in the Content

Many of us who professionally edit manuscripts spend a great deal of our time providing our clients with query letter assistance. And happily so. Because if we're not coaching those who use our services on how to write effective query letters, a lot of very good authors are often unaware of some of the more critical nuances.

It's a lot More Than Eschewing Adverbs and Running Adjectives

Forever, it seems, we have been warned against using adverbs in queries, the mind-set being that an agent will think that adverbs are indicative of the writer's overall style. Hence, the novel will be teeming with "stopped suddenly" and "smiled broadly" and all sorts of other superfluous couplets. Or that there will be a plethora of "irregular, big, burgeoning, brown spots" or "loud, cantankerous, feeble, wrinkled, old people" lurking somewhere. These are givens in the realm of query letter writing, but what is to follow is not.

Avoid the Temptation of Comparing Your Writing to That of Another Author's

First and foremost is the necessity for crafting a query that highlights the salient aspects of the story and not to permit the letter to come across as an overzealous personal pitch for its author.

For example, if a query says that the work is written like a Pat Conroy novel, an agent can and often will infer that the author is stating that he or she writes as well as Mr. Conroy, a lofty goal indeed. If comparisons to other works are desired, it is much better to simply imply that the novel is written in the style of a particular noted author—and not that your ability compares to that person's skill sets, regardless of how you or others in your circle of friends and acquaintances might rate your talent.

Humility is a big plus; conversely, braggadocio is a sure way of turning off an agent, since how you comport yourself by the content and tone of the query can have a great deal to do with how this person will perceive working with you.

Be Certain to Write the Query in a Way That Is Indicative of How You Wrote Your Novel

The well-respected literary agent and oft-published author Noah Lukeman wrote about how too much information via a writer's bio can be more damaging that helpful. And so much so that the bio can serve as the means for rejection—and not the text of the manuscript itself.

When I first read Mr. Lukeman's position on this I was appalled and offended, but as I thought about it more I decided not to blame the messenger. If a writer is an academician in a scientific field, and that person's query letter style, for a Mystery for example, doesn't indicate anything to the contrary, why should the agent believe that the book is not written like a professorial thesis? In the same vein, if someone has been designing advertising copy for 20 years—and that individual's query for a Police Thriller is rife with overblown rhetoric—why would the agent think any differently about the condition of the narrative he or she is being asked to read?

There Are Facts About an Unpublished Writer's Background That Can be Advantageous

In line with what I just discussed, I suggest that unpublished authors write sparingly about their credentials, except should their CV include writing honors they've received, and only if these pertain to the genre in which the book they are presenting happens to be written. Workshop or symposium awards, and book competitions in which germane work was singled out for excellence, are what the author would want to present at the close of the query. Forget everything else. Just thank the agent for his or her time and rest your case.

Give Yourself a Chance

If you're careful about hype, watch the obvious benchmark rejection issues such as unnecessary adverbs and running adjectives, and keep you CV pertinent to the novel you are presenting, you'll allow the description of your story's features to dictate if the agent is going to request your manuscript. And you won't be rejected for reasons that may well have nothing to do with the quality of your work.

Query Letter Writing
Differs From Writing a Synopsis

Query Letter Writing–a Daunting Dilemma

Some years ago, to add to a discussion I was encouraging related to the nuances of query letter writing, a woman who had just received a contract for her first novel–and from Simon & Schuster no less–wrote me to lament how arduous she had found the task of crafting her missive to appeal to agents. She admitted that she considered the query more difficult than writing the actual work, and had spent more than a year on her letter. For discretion's sake, I won't reveal the name of the author, but many people would recognize this now well-known Ph.D., and her breakthrough novel.

The Synopsis Syndrome

I chuckled at her comment, not out of derision but from empathy, since I have often felt the same way about my own queries. While I haven't spent a year on a letter to attract an agent, at times I wish I had. One of the problems is that I have often found my query turning into a synopsis. And in parsing the query letters of others, "the synopsis syndrome," as I call it, seems to be the most chronic malady that inhibits the presentations.

For a Successful Query Letter for Fiction, Less Is Generally Better Than More

A writer desires to tell as much as possible about the story of which he or she is so passionate, and is often influenced by an industry success story in which someone has crammed as much as possible onto one page, even to the point of reducing font size to make the text fit. Unfortunately, the end result for most is invariably a synopsis and not a presentation of the subtle plot and character elements that accurately depicts the writer's skill and which sets the work apart—and what will influence an agent to request the manuscript.

Think of a Query Letter As an Advertisement; Hence, Sell the Sizzle and Not the Steak

When I began writing seriously back in the days of the covered wagon, an agent once railed at me about a poor query I had sent him because it told too much of the individual aspects of the story and not about the work as a whole. He said to write the query as if I was designing the liner notes for the novel. I found this to be some of the best advice I have ever received. As a comparison, if one wants to be successful in sales, one of the time-worn axioms is to "sell the sizzle and not the steak." It might be suggested to apply the same maxim to writing a query letter. This can be like grasping "showing versus telling" the first time around (or the tenth), but it has to be understood if a query is going to work.

Write a Query from the Gut, Not the Heart

It might help to think of your work in visceral terms; meaning, what are the hard-hitting aspects of your story from an overall perspective. This will take your thinking beyond the brick and mortar. And remember most of all that you are wanting to provide the agent with just enough knowledge of your work (and ability) to foster interest. If you do this by carefully choosing words to create the most impact, would it not be logical that the agent might assume your novel is written at the same level? Should you review queries that have been effective (and I can't suggest this strongly enough), please notice how little is told about the actual stories–but how much the successful letters indicate the respective author's competence for writing quality prose.

Query Letter Writing Fact and Fiction

Fact: Query letter writing is an art form.

Make no mistake about it, writing queries that produce results is a craft.

Fact: A query should not be written like a synopsis.

I devoted an entire article to this, yet writers who have read the piece continue to send me sample queries that ignore this premise. Yes, there are exceptions. There are exceptions to everything in publishing. But if an author wants to entice an agent to stand up and take notice, as I said in the article, sell the sizzle and not the steak. Pure and simple, for fiction it's best to write a query the same is if creating liner notes.

Fact: A writer has to know the genre in which the work is written.

If the author doesn't know the genre in which his or her work is written, any bona fide editor can explain it. A writer who doesn't take the time to figure this out has virtually no chance. Genre identification is paramount. And while critique groups, etc., are a wonderful sounding board, they are historically populated by amateurs, and as such not the place to learn about genre specificity in today's complicated and ever-changing market.

Fact: Structurally, a query can be designed like a short theme.

Yes, a simple but effective way to structure a query is like a theme. Begin with a core thought that highlights two or three critical plot elements. Justify these issues in the next paragraph, then close the letter with why readers will gravitate to the story. Personal credentials if they pertain directly to the work can be added in a final brief sentence or two, along with a statement of appreciation for the agent's or publisher's time.

Fiction: Copying the words or phrases from a successful query will assure another query's success.

Nothing could be further from the truth. A query should define the voice and strength of the writer and the project. An experienced agent or publisher can pick up the nuances of a writer's style. Counterfeiting doesn't work.

Fiction: Query letters should never contain questions.

This farce has been bandied about for some time and is ridiculous. No one likes a query that reads like a movie opening: In a world . . . followed by a "what if" scenario. But there is nothing at all problematic about asking an agent or publisher to consider a novel's most poignant issue or issues. And if some agent has written to the contrary, so be it. Hundreds of other agents, and all of those I know and work with, think differently.

Fiction: A query should fill as much of the page as possible.

It's quality not quantity that matters. A query with 500 words jammed on a page is not going to be perceived to be any better than 300 words that clearly and concisely demonstrate the writer's skill and the "hot points" about the story he or she has written. An overwritten query can plant the thought that the novel is structured in the same manner.

What can distort this last remark are the bloated query examples posted by some writers whose work has been accepted for publication. But when a query turns into a synopsis, which is almost always the tendency in longer efforts, it's generally a quick reach by the agent or publisher for the SASE or the rejection template on the computer file.

Fiction: If my query doesn't work the first time, I can write another one later to the same agent for the same book.

Agents keep records. At least many of the good ones I know do. And, universally, as I've experienced it, agents never want to see a query about the same material a second time any more than they will consider a manuscript they previously rejected. So it is imperative to get it right the first time.

A final thought: A poor query will never get a book in front of an agent; however, a great query can influence an agent to look at a novel that might require just a touch-up. And critical feedback can often be gleaned from an agent. For anyone not using a professional editor (curses), I cannot think of a better way to receive professional advice without having to pay for it. However, most authors would be way ahead of the game if they sought professional direction to assure a quality query before bombarding a highly selective marketplace with less than sterling requests to review material.

Querying an Agent – Make Certain Your Manuscript Is Ready

As an independent book editor who freely solicits outside material to edit, I receive a great many manuscripts with this caveat: "I have sent my manuscript to a lot of agents but received rejections that indicated my work needs editing by a professional. If I have you edit my manuscript, should I send it back to agents who have previously rejected it?"

Agents Don't Want to See the Same Material a Second Time

At least this has been my experience for more than 20 years, during which time I've queried a half-dozen of my own novels. There are exceptions, but an editor for whom I carry great respect told me early-on that he had never heard of an agent representing a book from a heretofore unpublished author he or she had rejected earlier. And while I've had a well-regarded submissions editor refute this, until a previously unpublished writer tells me his or her personal book was accepted by the same agent after it was rejected, I'm sticking with my original statement and what the first editor told me eons ago. If someone was already published and has a following, this is a horse of a different color, but for industry unknowns, again, once a draft is rejected I suggest moving on to fresh territory.

A Writer Can't Be Faulted for Not Knowing the Nuances of the Business

There is no handbook on how to deal with agents or to what level an author's representative will go to support a draft. Most novice writers think that if their work is good enough an agent will accept the manuscript and polish it for them. My experience is that it doesn't work this way, as in-house editing relates entirely to where the writer is on the "usefulness curve." If a writer is an established property, an agent might well edit a draft. And many publishers send drafts written by their franchise writers to editors for extensive revision. These editors are not often listed in the acknowledgments, but in some instances they do more writing on the work than the author. It's just the way the business works.

Publishers Do Indeed Edit

To reinforce what I just wrote, when a problem is discovered quite often the publisher will revise the text (or have it sent out to an editor the company contracts with), and sometimes this can entail major effort. But this is likely not going to involve a new author's material unless that work is thought to have blockbuster potential. And even though every publisher wants "the next big book," none are naive to the reality of the likely sales numbers for the material they have agreed to publish for a heretofore unpublished writer.

There Is a Moral to This Story

Few writers I have come in contact with, and I'm included in this lot, have not sent out material that wasn't ready. We all think we wrote something really good, and if it needs a little touch-up this will be provided at the agent level.

Unfortunately, an average agent's workload consists of upwards of 50 queries each day, along with several manuscripts each week. Add to this the existing clients they represent (and specifically their needs) and how much time does an agent have left to edit material? Sure, the larger agencies have personnel to assist with the day-to-day chores and even to edit, but most employ or use interns as readers and do not have the capacity to hire a bevy of high-end, in-house editors.

However, there are agencies that do claim to provide extensive editing services for their clients at no charge. And while this might well occur, I have no personal knowledge or experience with any agencies that offer these services to previously unpublished writers. All I know about are the crooked outfits that have scammed unsuspecting authors, and I've done my best over the years to alert writers to who these are so they can be avoided.

Same Old Same Old

My harangue is identical to what it has been for years. For all practical purposes, a draft gets one chance with an agent or publisher—and that is all. So I don't think it's out-of-line to suggest having a professional critique material before sending out queries for it. Because, in addition to the moon and the planets needing to be aligned in a precise syzygy, the one indisputable fact, if there is one in the publishing industry, is that a manuscript should be in the best possible shape the author can get it in, period, before submitting it to an agent or publisher.

Reference Manuals
Aren't Always Accurate or Pertinent

Sometimes the Most Respected Reference Manuals Don't Provide Pertinent Advice

Most often the reason for the error is the time that has passed since some rule was written. An example of this is a reference in THE CHICAGO MANUAL OF STYLE that allows for placing thoughts in quotations. This has been eschewed for decades, but in one of my writing workshops not long ago I had a participant cite section 10.42 from TCMOS and the following text: "I don't care if we have offended Morgenstern," thought Vera.

Fortunately, TCMOF illustrates four other ways to handle thoughts, and I believe any contemporary writer will be well advised to choose one of the last two, which means either straight interior monologue without any quotation marks or the use of italics.

THE CHICAGO MANUAL OF STYLE Also Approves of Dual Punctuation Ending a Sentence

Every so often I'll receive a draft from a client with both a question mark and an exclamation point at the end of a sentence. Never write like this. If a question is exclaimed with such force that an exclamation point is deemed necessary as well, use this as the only punctuation to end the sentence. Again, never both—no matter how tempting it might be.

Strunk and White Are at the Top of the List of Style Enemies

I believe it's fair to state that almost every college student who has ever taken an English 101 course was informed via the syllabus to acquire a copy of THE ELEMENTS OF STYLE by Strunk and White. A while ago I was sent a very clever article about all that was wrong with this manual from the perspective of grammar, and while I could credit the author and replicate what I was provided, it would consume pages. So let me instead offer one example that stood out for me from my first reading of THE ELEMENTS a light year ago. It dealt with avoiding unnecessary adjectives and reads as follows: "The adjective hasn't been built that can pull a weak or inaccurate noun out of a tight place." The sentence contains three adjectives and certainly stronger nouns could be found to eliminate the need for at least two of the adjectives.

THE ELEMENTS OF STYLE is rife with misstatements about grammar that are evident to anyone who studies English. A great many of the problems are related to pompous drivel from Mr. Strunk (and later never corrected by Mr. White when he lent his time to the text) and have nothing to do with style or grammar. This involves questionable advice about when not to apply commas in a series (hence fomenting the "running comma" debate), to the absurd rationale for eschewing passive voice except in extreme circumstances, exacerbated by the inaccuracy of three of their four examples of passive voice that are in fact active! No wonder so many people who took an English 101 course became confused about passive voice—and stayed that way forever.

It's Important to Recognize Words That Don't Convey Their Intended Meaning

"Moot" means debatable, yet many people think it refers to the opposite. And sentences designed as aids to illustrate the word's correct usage serve to advance this misconception. Here is a sentence taken directly from Dictionary.com: "If you cannot repay your friend right now, the question is moot." With an example like this, what is someone supposed to think is the definition of "moot"? Yes, a second definition for moot is "of little or no practical meaning," but either definition is a stretch when trying to apply it to the sentence used for illustration. The word's meaning has been bastardized to the extent that I'm of the opinion it should apply solely to a moot (debate) court.

Understand the Time Frame of a Work's Publication

Reference manuals that pertain to rhetoric—as well as the words that compose the English language—must all be viewed in a contemporary context. This is no different from reading a work such as Kafka's METAMORPHOSIS, which was published in the '20s, and assume in 2012 that any of us can mimic that style and place our protagonist's thoughts in quotations.

Read Contemporary Bestseller Material to Develop a Comfort Zone

This isn't surefire, but a writer can generally get a feel for what's acceptable by reading a contemporary novel that has become a success—and especially if this is debut material published by a major imprint. Most of these "first-time" authors have had to follow accepted convention quite closely, and this will often give an aspiring writer a decent idea of what will pass muster, as this book certainly had to make it through the publishing gantlet or it wouldn't be on the bookshelf.

Revision Suggestions and How to Deal With Them Effectively

When I first started editing for a living, the most difficult part of my job was having to tell a writer that something was not working, which could be anything from a plot element to a character to a run of dialogue to a passage of exposition. But I soon learned that I had a greater challenge, which was really a responsibility, and this was to dissect the job of an editor so the writer could correctly interpret revision suggestions.

Revisions Are Suggestions and Concepts

My critiques are littered with the words "I suggest." The reason is not because I'm not sure of the advice I'm offering, nor is this phrase meant to mollify. Instead, the words are provided as a statement of fact, since editing is largely subjective and editorial opinions should be treated as such.

A Revision Suggestion Is a Call to Action

Simply stated, a suggestion to revise text is designed to get the writer to consider alternatives, not that the editor's idea is the only way something can be written. Often I'll give a client several methods to face down an issue. In this manner, the writer can make a decision based on more than one option, and it also shows that there are indeed many ways to resolve the problem.

However, Every Suggestion Doesn't Demand an Action

No editor should ever be offended if a writer chooses to eschew a suggestion, just as no author should be distraught by editorial opinion. It's the thought processes that matter, and if an editor substantiates a contention, the writer can make an educated assessment of what, if anything, should be done to improve the text, always knowing that there was an "issue" or the editor would not have broached the subject in the first place. The ultimate decision should always rest with the author, and I believe this is the one inviolable aspect of the entire editorial process.

Screenplay Writing – Turning a Book Into a Screenplay, and the Cold, Hard Facts About Options

With a certain degree of frequency, I'll be approached by a client about having his or her work turned into a screenplay, as there is confidence from some quarter, if not directly from the author, that it will make a great movie, TV show, miniseries, etc. And I've been asked, since I've worked with this client's material, if I'd be willing to write the screenplay. Invariably, it also comes up if I'd consider becoming a "partner" and write the screenplay without payment but with the prospect of a split of the profits when the work is purchased. This is when I split, and what follows explains why.

Screenwriting Is an Art Form All Its Own

Above all else, I do not take any work on consignment related to a project's being signed by any medium. If I did this, I would have a library full of unpublished manuscripts sitting next to my cardboard house abutting a Dumpster.

Ignoring the necessity of shelter and food, the next reason is because I have never felt qualified to write a screenplay, as it is a separate discipline from crafting a novel. Screenplays have their own set of requirements related to layout and structure, and I'm not versed in any of them.

But of greatest importance, spending the funds to turn a manuscript into a screenplay in my opinion is a colossal waste of money.

It's Important to Understand the Process

Once a producer likes a storyline, the normal modus operandi is for that studio executive to commission a respected screenwriter to design the screenplay. And since any screenplay submitted by a layman would be revised substantially, it would be just as easy to work from the manuscript. One big reason it's done this way is because an experienced screenwriter has knowledge of what can or can't be converted to film based on an estimated budget, which is no minor detail and something the average individual would not know much if anything about.

How an Option Plays Into This

An option to purchase a work is not a contract for the material but essentially buys time for the studio to consider the project. This sort of "wait and see" agreement generally ranges from 12 to 18 months, and an unknown writer can earn on average from $500 to $5,000 for granting this right, which is aptly referred to as "the option payment." The lower range is more common, and any previously un-published writer getting $5,000 should run around the town square naked at noon.

The Purchase Option

If the option is executed, this means the writer would be entitled to "the purchase price" established by the original options agreement, and is why an experienced agent or lawyer (or both) is mandatory. Fees for the exercising of the option are often tied to a project's budget, and as it increases so does the writer's stipend. But this is all over the place, ranging from the low five figures to breaking seven.

One Definite Author Advantage Provided by Options

If the work is not "greenlighted" within the option period, the nice thing about a properly structured option agreement is that the rights are returned to the author and the writer is allowed to keep the original option fee. And at this point the work can be shopped around without any fear of legal repercussions.

Author Realities

How many times have you heard of a writer's work being reop-tioned? And how often have you learned of a writer, whom you know, whose material has been turned into a movie, TV series, or miniseries? During the past 20 years, one associate of mine had a short run with a cable TV show, and I know a lot of people who write.

To put this in perspective, some insiders say having an option exer-cised is 10,000 times more difficult than getting a book published by a major imprint, and how hard is that in today's sardine-crowded market? The poor odds, as much as anything, are why I never had the urge to learn how to write screenplays.

I won't accept work to edit unless I believe in my heart of hearts the story has a shot at finding an audience in some milieu. And I'm okay with this even if the odds are 1,000 to 1, as my clients at least have a chance at success at some level.

The Cold, Hard Facts

But when the odds become 10,000,000 to 1, I have to bow out, as I can't take a person's money when the possibility of success is right up there with getting bitten by a mountain lion in Manhattan, killed by lightning in Death Valley, or hitting 10 of 10 numbers on a keno card. This last example is around 9,000,000 to 1, but who's counting at this point, right? And it's what I'm really getting at in all of this.

Word Count for a Novel and How It Applies to Genre

Does Word Count Matter?

Word count is a common question writers ask, and not one that can be easily answered, if at all, but I'll attempt to offer at least some degree of clarification. However, it must be kept in mind that much of what is written in this article will be nugatory if in ten years almost every book is published in an e-book format. It's also important to understand that some people say that word count doesn't matter. But I say it does, and what follows are my reasons.

The First Issue to Consider Is If a Writer Is Presently Unpublished

Previously unpublished authors are scrutinized much more closely than well-known writers with an established readership. A 150,000-word book by an unknown has one obvious thing going against it from the outset, and this is the cost to publish the book if it's twice the size of an average work in the same genre. This would likely entail a higher retail price point and the immediate concern that the buying public will be reluctant to pay more for a book by someone who is not yet "branded" (with an e-book, this of course is a nonissue).

So What About the Previously Published Writer?

This seems to be what causes the most confusion. Some people might love to read Joe Jones so much that every word is a trip to Nirvana and therefore the more text the merrier. Also, publishers might be reluctant to come down too hard on their strong revenue-producing writers, and leave their overwriting alone. Or, simply, publishers aren't editing their successful writers' works, and what is submitted is essentially what is going to be put into print and word count never enters the equation.

There Are Some Quantifiable Answers

And these relate to genre. In Literature, for example, how can any book be too expansive? Yet, in the Police Thriller world, there is a model in the 100,000-word range, give or take 10,000 words either way, that seems to work best. Perhaps the rationale is a ten-hour or so read for the average individual taking part in a round trip, coast-to-coast flight. This might be a silly analogy to some, but look at 80 percent of the novels in an airport bookstore and get back to me if you think I'm altogether wrong.

Asking About Word Count Is Normal

I also find myself looking at word count whenever someone presents me with a novel to edit. And there is good reason. If a writer has a 250,000-word Science Fiction first draft, I know right away this is not the project for me. On the other hand, if someone has a work of commercial fiction that is 125,000 words, and even though I can almost always assume the novel is going to be 25,000-35,000 words too long, its length doesn't concern me.

Don't Be Put Off By Word Count

Some of the word-count "hoopla" is just that, in my opinion. I remember an absurd situation a dozen years ago that was the result of sending a manuscript of mine to a well-known agent. My book was

78,000 words in length and contained a light romantic element that was significant to one of the story's developmental arcs. The august agent informed me that a novel needed to be in the 120,000-word range to allow enough rhetoric for a "juicy enough romance to develop." Go figure, as I'm still scratching my head on that one.

The bottom line is that nothing is more subjective than word count, but if you're trying to become published for the first time, I think you'll find it a good idea to try to fit your story within the current parameters for the genre in which you write.

Writing New Material –
When It's Time to Write Something Else

This might well be the single most important issue I will ever discuss, as it really is about letting a project go and beginning another.

Dragging Along a Corpse

Before "retiring" and editing for a living, I spent my entire career in sales. And by most standards I was considered successful, sometimes even highly so. One manager analyzed why I was effective at consistently posting strong numbers against stiff competition, and his comment was that I never dragged along a corpse. Truer words were never spoken.

The Time Comes When a Writer Must Move On

In no world I know of does hope spring more eternal than for a budding author. Every writer I know personally, including me, has hung on much too long to a manuscript that wasn't signed right away by an agent or publisher.

Give It Your All

Yes, do give it your all, but then give your all to something else. The best advice I ever received that pertained to my writing was when my agent told me to write something else. He wasn't telling me that my current story wasn't any good, which was my initial reaction, but that waiting on the current work to be signed by a publisher could indeed take a long time.

Doing Nothing Creates All Sorts of Bad Habits

I've known excellent writers who became downright bitter at not having their first project signed—and then threatened never to write another word. Some unpublished authors decide moping and whining will get their book published, while others go the denial route and complain about everything and everyone associated with the industry.

Hitch Up Your Britches and Move On

Grab hold of the keyboard and write something new. Nothing I know of can get a writer out of the doldrums quicker than crafting fresh material. For writers who care about their sanity, text is the ultimate elixir, and it always amazes me at how quickly most of us can "recover" once we get the creative juices flowing once more.

New "Life" Is Only a Few Keystrokes Away

The solution is in taking the initiative to put aside the now dusty manuscript, if only figuratively, and begin working on another project. In as little as a few days (a few hours, for some), the old material will be thought of as just that, and the new concept will be consuming every waking moment.

Putting a Draft Aside Doesn't Mean Giving Up the Ghost

As with what my agent told me, the main issue I always keep in front of my clients is that working on a new book doesn't imply giving up on an old one. It simply means that time is once again being utilized in a constructive manner. If a person spends six months creating a new work or holding onto an old manuscript and moping around like death warmed over, a half-year is still going to have passed. Which option makes the most sense?

The answer is obvious, but the real point is that the time comes when a person has to take stock of the situation and realize that the best option is to write something else. Maybe the phrase "something else" is offensive to some people, as this could be misconstrued to imply that the initial material wasn't good enough. So, I'll offer revised rhetoric: write something more. You'll be happy you're occupying your mind with a new story, and so will the future audience for your work.

Afterword

Anyone concerned about the liberties I might have taken within the hallowed halls of language stricture, and who believes a cardinal premise was violated along the way, must remember this book is titled HOW TO WRITE WHAT PEOPLE WILL PAY TO READ! It was never intended as a book on grammar, and it's not marketed as such. I am certainly not an academician or educator, and this material is not designed to substitute for, or in any way refute, what has been or is being taught in our school systems.

But I believe in what I'm saying in these articles, and it's the educators attending my creative writing workshops over the years who have given me confidence that I'm providing something worthwhile. Historically, my programs are populated by more English teachers with graduate degrees, including Ph.D.s, than any other demographic. I generally have newspaper journalists and magazine writers in attendance, as well, and many times these folks are retired and want to write a novel for the first time. And I'm proud to state that I've also had a number of writers participate who have been published by major royalty imprints.

When I've asked workshop participants why they attend my classes, I'm told it's in large measure because of my enthusiasm for literature. However, they also tell me that I provide information they haven't received anywhere else. I have no idea what this encompasses, but my hope is that those of you who have taken the time to read my articles will have come across something you might not have known, or perhaps you'll see an aspect of prose writing in a fresh light that you can apply to your advantage. And if you have questions or comments about anything you've read in the material, please feel free to contact me at theperfectwrite@aol.com.

About the Author

Robert L. Bacon facilitated creative writing workshops sponsored by the Palm Beach County Library System and the prestigious Weiss School. A Newsletter he began in 2009 to provide continuing education for library workshop participants, as of January, 2015, is broadcast to writers in forty-five countries. To accompany each Newsletter, Mr. Bacon designs an article that focuses on writing prose at a level people will pay to read or the publishing industry as he's come to know it during the past twenty-plus years as both a novelist and an editor. It is at the behest of subscribers to The Perfect Write® Newsletter that he has assembled more than 120 of his articles in this single volume. Mr. Bacon's Newsletters are free and available by filling out the simple two-step form at the bottom of any page on his Web site at theperfectwrite.com.

Index

A

B

C

D

E

F

G

H

I

J

M

N

O

P

Q

R

S

T

Y

Z

www.ingramcontent.com/pod-product-compliance
Lightning Source LLC
Chambersburg PA
CBHW060448290526
45791CB00001B/31